# Women
## and the
# Value of Suffering

## AN AW(E)FUL ROWING TOWARD GOD

~

*Kristine M. Rankka*

A Michael Glazier Book
THE LITURGICAL PRESS
Collegeville, Minnesota

A Michael Glazier Book published by The Liturgical Press

Cover design by Greg Becker

The Scripture quotations are from the Revised Standard Version Bible, Catholic edition, © 1946, 1952, and 1971 by the Division of Christian Education of the National Council of Churches of Christ in the U.S.A. Used by permission. All rights reserved.

| 1 | 2 | 3 | 4 | 5 | 6 | 7 | 8 |
|---|---|---|---|---|---|---|---|

Library of Congress Cataloging-in-Publication Data

Rankka, Kristine M., 1951–
    Women and the value of suffering : an aw(e)ful rowing toward God / Kristine M. Rankka.
        p.     cm.
    "A Michael Glazier book."
    Includes bibliographical references (p.   ) and index.
    ISBN 0-8146-5866-0 (alk. paper)
    1. Suffering—Religious aspects—Christianity.   2. Feminist theology.   I. Title.
BT732.7.R35   1998
248.8'6—dc21                                  98-29485
                                                        CIP

*For*
*Irene, Helja, Alina, and Sigrid,*
*in gratitude and loving memory,*

*and to*

*Mary Jo, Monica, and Tri-umph-ity,*
*in celebration of your lives.*

# Contents

ACKNOWLEDGMENTS . . . . . . . . . . . . . . . . . . . ix

PREFACE . . . . . . . . . . . . . . . . . . . . . . . xiv

1. INTRODUCTION . . . . . . . . . . . . . . . . . . . 1

   The Search for Meaning in Suffering . . . . . . . . . . . 2

   Purpose of This Study . . . . . . . . . . . . . . . . . 5

   Reasons for Focusing
   on Women's Experiences of Suffering . . . . . . . . . . . 6

   Methodology . . . . . . . . . . . . . . . . . . . . . 8

   The Aw(e)ful Rowing Toward God . . . . . . . . . . . . 11

2. ATTEMPTS TO DEFINE THE EXPERIENCE
   OF PAIN AND SUFFERING . . . . . . . . . . . . . . 14

   Suffering's Inexpressibility and Unsharability . . . . . . . 15

   An Experience of Loneliness and Isolation . . . . . . . . 16

   Suffering as Mystery . . . . . . . . . . . . . . . . . . 17

   Attempts to Evade Suffering . . . . . . . . . . . . . . . 18

   Desire to Control Suffering and Apathy . . . . . . . . . . 19

   Suffering as Limit Situations . . . . . . . . . . . . . . 20

   Definitions . . . . . . . . . . . . . . . . . . . . . . 21

   Pain and Suffering . . . . . . . . . . . . . . . . . . . 24

   Pain as Perception and Interpretation . . . . . . . . . . 25

   Pain Process and Meaning . . . . . . . . . . . . . . . 26

"Persons" Suffer . . . . . . . . . . . . . . . . . . . . . . 27

Role of the Future . . . . . . . . . . . . . . . . . . . . . 28

Purpose and Self-Identity Affected . . . . . . . . . . . 29

Self-Conflict . . . . . . . . . . . . . . . . . . . . . . . . 29

Suffering as Individual Loss, Self-Hatred, and Guilt . . . . 30

Affliction . . . . . . . . . . . . . . . . . . . . . . . . . . 32

Religious/Theological Responses
to the Experience of Suffering . . . . . . . . . . . . . . . 35

Injustice . . . . . . . . . . . . . . . . . . . . . . . . . . 36

Power/Powerlessness . . . . . . . . . . . . . . . . . . . . 36

Theodicy . . . . . . . . . . . . . . . . . . . . . . . . . . 37

Typology of Traditional Theodicies . . . . . . . . . . . . 37

Additional Perspectives
on Theological Responses to Suffering . . . . . . . . . . 43

    Process Theology . . . . . . . . . . . . . . . . . . . . 43

    "Suffering God" Approach . . . . . . . . . . . . . . . 44

    Liberation Theologies . . . . . . . . . . . . . . . . . 46

Conclusion . . . . . . . . . . . . . . . . . . . . . . . . . 50

3. SELECTED WOMEN'S EXPERIENCES AND
   THEOLOGICAL REFLECTIONS ON SUFFERING . . . 53

Feminism/Feminist Defined . . . . . . . . . . . . . . . . 56

A Schema of Women's Writings on Suffering . . . . . . . 58

Reconsiderations of Evil . . . . . . . . . . . . . . . . . . 59

    Cultural/Social Evil . . . . . . . . . . . . . . . . . . 60

    Sexism and the Fall . . . . . . . . . . . . . . . . . . 63

    Disobedience and the Patriarch . . . . . . . . . . . . 69

    Some Additional Views of Evil and Sin
    from the Perspective of Women . . . . . . . . . . . . 72

    Sands' Typology of Feminist Responses to Evil . . . . . 78

    Summary . . . . . . . . . . . . . . . . . . . . . . . . 84

Critiques of Traditional Theodicies and Reflections
on the Paschal Mystery . . . . . . . . . . . . . . . . . 85

   Augustinian/Irenaean Theodicies Critiqued . . . . . . 86

   Redemptive/Atonement Theodicies Critiqued . . . . . 89

Theological Reflections That Uncover Areas
Not Formerly Considered in Theology . . . . . . . . . . 99

"Wrestling with God" Writings . . . . . . . . . . . . . 109

   Pamela Smith . . . . . . . . . . . . . . . . . . . . . 109

   Melanie May. . . . . . . . . . . . . . . . . . . . . . 113

   Jean Blomquist . . . . . . . . . . . . . . . . . . . . 117

Extensive Theological Inquiries into Suffering
That Incorporate Women's Stories and Experiences . . . 120

   Dorothee Sölle's Study of Suffering. . . . . . . . . . 120

   Wendy Farley's Tragic Suffering. . . . . . . . . . . . 134

   Womanist Contributions . . . . . . . . . . . . . . . 140

Writings Pointing Toward the Development
of a Feminist Theology of Suffering . . . . . . . . . . . 149

Summary . . . . . . . . . . . . . . . . . . . . . . . . 151

   General Trends . . . . . . . . . . . . . . . . . . . . 152

   Any Value to Suffering? . . . . . . . . . . . . . . . . 159

   Areas That Are Troubling or Missing
   from These Discussions . . . . . . . . . . . . . . . . 159

4. TRAGIC VISION AND SUFFERING . . . . . . . . . 161

Themes . . . . . . . . . . . . . . . . . . . . . . . . . 163

The Tragic Structure of Reality . . . . . . . . . . . . . 174

   Wendy Farley on This Tragic Structure. . . . . . . . 175

   Tiina Allik on This Tragic Structure . . . . . . . . . 181

   Paul Ricoeur on This Tragic Structure . . . . . . . . 184

An Excursus on Job as an Example
of a Tragic Sufferer . . . . . . . . . . . . . . . . . . . 189

Importance of Tragic Vision
to Theological Discussions of Suffering . . . . . . . . . . 195

5. ELEMENTS OF A PROPOSED
   SPIRITUAL RESPONSE TO SUFFERING . . . . . . . 205
   Spirituality Defined . . . . . . . . . . . . . . . . . . . 206
   A Proposed Spiritual Response
   to Some Forms of Women's Suffering . . . . . . . . . . 210
   Concluding Remarks. . . . . . . . . . . . . . . . . . . 223

6. CONCLUSION. . . . . . . . . . . . . . . . . . . . . . 226
   "The Rowing Endeth" . . . . . . . . . . . . . . . . . . 237

BIBLIOGRAPHY . . . . . . . . . . . . . . . . . . . . . 239

INDEX. . . . . . . . . . . . . . . . . . . . . . . . . . 248

# Acknowledgments

NO WORK IS EVER THE PRODUCT OF ONLY ONE PERSON'S EFFORTS, and this study is no exception. My gratitude in this collaborative effort begins with three scholars at the Graduate Theological Union in Berkeley: to George Griener, S.J., for the generosity of his time and for his unerring example of a rigorous scholar, inspiring teacher and theologian, and courageous soul for taking on this project with me; to Dr. Sharon Thornton, for her pastoral sensibilities, keen eye, insightful responses, and enthusiastic support; and to Dr. Leanne VanDyk, for her willingness to share in this venture during a particularly demanding time, for her collegiality, incisiveness, and deep faith. To these three—my unending gratitude that they all "got it," and then some.

I am also not only indebted to the scholars and writers encompassed in this work but also to my own teachers over the years, including Diana Behler, Eugene Webb, Constantine Christofides, Benjamin Page, Marcus Borg, Nick Yonker, Annette Moran, Joseph Driskill, Steven Chase, and William Countryman.

I extend my gratitude for much-needed laughter, critical feedback, and ongoing help in maintaining my sanity to members of my writing support group (a.k.a. the Unbalanced Load): Bula Maddison, Carla Kovack, O.P., Carrie Rehak, and Walter Munton. This work has also been supported in innumerable ways by dear friends and colleagues, including Patricia Heinecke for her thoughtful feedback and outstanding editorial skills; Sarah Connor, Jane Grovijahn, and Mary Jo McCann for our thought-provoking, God-centered, grace-filled discussions over the years; Linda Rober, Marilyn Guin, Connie Gilmore, Jim Naumann, and Paul Keoppel for their examples of how to live with passion and delight in the midst of great suffering; Robin Kokemor, Lori

Brown, Mary Lynn Sepkowitz, Mary Hardy, Myra Binstock, Paul MacLennan, Leslie Elledge, Robert Lawrence, Susan Buresh, Aida Merriweather, and Louise Saylor for being there with words of encouragement, a listening ear, or a helping hand throughout this process. I am also especially thankful for the parish community of the Episcopal Church of the Good Shepherd in Berkeley, with whom I have had the joy of worshiping for the past few years.

My special thanks go to Linda Maloney of The Liturgical Press, Carrie Rehak, Mary Frances Michaels, and Monica Kaufer, r.c., for without them this book would never have come to fruition; to Viljo Rankka and Sigrid Wallin, for their longtime support of my educational endeavors and for their loving hearts; and finally, to my parents, Irene and Neilo Rankka, for their gifts of *sisu* and enduring love.

God's blessings on them all.

I am also grateful to the following authors and publishers for permission to quote from the works noted below:

- Augsburg Fortress Publishers for excerpts reprinted from *Suffering* by Dorothee Soelle, © 1975 Fortress Press, and from *Escape from Paradise: Evil and Tragedy in Feminist Theology* by Kathleen M. Sands, © 1994 Augsburg Fortress. Reprinted by permission of Augsburg Fortress.

- The Rev. Joy M. K. Bussert for excerpts from her work *Battered Women: From a Theology of Suffering to an Ethic of Empowerment,* published by the Lutheran Church in America's Division for Mission in North America, 1986.

- The Continuum Publishing Company for excerpts from *A Body Knows Best: A Theopoetics of Death and Resurrection* by Melanie May, © 1995 by Melanie May. Reprinted by permission of The Continuum Publishing Company.

- *Currents in Theology and Mission,* Lutheran School of Theology at Chicago, for excerpts from "On Suffering, Violence, and Power" by Lou Ann Trost, published in *Currents in Theology and Mission* 21 (1994).

- *Horizons: Journal of the College Theology Society,* Villanova University, for excerpts from "On Feminist Spirituality" by Anne Carr, published in *Horizons* 1982, and reprinted in

*Women's Spirituality: Resources for Christian Development,* edited by Joann Wolski Conn, Paulist Press, 1986.

- Houghton Mifflin Company for excerpts from "Rowing" and "The Rowing Endeth," from *The Awful Rowing Toward God* by Anne Sexton, © 1975 by Loring Conant, Jr., Executor of the Estate of Anne Sexton; and for "Big Boots of Pain," from *45 Mercy Street* by Anne Sexton, © 1976 by Linda Gray Sexton and Loring Conant, Jr. Reprinted by permission of Houghton Mifflin Company. All rights reserved.

- Marquette University Press for excerpts from "Narrative Approaches to Human Personhood: Agency, Grace, and Innocent Suffering" by Tiina Allik, published in *Philosophy and Theology* 1 (1987), © Marquette University Press.

- W. W. Norton & Company for the lines from "Splittings," from *The Dream of a Common Language: Poems 1974–1977* by Adrienne Rich, © 1978 W. W. Norton & Company, Inc. Reprinted by permission of the author and W. W. Norton & Company, Inc.

- Orbis Books for excerpts from M. Shawn Copeland's "Wading Through Many Sorrows: Toward a Theology of Suffering in Womanist Perspective"; Clarice J. Martin's "Biblical Theodicy and Black Women's Spiritual Autobiography: The Miry Bog, the Desolate Pit, a New Song in My Mouth"; Emilie M. Townes' "Living in the New Jerusalem: The Rhetoric and Movement of Liberation in the House of Evil"; and Delores S. Williams' "A Womanist Perspective on Sin"; published in *A Troubling in My Soul: Womanist Perspectives on Evil and Suffering,* edited by Emilie M. Townes, © 1993. For excerpts from Patricia L. Wismer's "For Women in Pain," published in *In the Embrace of God: Feminist Approaches to Theological Anthropology,* edited by Ann O'Hara Graff, © 1995.

- The Pilgrim Press for excerpts from Joanne Carlson Brown and Rebecca Parker's essay "For God So Loved the World?" and Marie Fortune's "The Transformation of Suffering." Used by permission of The Pilgrim Press, Cleveland, Ohio, © 1989. *Christianity, Patriarchy, and Abuse: A Feminist Critique,* edited by Joanne Carlson Brown and Carole R. Bohn.

- The Putnam Publishing Group and G. P. Putnam's Sons for excerpts reprinted by permission of G. P. Putnam's Sons, a division of Penguin Putnam Inc. from *Waiting for God* by Simone Weil, © 1979 by G. P. Putnam's Sons.

- *Theology Today* for excerpts from "Beyond Moral Influence to an Atoning Life" by Pamela Dickey Young, published in *Theology Today* 52 (1995).

- University of California Press for excerpts from *The Culture of Pain* by David B. Morris, © 1991 The Regents of the University of California, and from *Women and Evil* by Nel Noddings, © 1989 The Regents of the University of California.

- University Press of America Inc. for excerpts from Isabel Carter Heyward's *The Redemption of God: A Theology of Mutual Relation,* published in 1982, and "Chronic Pain and Creative Possibility: A Psychological Phenomenon Confronts Theologies of Suffering," published in *Broken and Whole: Essays on Religion and the Body,* edited by Maureen A. Tilley and Susan A. Ross, 1995.

- Westminster/John Knox Press for excerpts reproduced from *The Dictionary of Feminist Theologies,* edited by Letty Russell and Shannon Clarkson, © 1996 Westminster/John Knox Press, and from *Tragic Vision and Divine Compassion,* © 1990 Wendy Farley. Reprinted by permission of Westminster/John Knox Press.

- Excerpts from "Pain and Suffering" by Eric J. Cassell, vol. 4, pp. 1897–1905, and from "Tragedy" by Larry D. Bouchard, vol. 5, pp. 2490–2496. Excerpted with permission of Macmillan Library Reference USA, from the Encyclopedia of Bioethics, rev. ed., Warren Thomas Reich, editor in chief, vols. 4 and 5, © 1995 by Warren T. Reich.

While every effort has been made to secure permission from additional publishers and authors, I may have failed in a few cases to trace or contact the appropriate copyright holder, or receive permission by time of publication. I am very grateful for use of all material quoted herein, and refer the reader to the footnotes and bibliography for information on the original sources of those materials.

I WILL GO BEFORE YOU
  and level the mountains,
I will break in pieces the doors
      of bronze
and cut through the bars of
      iron,
I will give you the treasures of
      darkness
and riches hidden in secret
      places,
so that you may know that it is I,
      the LORD,
the God of Israel, who call you
      by your name.  .  .  .

I arm you, though you do not
      know me,
so that they may know, from the
      rising of the sun
and from the west, that there is
      no one besides me;
I am the LORD, and there is
      no other.
I form light and create darkness,
I make weal and create woe;
I the LORD do all these things.

Shower, O heavens, from above,
      and let the skies rain down
      righteousness;
let the earth open, that salvation
      may spring up,
and let it cause righteousness to
      sprout up also;
I the LORD have created it.

                    –*Isaiah 45:2-8* (RSV)

                    ⌒

  Give me to be in Your presence,
God, even though I know it
                only as absence.
  —May Sarton, *Journal of a Solitude*

# Preface

THE ORIGINS OF THIS BOOK THAT YOU HOLD IN YOUR HANDS stretch back to a small town near the coast of Washington State, where I grew up in the 1950s and '60s, a part of an even smaller Finnish-American community that made its living in one way or another related to the fishing and timber industries. My father was a fisherman and a millworker; my mother, a homemaker with an artistic spirit. Along with my older sister, we lived modestly yet comfortably (I always thought), a close-knit family embedded in a highly stratified community. As with most families, though, we had our prejudices and our difficulties—everything from racial and gender prejudices to debilitating illness and premature deaths.

Within an extended family whose members lived within walking distance of one another, both of my grandmothers stood out as significant figures at that time and subsequently, throughout my life. One, who died in her nineties after seven decades of living in the United States, refused to speak English. Tenaciously, she held on to her mother tongue. She also lived by a river that became my playground. My other grandmother, who also immigrated from Finland as a young woman, died when I was six—a woman I have always believed, even at such an early age, was one of my soul mates. Both women had gardens in which I spent much of my childhood concocting stories and dreaming of adventures beyond my small town life—imagination became a critical way of living for me.

From this milieu two persistent memories of those days have resurfaced over the many years since I have been away from my hometown and my family. These two memories have generated guiding images or metaphors for the work that follows. It may help you in your reading and evaluation of this work to know a bit more about these memory-metaphors that have shaped this endeavor for me.

The first memory is that of spending seemingly endless hours sitting around dining room and kitchen tables with the various women of my family and their friends—listening to their stories, confessions, and discussions of life's ups and downs. For many years, I was just that, a listener, an invited guest, as the older women talked and debated about everything from food to families to world affairs to "women's problems." All the while, there were the ubiquitous coffee cups, sometimes half-smoked cigarettes or a shot of whiskey, and always for me, a sense of being a part of a bigger, transforming conversation—one that helped these women (and me) know themselves and their lives differently than if they had remained totally separate or silent. Of course, some topics remained taboo, untouchable, even at these tables, and were often locked behind doors or hidden in hearts.

For many years I listened as a child from under the table, and then as an adolescent from close by, often seated on the floor with some project of my own to keep my hands busy. And, in later years, I have drawn my own chair up to the table, to join in the ongoing conversation, to wrestle with the events that have brought both sorrow and joy to our lives. This book is one aspect of my drawing up to that table with my grandmothers, my mother and my aunt, my sister and my cousins, and now, with the younger women of our family. This is a portion of my contribution to those discussions, one that brings to bear my academic and professional work as well as my personal experiences.

The metaphor that comes from this memory, that actually forms the underlying structure of the present work, is that of a house—more specifically, what I think of as the "house of suffering." As you read this work, if you do so sequentially, I invite you to think or imagine the chapters and sections forming a house. Through the introduction, for example, imagine yourself entering the house of suffering through a garden (very like my grandmothers'), a tangle of growing shoots, plants, trees, images, questions—a bit less structured than the "house" itself that follows with its more formal arguments and discussions. You are invited in via the garden, through questions and poetry, to bring yourself and your own experiences of pain and suffering, to enter into one house that one woman has constructed.

Enter in and explore the many rooms that several other scholars and practitioners have designed and hear their conversations, as I have interpreted them. Open up the closets and the cupboards, look into the corners where both light and shadow merge, and bring your own views to these rooms. Go down to the basement and up to the attic.

Then, come, join me at the kitchen table, in the last few chapters, where I hope to bring out some of my own views on the value of suffering for consideration and critique. My desire here is that this work might generate or provoke more exploration and discussion of suffering within women's private, social, and professional circles. So, let's then sit together around the kitchen table drinking coffee and smoking cigarettes with the women of my family, and speak specifically of suffering, and of hope. And finally, at the end of the work, leave this house of suffering going back through the garden of poetry—through a most profound poem by Anne Sexton.[1]

As I mentioned earlier, there is a second memory-metaphor that informs this endeavor. This one involves my father. He and I used to go fishing together. Sometimes, we would spend long hours on a cold, rain-soaked riverbank waiting for and coaxing a steelhead in all its fierce beauty to offer itself up as food for our family. Other times, we would launch the wooden rowboat that he had built out onto that river by my grandmother's house (or perhaps onto another river "up country") and fish, trolling up and down those waters. At these times, I often took up my favorite role—that of rower.

Secretly, I liked rowing better than fishing—still do. I have always loved the hard pull on the oars and the smooth glide of the boat as the oars gently feather the surface of the water and the boat pushes out into different, sometimes very deep and perilous wa-

---

[1]Sexton, who committed suicide soon after she completed this poem, perhaps never thought of herself as religious or spiritual, and might be loath to find her poetry used in a theological work. But, for me, some of her poetry is ultimately theological, as I hope the use of her poem here will illustrate.

ters. But, I have also found it tough going when working against the current to get to a favored fishing spot, or when racing home just ahead of a storm, or when rowing upstream. Sometimes, when rowing upstream, I would be inspired by those magnificent steelhead that I had seen literally leap waterfalls in their migration upstream from sea to home river for spawning. They taught me how to leap against all odds and how to rest periodically in the gentler pools along the way, before moving on against the swifter current. They taught me much about rowing, as did my father.

Generated from this memory, rowing has become a central metaphor for my own quest for God, for wholeness and connection, for home. My spiritual journey can be likened to that pull-glide-push, to the hard rowing upstream, to the getting stuck in whirlpools or becalmed by ennui or depression, and involves the surprising discoveries of places to rest or moor my boat, my soul. Sexton's "rowing poems" speak eloquently to me of my own rowing toward God, and so two of them frame this book at beginning and end.

With these two memory-metaphors as guides, I now welcome you into this work that has taken me many years to write, and has led me to explore such topics as feminist theory, gardening, psychology, tragedy, religious symbolism, Zen Buddhism, and Christian theology. If it does nothing else, may this book prompt you to think differently about your own suffering and that of the women you know. May it prompt you to write the next book or article or song or poem or story, or construct some creative work that keeps the conversation going around that kitchen table.

—Kristine Rankka
*Epiphany 1998*

# 1

# Introduction

PERSONAL AND COMMUNAL ANGUISH ARE NO STRANGERS TO those of any period in history while manifestations of suffering in our own time appear to have reached devastating proportions. According to the Weizmann Institute of Science in Israel, more than 1.3 billion people (or about one-fifth of the world's population) suffer hunger and poverty today.[1] Some 40,000,000 die per year from malnutrition and hunger, while 40,000 children under the age of five die *per day* due to lack of disease-preventing vaccines.[2] The most conservative estimates reveal that 1.4 to 1.9 million children in the United States are the victims of physical abuse each year, while the toll that emotional trauma exacts in cases where children witness violence between their parents still cannot be fully determined.[3]

Pain. Sorrow. Loss. Anxiety. Meaninglessness. Fear. Physical violence and torture. War. Disease—both physical and mental. Social conflict and interpersonal pain. Psychological harassment. Homelessness. Discrimination. Oppression. Affliction. Despair.

[1]*New Yorker,* 72 (November 18, 1996) 20.
[2]*Croissance* 8 (1992), Special Issue, as quoted in *The Scandal of a Crucified World: Perspectives on the Cross and Suffering,* ed. Yacob Tesfai (Maryknoll, N.Y.: Orbis Books, 1994) 1.
[3]Murray A. Straus, Susan K. Steinmetz, and Richard J. Gelles, *Behind Closed Doors: Violence in the American Family* (Garden City, N.Y.: Doubleday, 1981) 64; cited in Joy M. K. Bussert, *Battered Women: From a Theology of Suffering to an Ethic of Empowerment* (New York: Lutheran Church in America, Division for Mission in North America, 1986) 24.

. . . The media worldwide makes its "market share" by trafficking in the bombardment of such suffering on television and radio, in the print media, on film and video, and via the Internet. Everything from domestic violence to wars and civil unrest in an unprecedented number of countries, to drug-related crimes stretching from U.S. urban centers to the smallest midwestern town bombard us daily with the reality of our situation. The effects of earthquakes, volcanic eruptions, drought, flood, and famine in such areas as the Philippines, California, and Sudan; political oppression and full-scale wars in countries as far-flung as East Timor, Bosnia, Burma, Mexico, Northern Ireland, and Rwanda; racism, hate crimes, and human rights violations in Germany, the United States, China, and Guatemala; as well as the increasing rise to epidemic proportions of global diseases such as tuberculosis, AIDS, various addictions, and cancer are our constant companions. On some level, no one goes untouched—no matter how hard we try to fortify ourselves against these realities whether through a stoical acceptance (e.g., "that's just the way things are") or through a variety of self-absorbing means of survival and keeping the suffering "out there." Suffering is a hard fact of life in our postmodern times.

## THE SEARCH FOR MEANING IN SUFFERING

Accompanying this harsh reality, critical questions regarding the cause and meaning of suffering have persisted through time to the present—why must we suffer? Why my specific nation or group? And, why me, in particular? What did we (or I) do to deserve this? And, why is it that some are left debilitated by experiences of suffering while others are enriched, somehow made more whole, more human? Moreover, can we learn from suffering? Can there be a value to individual and corporate pain? Should we (as so much of our North American advertising directly or implicitly proposes) strive for a life that is pain free?

These and other questions have forced their way repeatedly into my own consciousness over the past four decades, for experiences of anguish, pain, and distress are no strangers to me either. Besides my own chronic physical and emotional ailments, numerous deaths and tragic accidents have haunted my family and friends, and just within the last few years I have lost several close companions to AIDS, cancer, and suicide.[4] Betrayal of trust, abuses of power, and oppression have made their ways into my life through my own experiences and those of members of my family and friends. Self-mutilation, eating disorders, and depression, as well as rape, wife battering, and sexism, have touched the lives of many women that I know. Some say that just by being born female, I come into the world suffering, and my own life has certainly exhibited common experiences of patriarchy's pernicious effects— from verbal abuse and physical assault clearly inflicted because of my being female, to sexual harassment in academe and in my work, to the economic realities of making less for the same work than my male colleagues with fewer skills and less experience (this even in a profession that is female-dominated!).

For me, Anne Sexton captures some of my own sense of the search for meaning in suffering in her poem "The Big Boots of Pain":

> There can be certain potions
> needled in by the clock
> for the body's fall from grace,
> to untorture and to plead for.
> These I have known
> and would sell all my furniture
> and books and assorted goods
> to avoid, and more, more.
>
> But the other pain . . .
> I would sell my life to avoid
> the pain that begins in the crib
> with its bars or perhaps
> with your first breath

[4]In a study published in the *Journal of the American Medical Association* in November 1996, researchers at the University of California at San Francisco contend that chronic ailments (any persistent, recurring illness that cannot be cured) afflict 100 million Americans—over one-third of the population. This number is expected to swell to 150 million by 2030. Currently, out of the 100 million, 32 million have some limitations due to their conditions, while over 9 million cannot carry out daily activities because of a chronic condition. Based on both indirect and direct health care costs, the annual social cost of chronic illness in 1990 in the United States grew to $659 billion. Reported by Sabin Russell, in "Chronic Sickness Epidemic," *San Francisco Chronicle* (November 13, 1996) A4.

when the planets drill
your future into you
for better or worse
as you marry life
and the love that gets doled out
or doesn't.

I find now, swallowing one teaspoon
of pain, that it drops downward
to the past where it mixes
with last year's cupful
and downward into a decade's quart
and downward into a lifetime's ocean.
I alternate treading water
and deadman's float.

The teaspoon ought to be bearable
if it didn't mix into the reruns
and thus enlarge into what it is not,
a sea pest's sting turning promptly
into the shark's neat biting off
of a leg because the soul
wears a magnifying glass.
Kicking the heart
with pain's big boots running up and down
the intestines like a motorcycle racer.

Yet one does get out of bed
and start over, plunge into the day
and put on a hopeful look
and does not allow fear to build a wall
between you and an old friend
or a new friend and reach out your hand,
shutting down the thought that
an axe may cut it off unexpectedly.
One learns not to blab about all this
except to yourself or the typewriter keys
who tell no one until they get brave
and crawl off onto the printed page.

I'm getting bored with it,
I tell the typewriter,
this constantly walking around

in wet shoes and then, surprise!
Somehow DECEASED keeps getting
stamped in red over the word HOPE.
And I who keep falling thankfully
into each new pillow of belief,
finding my Mercy Street,
kissing it and tenderly gift-wrapping my love,
am beginning to wonder just what
the planets had in mind on November 9th, 1928.
The pillows are ripped away,
the hand guillotined,
dog shit thrown into the middle of a laugh,
a hornet's nest building into the hi-fi speaker
and leaving me in silence,
where, without music,
I become a cracked orphan.

Well,
one gets out of bed
and the planets don't always hiss
or muck up the day, each day.
As for the pain and its multiplying teaspoon,
perhaps it is a medicine
that will cure the soul
of its greed for love
next Thursday.[5]

## PURPOSE OF THIS STUDY

So, many of the questions that I seek to explore in this work are
personally important to me, as well as to many of the people with
whom I have worked in spiritual direction or have shared moments of trial, as well as those who have experienced and shared
with me sufferings that I can only imagine. This study is one attempt to explore the complexity of suffering in our times, but
also to reflect on how one woman of faith, gripped by and responsive to God's expression of God's self in Christ and the Holy

[5]Anne Sexton, "The Big Boots of Pain," in *The Complete Poems* (Boston:
Houghton Mifflin, 1981) 547–9.

Spirit, attempts to come to terms with the enormity, diversity, and, at times, apparent senselessness of human suffering.

Some key questions underpin my interest in this study. Is Christianity at heart a religion that encourages and demands from its adherents a masochistic personal and collective suffering? If so, what does this say of the God of Christian proclamation? Where is the "good news" in all of this? How can we speak of life in abundance (John 10:10) when so massive is the suffering just of our own time, not even to mention the past? And, more specifically, how do these questions look from the varied perspectives of women today? How might the responses change because of women's experiences?

## REASONS FOR FOCUSING
## ON WOMEN'S EXPERIENCES OF SUFFERING

But, why focus on women? Surely, men suffer, too; but, while women share in the experiences of suffering reflected in the generalized statistics given above, we have additional situations of suffering with which to contend. It is not that women suffer "more," but differently than men. For example, according to the International Labour Organization, nearly half of the women in the world aged 15–64 work (most in low-wage, precarious employment), but on the average, even if they have higher-paying positions, they earn 75 percent what men do for the same work. Thus, not only are women poor, but even amongst the poor they make less.

Closer to home, in a report based on the federal government's biggest crime survey, the U.S. Justice Department's Bureau of Justice Statistics estimates that 500,000 sexual assaults on women occur annually.[6] Some sources estimate that a rape occurs every 45 seconds in the United States alone, and that one in four women is the victim of sexual assault.[7] Obviously, these statistics do not include the massive sexual assault that occurs worldwide as the result of war (as in Bosnia), young girls forced into prostitution as their only means of income (as in Thailand and Korea), and acquain-

---

[6]*Jet* 88 (September 4, 1995) 15–6.
[7]*Jet* 88 (November 27, 1995) 52–4; *Mademoiselle* 97 (December 1991) 149–50.

tance and "date rape" in countries that refuse to see this activity as "criminal." Nor do they describe the variety of suffering that is common to women that I have known and know—everything from physical abuse to the high incidence of depression, to breast and ovarian cancers, to the fear of walking down a street at night, to the silencing of the self in situations where we *do* have something to say but are afraid to say it. These are but a few of the gender-specific incidences of suffering that occur on a daily basis throughout the world that make a discussion of women's suffering imperative.[8]

Another reason for focusing on women is that the Christian tradition has accorded women a special place in some of its traditional reflections on suffering (e.g., one in which woman is believed to cause and continue evil and suffering and thus, deserves suffering as a just punishment and a means of expiation).[9] Because this traditional view has had untold destructive consequences for women and continues to persist, as a Christian woman, I am compelled to critique and respond to this view, and to begin constructing alternative ways of viewing suffering. By focusing on women, I do not seek to exclude men in this discussion (for I shall incorporate some male contributions as well), but to focus on some specific ways that suffering and theological responses to suffering affect women.

[8]E.g., the Minnesota Department of Corrections reported that between 1979 and 1981 an estimated 139,000 incidents of assault on women in that state alone took place *in the home*, in "Minnesota Programs for Battered Women Update" (St. Paul: Department of Corrections, 1982) iii; cited in Bussert, 22. Further, abusive behavior in the home is frequently viewed as acceptable by Americans, as reported in a study done at the University of Wisconsin which revealed that 25 percent of a sample of American adults approved of slapping one's spouse on "appropriate" occasions. Interestingly, the greater acceptance level was correlated with greater educational level. Also, many whites believe that domestic abuse is more common among Hispanic, African-American, Native American, or racially-mixed families, but many statistics, such as those reported by Bussert, indicate that Caucasian males are most likely to abuse their partners. See Bussert, 23. As reported in 1982, one out of five to one out of three female children (as compared with one out of eleven male children) were victims of child sexual abuse usually beginning in preadolescence, between the ages of six and twelve, in Judith Herman, *Father-Daughter Incest* (Cambridge: Harvard University Press, 1982) cited in Bussert, 24.

[9]See Elizabeth Clark and Herbert Richardson, *Women and Religion: A Feminist Sourcebook of Christian Thought* (New York: Harper & Row, 1977).

By concentrating on suffering in women's experience, I also do
not seek to glorify it or to advocate a passive acceptance of suffering as women's deserved plight, but to determine if theologically
and spiritually one can find value in what seems an inescapable
human experience. From my own perspective, to encounter or
confront suffering is not necessarily only to accept it but to regain
a sense of choice and agency regarding alleviating it when possible,
bearing with it when necessary, transforming it for ourselves and
others when feasible.

As Adrienne Rich notes in her 1974 poem "Splittings,"

> . . . Yet if I could instruct
> myself, if we could learn to learn from pain
> even as it grasps us    if the mind, the mind that lives
> in this body could refuse    to let itself be crushed
> in that grasp    it would loosen    Pain would have to stand
> off from me and listen    its dark breath still on me
> but the mind could begin to speak to pain
> and pain would have to answer. . . .
>
> I believe I am choosing something new
> not to suffer uselessly    yet still to feel. . . .
>
> . . . I am choosing
> not to suffer uselessly. . . .
> I choose to love    this time    for once
> with all my intelligence[10]

From this perspective, then, I hope to explore ways Christians
might respond theologically and spiritually in responsible and
creative ways to suffering in women's lives.

## METHODOLOGY

In order to focus these concerns, I shall explore in this work the
complexity of our experiences of what might be called "radical" or
"tragic" suffering (i.e., suffering which is both "innocent" or unmerited, and potentially debilitating to the human spirit), looking
particularly at recent writings of women speaking from within the

[10]Adrienne Rich, "Splittings," in *The Dream of a Common Language: Poems
1974–1977* (New York: W. W. Norton & Company, 1983) 10–1.

Christian tradition, and more specifically, what selected women's theological and spiritual responses have been. Through a phenomenological and critical approach to relatively recent writings by selected women on the subjects of evil and suffering, I hope to identify strengths and limitations to these discussions, as well as to discover characteristics of viable theological/spiritual approaches to suffering that do justice to the varied situations of women in the North American context.

I attempt this with some hesitancy due to my awareness of the diversity of experience that is expressed in the North American context. In looking at suffering through the lens of women's experience, I am aware of the potential hazard of reducing all women's experience to my own white middle-class view. As shown by numerous feminist studies, "women's experience" is not just one, discrete thing but as varied as the women who suffer.[11] Pain is always an experience embedded in a particular political, social, historical, and cultural setting. Thus, forms of and responses to suffering vary according to whether a woman is, for instance, African-American, Anglo, Japanese-Canadian, or Latina; according to income and educational level; and cultural context.

And yet, I also believe aspects of the experience of suffering cut across every ethnic, economic, social, and cultural division. We may experience and speak of our suffering differently, but is it possible to speak of any commonality in our suffering?[12] For instance,

[11]Susan A. Ross and Mary Catherine Hilkert, "Feminist Theology: A Review of Literature," *Theological Studies* 56 (1995) 337–9. Cf. Rebecca S. Chopp, "Feminism's Theological Pragmatics: A Social Naturalism of Women's Experience," *Journal of Religion* 67 (1987) 241–7.

[12]In seeking commonalities, I am following the thought of Rebecca Chopp, as in, "Feminism *does* make universal claims, and it argues that its universal claims are more true and more coherent to human experience than, for instance, the universal claims made in theology proper," Chopp, 256. And, as she further contends, "Many feminist theologians are cautious, even opposed, to universal claims. I think the issue is not the viability of universal claims per se but, rather, the relative adequacy of these claims in terms of their ability to speak to and represent the concrete, as well as in their hypothetical or prototypical nature. The problem with avoiding rendering explicit the universal claims of feminist theology is the resultant lack of any resources or principles for displaying a feminist vision for the world, one that is universal—the way things are and ought to be—and yet relatively adequate—open for appropriation and change. Within each critique of feminist theology and through each vision of feminist reflection

we all feel the pain of a physical ailment or the loss of a loved one; is there not a common desire to overcome or understand or find some meaning in these experiences?[13] Can we share with each other, across the differences, our knowledge of suffering? And, to push things a bit further, can there be for women a *value* to suffering—both individually and collectively? If so, how might that affect a woman's spirituality and lived response to the suffering in her life?

In attempting to respond to these questions, I shall pursue the following framework: Chapter 2 will look at attempts to define the experience of pain and suffering from some current and historical perspectives—primarily from the biomedical, psychological, and theological fields—in order to identify some features of suffering that any viable response must address. I shall also categorize various theological approaches, ranging from traditional theodicies to some current theologies that seek to correct the limitations of the traditional approaches. However, due to the inherent space limitations of this work, I shall not go into great depth in each, but attempt to tease out the most salient features of these approaches in order to provide a foundation for the subsequent discussions.[14]

Chapter 3 will survey how selected women within a Christian context have spoken about suffering, and how these expressions might be similar to or differ from the ways men theologize about suffering. Further, this chapter will look at how feminist theologians are discussing the role of evil and suffering in women's lives, what theological lens they use to view these experiences, and how well the traditional theodicies have articulated and responded to women's experiences of suffering. By placing these writings by

---

is a constructive claim. These constructive claims have the status of universal arguments though, of course, in a more prototypical manner than many other kinds of universal arguments." Ibid., n. 58.

   [13]As noted by Frances Bancroft in a conversation conducted on March 15, 1997: "For example, if I am sad and you are sad, we may be sad because of completely different things. But on some level, sadness is sadness and we are connected or united because of this experience."

   [14]For a listing of a variety of discussions on theological responses to suffering, see Barry L. Whitney, *Theodicy: An Annotated Bibliography on the Problem of Evil, 1960–1990* (New York: Garland Publishers, 1993), the American Theological Library Association's *Religion Indexes,* the *Catholic Periodical and Literature Index,* and *Religious and Theological Abstracts,* all available as CD-ROM databases.

women in conversation with one another, I hope to gain a greater understanding of the complexity of women's suffering and of possible ways to respond compassionately and responsibly to those who suffer in our contemporary world.

Chapter 4 will consider further how an incorporation of a tragic vision of reality, through which one comes face-to-face with human limitation, might enhance theological considerations on evil and radical suffering for women. It will look at such areas as human fallibility and fragility, vulnerability, and openness within a context of larger sources of significance in such a way as to be empowered to move through suffering to hope and compassion.

Chapter 5 will look at the implications of the above exploration and focus on a discussion of the role of spirituality in responding to the experiences of women's suffering. It is hoped that the previous discussions of a tragic vision will help identify aspects of a spirituality that lead one not to passivity and despair in the face of radical suffering but to a deeper connection with God, with one's own self, and with others who may not share the specifics of one's suffering but know suffering in their own lives. I hope to identify what I call a "mystical-political" spirituality, which might empower one to endure and work through suffering, to see life as containing choices even when one has little control over changing a situation, and to be responsive to the needs and contributions of others. This mystical-political spirituality might move one from the personal, private, and individual realm to the communal, interdependent, and interconnected realm. By so doing, this movement might break the experience of loneliness and isolation that is often such a key destructive element in the experience of suffering. This spirituality is characterized by solidarity, protest, and resistance; but is also characterized by an acknowledgment of our inherent lack of control over our lives, and thus, our need for and openness to God's activating presence in alleviating and/or transforming suffering.

## THE AW(E)FUL ROWING TOWARD GOD

Again, Anne Sexton's poetry provides a sense of this endeavor in her metaphor of "the awful rowing toward God," as depicted in an excerpt from her poem "Rowing":

. . . but I grew, I grew,
and God was there like an island I had not rowed to,
still ignorant of Him, my arms and legs worked,
and I grew, I grew,
I wore rubies and bought tomatoes
and now, in my middle age,
about nineteen in the head I'd say,
I am rowing, I am rowing
though the oarlocks stick and are rusty
and the sea blinks and rolls
like a worried eyeball,
but I am rowing, I am rowing,
though the wind pushes me back
and I know that that island will not be perfect,
it will have the flaws of life,
the absurdities of the dinner table,
but there will be a door
and I will open it
and I will get rid of the rat inside of me,
the gnawing pestilential rat.
God will take it with his two hands
and embrace it.

As the African says:
This is my tale which I have told,
if it be sweet, if it be not sweet,
take somewhere else and let some return to me.
This story ends with me still rowing.[15]

How, then, might we speak of human suffering responsibly and compassionately, particularly given the experiences of women in the church and society? Is there a way(s) to retrieve suffering as a legitimate category of theological reflection without falling into traps that blame a group of persons (e.g., women) as scapegoats for the pain that occurs in our world and lives? Is there a way(s) to speak of suffering without leading women into further denigration, abuse, masochism, and passive martyrdom, and therefore, without adding further justification for the trivialization and oppression of women? Are there ways of responding to suffering

[15]Sexton, "Rowing," in *The Complete Poems*, 417–8.

wherein women retain a sense of personhood and agency while also encountering and legitimately accepting the limits of what we can do to alleviate some types of suffering? Perhaps, all these questions boil down to one central query: Is there a value to suffering for women? Who is writing about these topics, what are they saying, and what are the difficulties of such an inquiry?

# 2

# Attempts to Define the
# Experience of Pain and Suffering

A CCORDING TO DOROTHEE SÖLLE, GERMAN FEMINIST THEOLO-
gian, all true theology begins in the experience of suffering. "Theology originates in our need for more, in our
sense of failure, in our awareness of life destroyed. Its locus is suffering or the disregard for life that we experience all the time."[1] For
her, Christian theology grows out of the paradox or contrast between life experienced as finite and constricted by negative forces
and the promise of abundant life given in the Gospels (e.g., John
10:10):

> Theology begins with experience and sets experience over
> against the promise of a whole life, the promise of the
> Kingdom of God. It confronts these statements with the
> genuine life that has been promised to us, which is no more
> nor less than everything for all of us.[2]

For the person of faith, the experience of suffering leads to
critical questions about God, oneself, oneself in relation to God
and to others. As noted by Richard Sparks, for the believer, reflection on suffering ". . . involves one's concept of human nature
(anthropology) as well as one's image of God (theology). For

---

[1]Dorothee Sölle, *The Strength of the Weak: Toward a Christian Feminist Identity*,
trans. Robert and Rita Kimber (Philadelphia: Westminster Press, 1984) 90.
[2]Ibid., 91.

Christians, one also incorporates the message and person of Jesus (christology) and one's notion of redemption (soteriology)."[3] A primary task of theology, then, is to reflect responsibly on the meaning of suffering in light of "the good news" proclaimed by Jesus and spoken of in the Gospels.

## SUFFERING'S INEXPRESSIBILITY AND UNSHARABILITY

However, one aspect of the experience of suffering that makes this task more difficult is the problem of communicating what is meant by the word itself. Although most people would acknowledge that they experience suffering themselves or, minimally, know of others who have suffered, clear depictions of this experience are persistently elusive, especially when it comes to articulating physical pain.[4] Virginia Woolf, writing in an essay on being ill, notes, "The merest schoolgirl, when she falls in love, has Shakespeare or Keats to speak her mind for her; but let a sufferer try to describe a pain in his head to a doctor and language at once runs dry."[5]

In a detailed and erudite study on global torture, Elaine Scarry, too, highlights the difficulty of conveying an experience of physical pain to another when she contends "whatever pain achieves, it achieves in part through its unsharability, and it ensures this unsharability through its resistance to language."[6] What can be so difficult for sufferers is that while they experience their distress as a prime reality, as the very focus of their lives at times (as in the case of torture or domestic violence), others do not and truly cannot know what it is.[7] This inexpressibility of suffering and the split between one's sense of one's own reality and the reality of other persons is best shown by Scarry's own words, based on an extensive analysis of reports from Amnesty International on torture:

[3]Richard Sparks, "Suffering," in *The New Dictionary of Catholic Spirituality,* ed. Michael Downey (Collegeville: The Liturgical Press, 1993) 950.

[4]David B. Morris, *The Culture of Pain* (Berkeley: University of California Press, 1991) 71–8.

[5]Virginia Woolf, "On Being Ill," in *The Moment and Other Essays* (New York: Harcourt Brace Jovanovich, 1948) 11.

[6]Elaine Scarry, *The Body in Pain: The Making and Unmaking of the World* (New York: Oxford University Press, 1985) 4.

[7]Simone Weil, *Waiting for God,* trans. Emma Crauford (New York: Harper & Row, 1951) 120.

> So, for the person in pain, so incontestably and unnegotiably
> present is it that "having pain" may come to be thought of as
> the most vibrant example of what it is to "have certainty," while
> for the other person it is so elusive that "hearing about pain"
> may exist as the primary model of what it is "to have doubt."
> Thus pain comes unsharably into our midst as at once that
> which cannot be denied and that which cannot be confirmed.[8]

One can know that a person is in pain and is suffering, but not
what it is about this specific person that leads to the suffering.[9]

## AN EXPERIENCE OF LONELINESS AND ISOLATION

Moreover, whether we wish to acknowledge it or not, it is not unusual for humans to attack and/or blame the one who suffers. As
Simone Weil remarks:

> Men have the same carnal nature as animals. If a hen is hurt,
> the others rush upon it, attacking it with their beaks. . . .
> Our senses attach all the scorn, all the revulsion, all the ha-
> tred that our reason attaches to crime, to affliction. Except for
> those whose whole soul is inhabited by Christ, everybody de-
> spises the afflicted to some extent, although practically no
> one is conscious of it.[10]

In these ways, suffering is, perhaps, the quintessential solitary
experience. Consequently, this inherent loneliness heightens the
suffering in that isolation can become its outcome.

> Because the sufferer's loss of connection with the group is
> one of the most important aspects of suffering both from the

[8]Scarry, ibid.

[9]Eric J. Cassell, "Pain and Suffering," in *Encyclopedia of Bioethics,* vol. 4., ed.
Warren Thomas Reich, rev. ed. (New York: Macmillan Library Reference
USA/Simon & Schuster Macmillan, 1995) 1900.

[10]Weil, 122. "Research in the field of victimology reveals that the initial univer-
sal reaction of human beings to victims of violence is to reject them." Joy M. K.
Bussert, *Battered Women: From a Theology of Suffering to an Ethic of Empowerment*
(New York: Lutheran Church in America, Division for Mission in North America,
1986) 31. Cf. Marcia Alpert and Susan Schechter, "Sensitizing Workers to the
Needs of Victims: Common Worker and Victim Responses," *Victimology: An
International Journal* 55 (1979) 385–9.

> standpoint of its origins and its opportunities for relief, the
> loneliness of the sufferer is not only the feeling of being alone
> but an absence from the general "we-ness" of the world, from
> a shared participation in spirit.[11]

Connection and communication with others breaks down and
one enters into a state of alienation wherein one's condition is not
easily or totally conveyed to nor understood by others.

## SUFFERING AS MYSTERY

As with the experience of falling in love, suffering in its resistance
to language is more akin to a mystery that we encounter rather
than a puzzle to be solved. Writing in *The Culture of Pain,* David B.
Morris notes ". . . a mystery, as distinguished from a puzzle,
might be defined as whatever refuses to yield up all its secrets to
common sense."[12] Try as one might to find a "correct solution" to
a mystery (such as suffering) through the use of common sense
and reason, it consistently resists closure and retains an essential
open-endedness to definition and explanation. He elaborates:

> A true mystery, as opposed to a puzzle or riddle, cannot be
> known *apart* from the veil that separates us from a full under-
> standing. The veil in a sense is what makes the mystery vis-
> ible; it gives a presence or appearance to the unknown. . . .
> A mystery, then, is not something that exists principally to be
> solved. In fact, it transcends or eludes every normal tech-
> nique of solution.[13]

One might expect, then, in pursuing definitions of and responses
to the experience of suffering, that no one answer exists and that
any "solution" will have its inherent limitations.

Mysteries also disrupt accepted and familiar ways of handling
a situation, and often put one in a state of questioning everything,
including simple answers to profound questions. Perhaps, this native elusiveness of suffering is also one reason why so many in
search of religious meaning for suffering find many traditional

[11]Cassell, 1902.
[12]Morris, 152.
[13]Ibid., 24.

theological responses unsatisfying when juxtaposed beside the scale of massive suffering in this century.[14]

ATTEMPTS TO EVADE SUFFERING

Further, experiences of suffering, as with most mysteries, are those that life thrusts upon us in such a way that we cannot evade dealing with them on some level. In recalling the events surrounding the death of his father, Thomas Merton wrote:

> Indeed, the truth that many people never understand until it is too late, is that the more you try to avoid suffering, the more you suffer, because smaller and more insignificant things begin to torture you, in proportion to your fear of being hurt. The one who does most to avoid suffering is, in the end, the one who suffers most: and his suffering comes to him from things so little and so trivial that one can say that it is no longer objective at all. It is his own existence, his own being, that is at once the subject and source of his pain, and his very existence and consciousness is his greatest torture.[15]

It seems, as indicated by Merton, that the more one tries to avoid suffering, the more one becomes separated from one's self as a human person and falls into the banal and the trivial. If we try to evade suffering, perhaps we are trying to evade a basic human condition and a part of the reality of what it means to be human. Perhaps, then, suffering is constitutive of human persons.[16]

Interestingly, Morris also notes that painlessness may be more of a curse than a blessing, as indicated by the rare medical and psychological case studies of pain-free individuals. In these cases, pain-free children die early and are more prone to inflammation and infection, and often, the individual becomes more of an out-

---

[14]Lucien Richard, *What Are They Saying about the Theology of Suffering?* (New York/Mahwah, N.J.: Paulist Press, 1992) 5. Cf. Patricia L. Wismer, "For Women in Pain," in *In the Embrace of God: Feminist Approaches to Theological Anthropology,* ed. Ann O'Hara Graff (Maryknoll, N.Y.: Orbis Books, 1995) 138–58.

[15]Thomas Merton, *The Seven Story Mountain* (New York: New American Library, 1948) 86. My thanks to Eileen Haste for referral to this citation.

[16]Cf. Lucien Richard's discussion of Stanley Hauerwas's view of ethics and suffering, in *What Are They Saying about the Theology of Suffering?,* 104ff.

sider or sideshow wonder. A life immune from the pains that flesh is heir to can lead one to constant vigilance over minor physical activities, indifference to the pain of others, and social isolation.[17] So, the goal of a pain-free life may not be the ideal that one might assume.

However, as expressed by Lucien Richard, and many other theologians, sociologists, and cultural critics, characteristic of postmodern North American cultures is this very desire to evade and deny the experience of suffering in our midst—perhaps, due in part to our current awareness of the overwhelming degree of global suffering. Based on the work of Robert Lifton and Eric Olson, Richard notes the vast desensitization to suffering in our culture. This "psychic numbing," as it is often called, is characterized by an "overwhelming attempt to eliminate negativity . . . marked by the repression of pain and the consequent incapacity to suffer . . . incapacity to confront and appropriate the reality of suffering."[18]

### DESIRE TO CONTROL SUFFERING AND APATHY

Morris, studying pain from a cultural, historical, and psychosocial perspective, and Eric Cassell, conducting research in pain from a bioethics viewpoint, also both note the connection between this numbing and its reinforcement to the unprecedented development and use of a cornucopia of drugs and treatments to cope with pain, as well as the denial and separation of the experience of death from the everyday lives of most people in these times.[19] As pointed out by Morris, we try to control pain by anesthetizing it with pills, narcotics, and alcohol, as well as with pornography, televised violence, social isolation, and the endless pursuit of youth and pleasure.[20] Even more subtle are the ways we deny suffering by overwork, a constant search for achievement for ourselves and our children, and overindulgence in a myriad of ways.

[17]Morris, 12–4.
[18]Richard, 10.
[19]Morris, 48–51; 261–6. Cf. Eric J. Cassell, *The Nature of Suffering and the Goals of Medicine* (New York: Oxford University Press, 1991).
[20]Morris, 48.

Thus, even when we experience pain as a mystery, we *continue* to think of it—to our infinite perplexity—simply as an unsolved puzzle. . . . We might say it is the most earnest wish of almost every patient, ancient or modern, to be released not just from pain but from the requirement of dwelling within its mysteries.[21]

Furthermore, this contemporary condition of denial and avoidance is also characterized by personal and collective narcissism and a lack of empathy, which, when severe enough, becomes apathy on an individual, as well as a national, scale. Sölle also raises this concern regarding contemporary Western culture and defines apathy as the very inability to suffer. She understands it as "a social condition in which people are so dominated by the goal of avoiding suffering that it becomes a goal to avoid human relationships and contacts altogether."[22] When an individual or a whole collective avoids suffering, there is a corresponding lack of vitality, passion, and intensity, as well as a lack of awareness of one's own suffering and that of others. Not only does this lead to political apathy, cynicism, and alienation but also to an uncontrolled consumerism and a value system of self-indulgence, as noted by both Richard and Sölle.[23] One only needs to spend a day in the late-twentieth-century San Francisco Bay Area or to examine the history of post-World War II U.S. foreign policy to discover the validity of these claims.

## SUFFERING AS LIMIT SITUATIONS

Nonetheless, willingly or unwillingly we enter into and dwell within such experiences of suffering, into a realm where our familiar modes of thought and action do not suffice, nor do our efforts to define and explain exhaust the complexity of these experiences. As noted earlier by Sölle at the beginning of this chapter, we come face-to-face with our limitations and our finitude. However, if one agrees with theologian Walter Kasper, perhaps

[21]Ibid., 25.
[22]Dorothee Sölle, *Suffering,* trans. Everett R. Kalin (Philadelphia: Fortress Press, 1975) 36. Cf. Sölle, *Strength of the Weak,* 24–30.
[23]Richard, 22. Cf. Sölle, *Strength of the Weak,* 11–9; Ernest Becker, *The Denial of Death* (New York: The Free Press, 1973).

there is a greater mystery that we are led to through this experience of finitude:

> No one has experienced humanity to the full unless he or she has experienced its finiteness and suffering. But then experience becomes a way of leading into an open immensity, into a mystery that is ever greater and never to be completely plumbed.[24]

Morris also notes a potential value to suffering in that if we remain within this mystery, we can be introduced to new ways of thinking and unusual states of being. The human experience of pain, as witnessed by clinical reports, literary depictions, and sociological studies, involves not only the disruption of one's accepted modes of thinking, but also involves our encounter with meaning.[25] More on this will be discussed later in this study.

Part of the challenge, then, of dealing with suffering is that while it is reported as a common, if not universal, experience, one cannot easily identify, fully share, or explicitly categorize what is happening—e.g., what is labeled "suffering" by one person may not be so by another. What, if anything, can be said about the mystery of suffering in these times?

## DEFINITIONS

A simple way to enter into and begin an inquiry into any mystery is by consulting some knowledgeable source at hand. According to *Merriam-Webster's Collegiate Dictionary,* to suffer is "to endure death, pain, or distress," "to sustain loss or damage," or "to be subject to disability or handicap." The implication here is that one is vulnerable to that which is out of one's control, and this vulnerability can lead to an experience of pain or distress.

Further, to suffer is to take on that which is difficult, to "labor under" or "bear," as well as "to put up with that which is unavoidable or inevitable." Although experiences of suffering come unexpectedly, at times, and involve our vulnerability to the world, choice in how we react or respond to suffering is implied here. We

---

[24]Walter Kasper, *The God of Jesus Christ* (New York: Crossroad, 1984) 84.
[25]Morris, 26, 34–7, 267–90, etc.

can decide "to take on" or "to endure" versus to deny, evade, or suppress these experiences.[26]

Conversely, these definitions show that in some situations suffering is also associated with *loss* of choice, or agency, due to the necessity of submitting to or enduring something or someone more powerful than oneself—as in to suffer is "to submit to or be forced to endure," to be made to do what one does not choose or want to do because of another.[27] Examples of this can be seen in experiences as varied as the consequences of war to those of disease to those of discrimination of all sorts, as well as forced prostitution, rape, and domestic abuse.

The various connotations of these dictionary definitions range from a nagging or chronic pain caused by disappointment or the consequences of disease to a sense of longing over missed opportunities (e.g., associated with sorrow); from a deep sadness or regret to the unbearable quality of extreme suffering which involves anguish of body and mind (as with affliction, torture, anguish). Not only physical experiences, such as bodily pain, are involved, but also psychological distress, such as dread and anxiety or an inconsolable grief or misery (as depicted in the term "woe"). As can be quickly observed, a constellation of synonyms and related concepts is frequently associated with suffering, including pain, affliction, distress, anguish, sorrow, lamentation, woe, agony, torment, torture, grief, and a sense of loss and/or of being victimized.

Beyond these common dictionary definitions, both religious and non-religious alike have attempted to define and understand suffering. For some, "suffering can be any experience that impinges on an individual's or a community's sense of well-being."[28] It can

---

[26]Helen M. Luke elaborates on this definition by providing a sense of suffering as similar to the image of the undercarriage of a vehicle—that which bears the weight of one's life. "Suffering is that which carries the weight of the vehicle, distributing it over the fourfold wheels so that the driver may stand in safety and move toward her chosen goal." She sees this as "a weight we carry in full consciousness." See Luke, *The Way of Woman: Awakening the Perennial Feminine* (New York: Image Books/Doubleday, 1996) 56, 57, 59. My gratitude to Olivia Wax for referral to this work.

[27]*Merriam-Webster's Collegiate Dictionary*, 10th ed. (Springfield, Mass.: Merriam-Webster, Inc., 1994) 1177.

[28]Sparks, 950.

involve "the disruption of inner harmony" of an individual as the result of physical, mental, emotional, and/or spiritual forces.[29] In this sense, suffering is not just a physical sensation but is also a subjective experience involving the "whole" person. For some, this whole person can be defined as a composite of physical, historical, cultural, psychological, socio-political, and spiritual dimensions.[30] Rarely, for example, does the person in anguish suffer without some relation to her past, present, and future and/or to the social matrix of which she is a part. Accordingly, since the "whole" person is affected in the experience of suffering, authentic Christian responses to suffering must address not only one aspect or dimension of a person but the total person within her social/cultural context. So, if one addresses the suffering of women, one must consider not only that women might suffer differently than men in a patriarchal context, but that women will also differ amongst themselves in how they suffer because of their different socio-cultural contexts.

In addition, suffering afflicts not only individuals but entire communities. The "whole" community, as well as the "whole" person, can be involved, for example, in the effects of dropping the atomic bomb in Hiroshima on present and future generations. Racism provides another example of how not only an individual is affected by, say, a violent act, but how such an act ripples through an entire community—becoming an historical lightning rod for future acts of aggression and protest against such violent incidents. Thus, both personal and communal suffering can occur, and are often interwoven.

With the help of selected scholars who have looked closely at suffering from a variety of viewpoints, I hope to sketch more clearly the range of the human experience of suffering in the remaining sections of this chapter. By looking at these writings from socio-cultural, biomedical, philosophical, psychological, and theological viewpoints, I hope to identify particular features or characteristics of suffering not already mentioned above that any adequate theological or spiritual response must consider and address.

[29]Mary Ann Fatula, "Suffering," in *The New Dictionary of Theology,* ed. Joseph A. Komonchak, et al. (Wilmington: Michael Glazier, 1988) 990.
[30]Cassell, "Pain and Suffering," 1900.

Overall, some of the discussions of suffering noted below focus on physical and mental anguish and their consequences; others emphasize spiritual crisis and social isolation; while still others take a more holistic view incorporating physical, mental, emotional, social, and spiritual trauma. Regardless of the perspective, however, suffering is, most notably, an experience of isolation and threat to the very existence of the individual or the group.[31]

## PAIN AND SUFFERING

Although often considered synonymous and used interchangeably, the terms "pain" and "suffering" are actually viewed as quite distinct, though related, in the biomedical literature. Suffering is different from pain in that suffering is the resulting condition of distress or disruption of the person arising from pain or discomfort. Moreover, pain is not only the physical experience, but also the mental thoughts and emotional reactions ascribed to the physical sensation. Pain is frequently identified as the most common source of suffering while suffering can result from pain but also from other sources.[32]

In clinical studies, a number of interesting observations have been made which more clearly show the distinction between pain and suffering. For instance, people report suffering when a pain caused by an invasive medical procedure is overwhelming, while they may also tolerate extremely severe pain "if they know what it is, know that it can be relieved, or know that it will soon end."[33] Once, in a sense, the person has some control over her pain and is assured that relief is forthcoming, suffering often subsides even though the pain itself remains. Therefore, in some cases, there can be pain without suffering.

Another interesting point is that people may suffer even when pain per se is not present. For instance, those with a history of severe migraines or other chronic pain may suffer from the fear of the pain's return even when they are experiencing pain-free periods. One can become obsessed with the pain and its potential re-

---

[31]Fatula, ibid.
[32]Cassell, 1899.
[33]Ibid.

turn to such an extent that it blocks other aspects of life and is present even in "shadow" in pleasurable experiences. Thus, fear and anxiety can play a major role in intensifying or escalating the experience of suffering.[34]

Moreover, suffering may be present in the absence of *any* symptoms in the individual, as depicted in the experience of Chilean women subjected to the sight and sound of their children being tortured while they were made powerless to save them. Although not experiencing the pain of torture directly, they suffered grievously because of their children's plight. Long-standing poverty or the loss of one's life work can also be occasions of suffering without necessarily a specific pain attached. As can be summarized, one can have suffering without pain, as well as pain without suffering, while fear and anxiety can heighten the experience of both.[35] In further clarifying the distinction between pain and suffering, it might be helpful to survey some of the current thinking within biomedical research.

## PAIN AS PERCEPTION AND INTERPRETATION

According to Eric J. Cassell, a principal biomedical researcher of suffering, pain was believed, until very recently in medicine, to be a fairly mechanical process of transmitting noxious stimuli along neural pathways to the brain, where the stimuli are identified as "something that hurts" and an ensuing aversive response is initiated.[36] However, recent research indicates a far more sophisticated process in which pain is not only a *physical sensation* but also a *perception* involving cognition and judgment. Cassell states:

> The actions of humans in response to pain generally take into account the location, severity, cause, and anticipated course of the pain. . . . Pain is the entire process of sensing, interpreting, and modulating the nociceptive process, assigning cause, anticipating course, and determining response.[37]

[34]Ibid.
[35]Ibid.
[36]Ibid., 1898.
[37]Ibid.

Not only a physiological response in the human person, pain is also a complex interpretation of sensation—a type of hermeneutics of pain.[38] David Morris also agrees and puts it more provocatively:

> Here is perhaps the most difficult thought to accept about pain. We experience pain only and entirely as we interpret it. . . . In perceiving our pain, we transform it from a simple sensation into the complex mental-emotional events that psychologists and philosophers call perception.[39]

In addition, Morris points out the changing nature of the pain process, while also indicating the possibility that we may affect, more than we have given ourselves credit for, the way we experience pain:

> Pain, after all, exists only as we perceive it. Shut down the mind and pain too stops. Change the mind (powerfully enough) and it may well be that pain too changes. When we recognize that the experience of pain is not timeless but changing, the product of specific periods and particular cultures, we may also recognize we can *act* to change or influence our own futures.[40]

Thus, according to biomedical and socio-historical research, we are not solely passive victims of pain, but can profoundly influence our response to pain. How does this actually work in the body? A closer look at this pain process might be instructive.

## PAIN PROCESS AND MEANING

In the pain process (known as the nociceptive process), a noxious physical sensation (nociception) is generated by mechanical, thermal, and chemical stimuli received through nerve endings in the skin, muscles, and internal organs. The sensation is then transmitted along neural pathways that have not only the ability to transmit but also to modify the character of the nociceptive signal. Chemical messengers (including endorphins) and their receptors,

---

[38]Cf. Hauerwas's view that suffering always occurs in an interpretative context, discussed in Richard, 116.

[39]Morris, 29.

[40]Ibid., 4.

as well as neuro-transmitters, can also alter the message within the nervous system. Not only do externally administered pain relievers, such as morphine, affect the character of the signal, but the nervous system itself can enhance, diminish, or suppress noxious information. It appears, then, that the human body, in conjunction with the mind, can affect its own response to a noxious sensation. As Morris points out:

> Pain can be described as always a cerebral phenomenon in the sense that it is never simply a sensation but rather something that the time-bound brain interprets and . . . constructs: a specific human artifact bearing the marks of its specific human history.[41]

In Cassell's view, this "modulation of the noxious sensation occurs as part of the process of perception where meaning influences the original message."[42]

And, as Morris' book repeatedly shows, pain's meaning is constructed as much by gender, social class, cultural forces, and historical conditions as by the nervous system.[43] "Pain is always historical—always reshaped by a particular time, place, culture, and individual psyche. . . ."[44] Pain's meaning is also reinforced by psychological and emotional states, such as guilt, fear, anger, grief, and depression. For Cassell and Morris, then, pain's meaning, its significance and importance to any particular person, is constructed by a physical sensation, the mind and emotions, and the social/historical location of the person. In their view, meaning, constructed by these various factors, is pain's most important component because it can alter how one suffers.

### "PERSONS" SUFFER

Closely related to pain, suffering is defined by Cassell as

> a specific state of severe distress induced by the loss of integrity, intactness, cohesiveness, or wholeness of the person,

---

[41]Ibid., 28–9.
[42]Cassell, 1897.
[43]Morris, 20, 104, etc.
[44]Ibid., 6, 52–6. Cf. Mark Zborowski, *People in Pain* (San Francisco: Jossey Bass, 1960).

or by a threat that the person believes will result in the disso-
lution of his or her integrity. Suffering continues until integrity is restored or the threat is gone.[45]

Only persons (not bodies) suffer according to this view, and "person" includes not only the individual's body, but also her personal
history, beliefs, and associations with others (such as family and
friends). The society and culture in which she lives, at a given time
in history, are also a part of her personhood, including political
and social conditions that affect her and that she affects. Her secret
interior life, the unconscious, and her transcendent dimension are
all a part of her person, too. Any and all of these dimensions are
at risk to profound change that can threaten one's cohesiveness
and integrity, thus initiating suffering. Suffering, then, is always
individual and unique because the person experiencing pain and
ascribing meaning to pain is unique and particular.[46]

### ROLE OF THE FUTURE

Further, according to this definition, the sufferer not only experiences distress occasioned by an actual event (such as rape), but also
by the fear of potential future pain (such as the threat of rape oc-
curring again). In ascribing meaning to a pain event, the role of the
future in these situations of suffering is crucial; in a way, a sense
of the future is necessary to experience some types of suffering. In
cases of chronic pain, for example, part of the suffering that occurs
is tied to thoughts about possible futures—say, the possible inability to withstand this pain in days and years to come, how this pain
may change one's quality of life, and/or that the pain will become
increasingly worse and create a breakdown of relations with others. One suffers partially, at least, because one is aware that overwhelming pain may be never-ending and that one may not be able
to do anything to alleviate it, accompanied by the fear that there is
no hope for anything better. [47]

[45]Cassell, 1899.
[46]Ibid., 1900.
[47]Ibid., 1899.

## PURPOSE AND SELF-IDENTITY AFFECTED

Another aspect of suffering that needs to be considered is that of the destruction of purpose. As Cassell says, "to be whole and able to suffer is to have aims or purposes."[48] Part of one's personhood involves the preservation and continued development of who we know ourselves to be—our self-identity, which includes these purposes and our ability to act to achieve them (what I call "agency"). Illnesses and other sources of suffering can interfere with our ability to act out our self-defined purposes, thus damaging the intactness and integrity of the person, leading to a sense of defeat and suffering. In some cases, the pain event may become so intense that the person's attention is totally focused on the situation to the exclusion of all other purposes, including preserving and developing the self.

## SELF-CONFLICT

Suffering, for Cassell, also always involves self-conflict, even if the source of suffering is usually seen as outside the sufferer. What I believe he means by this is that even if the origin of pain and suffering is usually considered external to the person (e.g., repressive governments, fate, earthquakes, loss of a loved one), what arises in suffering are the questions of meaning that only the individual person, in her own particularity, can ask. The meanings one attaches to the pain or the beliefs about its origin or consequences are what really sustain or threaten the integrity of the person, and thus, initiate and reinforce the suffering.[49] So, for Job, as an example, self-conflict is set up when he must face two strongly held beliefs within himself—that God is always aware of everything happening to him and is just, and that part of himself that believes his friends are right in saying only the wicked are punished even when he knows himself to be innocent. Job would not suffer, according to Cassell, if he were not a believer in both.

The threat to the person's integrity, as highlighted in this definition of suffering, lies in the meaning of the pain event or beliefs about its consequences. It is not necessarily the quantity of pain

[48]Ibid., 1900.
[49]Ibid., 1901.

but its meaninglessness that can pose the deepest threat to the person. Thus, meaning is what is most important in the treating of pain and the reducing of suffering for, according to Cassell, "suffering can sometimes be controlled merely by changing the meaning of the pain."[50]

## SUFFERING AS INDIVIDUAL LOSS, SELF-HATRED, AND GUILT

How suffering and meaning are interrelated also plays a major role in the writings from psychotherapists and pastoral counselors on suffering. How one endures and/or learns from personal loss dominates much of these pastoral and secular psychological discussions. According to one author, this literature emphasizes suffering as individual human brokenness and despair—reflecting on suffering as experiences of grief and loss, as well as those involving self-hatred and personal guilt. Loss, from this perspective, and the suffering it creates are real and intrinsic to humanity's finitude. Ideally, one must "move through" loss and learn to accept it in order to maintain contact with reality. In this literature, then, the focus centers on the acceptance of one's limits, yielding to the reality of suffering, and compassion for oneself in the process of moving through suffering. In so doing, one gains a deepened appreciation of life through the suffering experience.[51]

This focus, until recently, in the psychological literature on the individual has minimized the social/political context of the sufferer—neglecting how "objective factors such as discrimination intertwine with the subjective despair they engender."[52] However, especially in work with minority clients, the importance of incorporating an understanding of social and structural evil into therapeutic views of suffering has gained recent attention. Moreover, the individual, in some instances, is seen within a larger context of

[50]Ibid., 1899.
[51]L. Bregman, "Suffering," in *Dictionary of Pastoral Care and Counseling,* ed. Rodney J. Hunter (Nashville: Abingdon Press, 1990) 1231. Cf. Frank Gruba-McCallister, "Becoming Self through Suffering: The Irenaean Theodicy and Advanced Development," *Advanced Development Journal* 4 (1992) 51.
[52]Ibid. Cf. Polly Young-Eisendrath, *The Gifts of Suffering: Finding Insight, Compassion, and Renewal* (Reading, Mass.: Addison-Wesley Publishing, 1996).

oppression in which the same individual (e.g., a white woman) or group (white women in general) can be both a victim of injustice (e.g., sexism) and a perpetrator of it (e.g., as beneficiaries of a prosperity built at the expense of, say, women of color).

Regardless of the particular therapeutic orientation, many psychotherapists and counselors now note also the pervasiveness of suffering as self-hatred and guilt in contemporary individuals. As L. Bregman states, this "self-hatred may arise from internalization of injustice and oppression," or from "the pervasive anomie of modern society," either of which leads to "a sense of inner emptiness and worthlessness, often conjoined with barely suppressed narcissistic rage."[53] Similar to Cassell's views, suffering can clearly challenge the self-worth and integrity of the person to the point of despair.

Writers in this field also attempt to determine whether guilt is ever valuable for the development of self. Some question whether it is the therapist's role to help alleviate all guilt feelings, or if suffering in the form of guilt functions to bring about a change in the person that nothing else could. Other psychological theorists and practicing therapists contend that religion's focus on guilt, sinfulness, and self-denial has often been more a source for further suffering rather than a mechanism for alleviating it. Nonetheless, especially for pastoral psychologists, guilt is frequently seen within the context of humanity's need for redemption so that "not all self-hatred is unwarranted. . . ." Moreover, by advocating the value of some forms of guilt, while attempting to counter a potential descent into masochism, pastoral counselors often point out that "the suffering of self-hatred and guilt is what God redeems us *from;* it is not in itself 'redemptive.'"[54]

As can be seen in this brief survey, the psychological literature not only considers suffering from the standpoint of physical pain and its psychological effects, but predominantly in terms of loss and grief, self-hatred and guilt, and more recently, oppression and injustice. The focus, however, remains on the individual in these discussions, the effects suffering has on the individual psyche, and how one can cope and/or overcome suffering in one's life.

[53]Ibid., 1231–2.
[54]Ibid., 1232.

## AFFLICTION

Additional insights regarding suffering come also from a discussion of another term that is often associated with it—"affliction." Simone Weil, French philosopher and spiritual writer, distinguishes between "affliction" and "suffering" in a short chapter of her work *Attente de Dieu.*[55] For her, the French *malheur,* which connotes a sense of inevitability and doom, is a severe and prolonged form of suffering, inseparable from physical pain but at the same time quite distinct.

> Affliction is an uprooting of life, a more or less attenuated equivalent of death, made irresistibly present to the soul by the attack or immediate apprehension of physical pain. If there is complete absence of physical pain there is no affliction for the soul. . . .[56]

Furthermore, not only physical pain is essential in her definition of affliction, but also, as with Morris and Cassell discussed above, psychological, mental, and social consequences are involved.

> There is not real affliction unless the event that has seized and uprooted a life attacks it, directly or indirectly, in all its parts, social, psychological, and physical. The social function is essential. There is not really affliction unless there is social degradation or the fear of it in some form or another.[57]

While affliction is inseparable from physical suffering (due to pain's ability to grab our attention and harness our thoughts), for physical suffering to be affliction it must be prolonged or frequent and affect a number of personal and social networks. This sounds almost like an early depiction of the distinction between acute and chronic pain, as identified by Morris:

> . . . we nonetheless need to distinguish carefully between two essentially different *kinds* or classes of pain . . . acute pain descends in a sudden storm. The misery that lingers months and years later belongs to the class of pain that doctors call

[55]Weil, "The Love of God and Affliction," in *Waiting for God,* 117–36. Cf. Sölle, *Suffering,* 13–6.
[56]Ibid., 118.
[57]Ibid., 119.

> chronic. . . . Chronic pain is the medical term for a pain
> that, perversely, refuses to disappear or that reappears over
> extended periods, in episodes . . . unlike acute pain, chronic
> pain simply will not go away and stay away. . . . Acute pain
> . . . serves a recognizable function in protecting us from fur-
> ther harm. . . . Chronic pain solves nothing. It is sheer hell.
> . . . We enter into a very different state of being when our
> pain passes, at whatever arbitrary point, from acute to
> chronic.[58]

Affliction, for Weil (and, perhaps, chronic pain for Morris),
hardens and discourages the innocent, and brands one with scorn,
disgust, self-hatred, and a sense of guilt and defilement that nor-
mally would be reserved for a criminal. "Everything happens as
though the state of soul suitable for criminals had been separated
from crime and attached to affliction; and it even seems to be in
proportion to the innocence of those who are afflicted."[59]

According to Weil and echoed in the psychological literature
mentioned above, the person afflicted internalizes this self-
loathing and one's soul is poisoned to such a degree that one may
never totally think or see oneself otherwise. If the affliction has
sunk deep enough into one's soul, the individual may always feel,
to some degree, "accursed."[60] Furthermore:

> In anyone who has suffered affliction for a long enough time
> there is a complicity with regard to his own affliction. This
> complicity impedes all the efforts he might make to improve
> his lot; it goes so far as to prevent him from seeking a way of
> deliverance, sometimes even to the point of preventing him
> from wishing for deliverance . . . [or to] shun the means of
> deliverance.[61]

This point seems particularly exemplified in such situations as domestic violence in which abused children and spouses often seem
unable to extricate themselves from an abusive situation. Moreover, although Weil does not specifically address this, I believe the
foregoing can also be true with respect to a variety of marginalized

[58]Morris, 69–71.
[59]Weil, 121.
[60]Ibid., 122.
[61]Ibid., 122–3.

groups (such as in conditions of racism, sexism, homophobia, and other forms of discrimination). If, then, suffering is prolonged and severe, it can be quite difficult, if not impossible, to truly see oneself or one's afflicted group as different than the negative image affliction bestows.

It is notable that Weil also sees affliction as "taking possession" of the soul, "marking" and "binding" the soul to itself like a slave. Unlike simple physical pain, which she believed "leaves no trace on the soul" and can be eliminated by an appropriate adjustment of the mind, affliction controls us like a "sovereign lord." In a sense, because of the debilitating effects of affliction noted above, we are no longer able on our own to be free agents, working on our own behalf.[62] We are not only unable to fulfill our aims and purposes, but those damaged by affliction are also in no state to help others, according to Weil. Another potential effect of affliction's slavery, then, is the loss of one's ability to show compassion for others in concrete ways.[63]

Most seriously, affliction also drives us into spiritual trauma, in that

> affliction makes God appear to be absent for a time, more absent than a dead man, more absent than light in the utter darkness of a cell. A kind of horror submerges the whole soul. During this absence there is nothing to love. What is terrible is that if, in this darkness where there is nothing to love, the soul ceases to love, God's absence becomes final.[64]

Affliction damages the soul by its cold indifference, which dehumanizes the person and leads the soul to loss of hope and desire for something better.

> Affliction is anonymous before all things; it deprives its victims of their personality and makes them into things. It is indifferent; and it is the coldness of this indifference—a metallic coldness—that freezes all those it touches right to the depths of their souls. They will never find warmth again. They will never believe any more that they are anyone. . . .[65]

[62]Cf. discussion on Cassell above, 16–7.
[63]Weil, 120.
[64]Ibid., 120–1.
[65]Ibid., 125.

For Weil, suffering is not the mystery but affliction and what it can do is. It does not surprise her that the innocent are killed or tortured—because that is what is to be expected when humans interact—or that disease strikes someone down—because nature is at the mercy of blind mechanical necessity. What *is* an enigma for her is "that God should have given affliction the power to seize the very souls of the innocent and to take possession of them" in such a way.[66] With this, Weil enters into the age-old questions of religion and suffering.

## RELIGIOUS/THEOLOGICAL RESPONSES TO THE EXPERIENCE OF SUFFERING

Central to any religion is the question of meaning, so it comes as no surprise that all major religious traditions have attempted to grapple with the meaning of suffering. Religion, however, brings a particular slant on the questions raised by suffering, as noted by anthropologist Clifford Geertz:

> As a religious problem, the problem of suffering is, paradoxically, not how to avoid suffering but how to suffer, how to make of physical pain, personal loss, worldly defeat, or the helpless contemplation of others' agony something bearable, supportable—something, as we say, sufferable.[67]

Traditional theological discussions regarding suffering have centered around what is often articulated as the "problem of suffering," or the "problem of God in suffering."[68] Such discussions are inevitably linked with the problem and mystery of evil—its origin or source, what or who is responsible for it, and why it exists. In the eighteenth century David Hume formulated the central concern succinctly as similar to the following: Is God willing to prevent evil, but not able? Then God is impotent. Is God able, but not

[66]Ibid., 119-20.
[67]Clifford Geertz, *The Interpretation of Cultures* (New York: Basic Books, 1973) 103.
[68]Kenneth Surin, "Evil, Problem of" in *Blackwell Encyclopedia of Modern Christian Thought,* ed. Alister E. McGrath (Oxford, England/Cambridge, Mass.: Blackwell Publishers, 1993) 192.

willing? Then God is malevolent. Is God both able and willing to prevent evil and suffering? Then why is there evil in the world?[69] The locus of many Christian theological reflections centers on this question of how a good, loving, just, and omnipotent God can allow or permit evil and suffering to occur in a basically good creation. If there is such a God, why do humans suffer—what is the purpose of suffering? Equally important, does God cause or will our suffering, and, if so, what does that mean about God and about our relationship with the Divine?

### INJUSTICE

Furthermore, the unfairness and injustice of suffering is often raised in the question, "why me?" While some appear to suffer in excess of their deeds and actions, others seem not held accountable for their misdeeds and cruelties. The innocent and the "best" suffer alongside the evil and the "worst," and sometimes, it seems, even more so than those who perpetrate destruction, malice, injustice, and discrimination. Disease and natural disasters are no respectors of the ethical or moral quality of a person's life. Thus, one's expected "equal accounting" in life does not occur, and the individual or community is pushed into a place of mystery and questioning.

### POWER/POWERLESSNESS

Issues of power and powerlessness are also raised in the experience of suffering, as noted in the earlier section on dictionary definitions and throughout the foregoing discussions on pain's meaning and affliction. Old Testment scholar Walter Brueggemann also discusses these in relation to the biblical witness of suffering in the psalms. For him, not only does suffering raise questions about God, but also about the way in which society is ordered or structured that can lead to experiences of personal or communal suffering. Theological responses to suffering inevitably have much to do with "the rationale or legitimacy for the way in which society

---

[69]David Hume, *Dialogues Concerning Natural Religion* (New York: Harper, 1948 [1779]) 66.

is ordered,"[70] and need to be concerned with "the character of God as practiced in the system of values in a social matrix."[71]

## THEODICY

To respond to these crucial questions, theologians have traditionally constructed what are known as "theodicies," from the Greek *theos* (God) and *dike* (justice). Hence, theodicies are theoretical discussions or explanations demonstrating that, despite the existence of evil and suffering, God is just.[72] Less formally, theodicies also attempt to explain why a loving and all-powerful God allows evil and suffering to exist in the world, and what God does to overcome such situations. In short, according to Brueggemann, "theodicy is concern for a fair deal."[73]

### TYPOLOGY OF TRADITIONAL THEODICIES

Generally speaking, most traditional theological approaches have distinguished between two types of suffering—(1) that which is the result of "natural evil" (e.g., earthquakes, disease, accidents) and (2) that which is the result of "moral evil" (e.g., the result of human action, historical evil, and sin). More detailed elaborations have been developed over the centuries to answer the questions posed by theodicy. Based on a useful typology developed by Richard Sparks, traditional approaches to these questions can be organized into categories or types of theodicies, as outlined below.[74] While many possible typologies have been proposed, I have selected Sparks' because of its comprehensiveness and detail. In addition, while using his typology as a foundation for organizing the various traditional theodicies, I have also modified it by incorporating contributions from other proponents and critics of these theodicies.[75]

[70]Walter Brueggemann, *Message of the Psalms* (Minneapolis: Augsburg Publishing, 1984) 169.
[71]Ibid., 170.
[72]Surin, ibid.
[73]Brueggemann, 21.
[74]Sparks, 950–2. Cf. Cassell, 1903–4.
[75]Cf. John Hick, *Evil and the God of Love* (San Francisco: Harper, 1977); S. Paul Schilling, *God and Human Anguish* (Nashville: Abingdon, 1977); Duffy, Tilley, Surin, Brown and Bohn, Rahner, etc.

(1) The *dualistic model* sees suffering as resulting from an ongoing cosmic struggle between the forces of light and darkness, good and evil or chaos. Humanity is caught in the midst of a conflict between either two countervailing deities (as in the ancient Middle Eastern mythologies) or between a benevolent god and the created powers of evil (as in God vs. Satan, the Devil, demons, evil spirits). Such an approach underscores a distinct separation of the world and cosmos into opposing, polarized camps, and suffering occurs as humanity is balanced between and affected by these two polarities.

As can be seen, this model, prevalent in such writings as the book of Revelation, the Gospel of John, and in apocalyptic writings from Judaism and Christianity, suggests that God is not the only powerful force in the universe. Usually, these additional powers are specifically evil and potentially, at least, as powerful as God. In some cases, the opposing force can be viewed as totally independent of God, which, for some critics of this theodicy, breaches the basic doctrine of the unity of God. One variant of this approach implies a limit to the power of God in containing and eradicating suffering.[76] Whether this limit is self-imposed by God or imposed by the other polarity in the cosmos depends on the writer. Thus, the attribute of God that is sacrificed in determining why suffering and evil exist is that God is not all-powerful or that, at least, a limit of some sort is placed on God's power. What is maintained is God's benevolence and justness.

(2) The *"Augustinian"*[77] (or classical free-will) *theodicy* traces the origin of evil to human sin, manifested by destructive human choices that lead to negative consequences and subsequent suffering. Resulting from the Fall, evil exists because of the decisions and actions of free, rational, and fallible human beings, and is not willed by God. Humans' disregard for God's intended and good purposes in creation leads to evil and suffering. God only permits

[76]See Harold S. Kushner, *When Bad Things Happen to Good People* (New York: Schocken, 1981).

[77]According to Kenneth Surin, a question exists whether this theodicy can actually be attributed to Augustine given, Surin contends, that what we know as theodicy is really an Enlightenment/post-Enlightenment construction. "The modern theodicy problem . . . simply could not have posed itself to Augustine," Surin, 193; therefore, I have placed this attribution in quotes.

people to choose evil and evil to happen to them. Examples of this type of theodicy include biblical exhortations to turn from sin in both the Hebrew Scriptures and the New Testament, chapters 4–7 of Augustine's *Confessions,* and aspects of the writings of Thomas Aquinas, the early C. S. Lewis,[78] Paul Tillich, Alvin Plantinga, and Richard Swinburne, to name but a few.

(3) A variation on the preceding category, and often combined with the "Augustinian" theodicy, is that of the *punishment/retribution model,* in which is incorporated an explanation of those experiences of suffering that are not necessarily a result of conscious free choice, but still result from human sin (either personal or communal). For example, natural disasters are frequently included in this model as just retribution for sinful acts of humanity, however unintended. God is understood as One who keeps track of individual and group actions and intercedes in history to exact punishment or retribution from sinful humanity.

Old Testament stories of the flood, plagues, and disease, as well as the theologies of John Calvin and Karl Barth, reflect aspects of this perspective. See also Num 12:1-15 (the punishment of Miriam); Deut 8:19-20; 2 Sam 24:10-17; Ezek 31:1-18.

As can be seen, what is emphasized in this model, combined with the "Augustinian" theodicy, is God's justice and power, whereas God's goodness and love are viewed as mysterious, if not questionable and even, for some, highly suspect. For instance, this particular penal explanation raises further questions regarding the suffering of the innocent, such as in the book of Job, wherein people and communities suffer severe anguish and untold atrocities through no apparent fault of their own. As depicted even in writings in the New Testament, the faithful note that Jesus cautions against interpreting each evidence of suffering as the consequence of someone's sins, although it is clear that individuals and groups are called to repentance.

> And he answered them, "Do you think that these Galileans were worse sinners than all other Galileans, because they suffered thus? I tell you No; but unless you repent you will all likewise perish. Or those eighteen upon whom the tower in

[78]Ann Loades, "C. S. Lewis: Grief Observed, Rationality Abandoned, Faith Regained," *Journal of Literature and Theology* 3 (1989) 107–21.

Siloam fell and killed them, do you think that they were worse offenders than all the others who dwelt in Jerusalem? I tell you, No. . . ."[79]

(4) A fourth traditional response to the questions raised by suffering, the *redemptive suffering/atonement theodicy,* finds expression in the Suffering Servant Songs of Isaiah (chapters 40–55); and in the atonement theories of Anselm and Abelard. As a remedy for the consequences of the Fall, salvation is found in the suffering, death, and resurrection of Jesus Christ, as conveyed in the Gospels. Jesus' redemptive suffering and death are seen as vicarious atonements for the sin of the entire human race. He suffered and died to "pay the price" or "bear the punishment" for human sin, and thus, to satisfy God's sense of justice and remove God's wrath against humanity.

Following the example of Jesus, human suffering is also seen as expiatory, for one's own sake but usually for that of others. The Christian is to be like Jesus, and this imitation of Christ finds its foremost expression in the obedient willingness to endure suffering. One's suffering can take the form of personal sacrifice or selfless service to others, which, it is believed, can lead to some greater good.

In this theodicy, usually a "guiltless one" willingly accepts abuse, and even death, on behalf of others in payment for a debt owed to or demanded by God. Here again, God's justice and might are emphasized, while, for some critics, God's love and goodness are seriously called into question. Why would a truly loving God demand such payment or sacrifice, for example?

(5) Sparks identifies a fifth approach, the *Irenaean model,* whose origins are traced to Irenaeus, the second century bishop of Lyons, and which is also associated with the Fathers and traditions of the Eastern Churches (e.g., Clement of Alexandria and Gregory of Nazianzus), Friedrich Schleiermacher, and modern liberal theology. This approach has also been called the *evolutionary* or *developmental model* of suffering, and depicts evil as an integral part of an environment in which God shapes souls in a perfect likeness of the Divine. Evil results from the misuse of our free will and from

[79]Luke 13:2-5 (RSV).

our disobedience to God since we have received the knowledge of good and evil and have the potential for learning to conform to the image of God. Evil can also be permitted by God in order to provide a moral contrast to the good, which can strengthen humanity's will and capacity to do good.[80] The meaning of human life, then, is development and growth toward the perfect image of God, in which we are made.[81]

In this view human suffering is an essential dimension of the rhythm of life, an outcome of humanity's movement toward perfection via trial and error. Suffering is a by-product of this natural maturation process of matter and spirit, culminating in the cosmos coming into fullness of being and/or in the kingdom of God coming into its fullness. The meaning or amelioration of suffering may not be revealed until a later, end-time, and is, therefore, eschatological in orientation.

> We know that the whole creation has been groaning in travail together until now; and not only the creation, but we ourselves, who have the first fruits of the Spirit, groan inwardly as we wait for adoption as sons, the redemption of our bodies.[82]

God's love and goodness are maintained in this approach, whereas God's power and justice in the present are deemphasized.

(6) A variant of the Irenaean model, combined with the retribution model, conceives of *suffering as remedial or instructive*—a test imposed by God for the refinement or strengthening of an individual or humanity as a whole. In this model, that which seems harsh, difficult, even unendurable is actually beneficial when seen in the proper light. Suffering can lead one back to righteousness, a stronger faith, a closer relationship with God, and according to John Hick, one of its proponents, is constitutive of a "soul-making" process. It acts as a stimulus to growth, offers the opportunity to learn humility, and reveals a greater depth of human experience and a richer understanding of the meaning of being human. Moreover, it can evoke in the sufferer a greater compassion and active concern for the suffering of others while helping one turn

[80]For example, see Irenaeus, *Against Heresies,* Book IV 37.
[81]For example, ibid., Book IV 38:4, 39:1.
[82]Romans 8:22-23 (RSV).

away from the superficialities of contemporary daily life. Such experiences, according to this perspective, are actually paths to wisdom, virtue, and greater strength and character, and suffering should be endured so that the benefits may be actualized.

> More than that, we rejoice in our sufferings, knowing that suffering produces endurance, and endurance produces character, and character produces hope, and hope does not disappoint us, because God's love has been poured into our hearts through the Holy Spirit which has been given to us.[83]

Self-imposed suffering, a permutation of this model, in the form of various ascetical and pious practices (e.g., fasting, abstinence, tithing) may also aid the person in reaching a greater level of refinement in the spiritual life. Thus, related also to the atonement model, this approach contends that the individual suffers for the purpose of something better in herself and/or ultimately, on behalf of others.

For many critics, the problem with this approach is that it raises all kinds of further issues—e.g., suffering as a situation of test and trial can actually diminish or destroy rather than ennoble the person. Despite all good will to endure or to grow from experiences of suffering, some are warped and damaged by the severity, diversity, and magnitude of suffering in their lives.[84] Thus, while God's justice and power may be maintained, God's love, goodness, and compassion toward creation may be questioned.

(7) A final theodicy in Sparks' typology is often known as the *faith solution,* which finds expression in the books of *Job, Second Isaiah,* the lament *Psalms,* the *Gospels* (e.g., Matt 26:36-46; Mark 14:32-42; and Luke 22:40-46), and in the works of such twentieth-century writers as Simone Weil and transcendental Thomist Karl Rahner.[85] Most characteristic of this approach is that when one fails to find resolution to the origin and purpose of evil and suffering in the other theodicies, one "must come face to face with the ultimate mystery of evil and the incomprehensibility of God."[86] In

---

[83]Romans 5:3-5 (RSV).

[84]Cf. discussion of affliction above, pp. 32–5.

[85]Karl Rahner, "Why Does God Allow Us to Suffer?" in *Theological Investigations,* vol. 19, trans. Edward Quinn (New York: Crossroad, 1983) 205–8.

[86]Sparks, 952.

this model there are no adequate rational answers or ironclad explanations to the questions of suffering. One surrenders in love to God's incomprehensibility. No justification is given for God's sovereign freedom or the opacity of God's love. One laments, protests, and responds, nonetheless, in trust and faith in God and God's ultimate power, justice, love, and goodness.

## ADDITIONAL PERSPECTIVES
## ON THEOLOGICAL RESPONSES TO SUFFERING

In dialogue and critique with these traditional views, a number of alternative theological approaches to the standard theodicies have surfaced in order to respond to the limitations inherent in each. Not as concerned with theoretical justifications for God's actions in relation to humanity, the priority in many of these alternatives is toward a more pragmatic, praxis-oriented approach. These alternatives often emphasize concrete experiences of suffering, which encompass not only the individual's experience but also the social and historical structures which enable such suffering to occur. Moreover, questions are posed that focus not only on the responsibility of God but also of humans in eradicating or overcoming evil and suffering. I shall cover briefly three of the most significant of these alternatives below—the approach from process theology, that from those who advocate a "suffering God," and from liberation theologies.

### Process Theology

Process theology, formulated by Charles Hartshorne and exemplified by John Cobb and David Griffin, has become popular in recent years. Its view with respect to suffering is often articulated as one in which God "cannot control finite beings but can only set them goals which this God then has to persuade them to actualize."[87] God is persuasive (vs. coercive) and benevolent, powerful and just, but also depends upon humans to effect the course or shape of divine action in the world. Cobb and Griffin demonstrate this view in the following:

[87]Surin, 194.

God seeks to persuade each occasion towards that possibility
for its own existence which would be best for it; but God cannot control the finite occasion's self-actualization. Accordingly,
the divine creative activity involves risk. The obvious point is
that, since God is not in complete control of the events of the
world, the occurrence of genuine evil is not incompatible
with God's beneficence towards all his creatures.[88]

What is surrendered in this approach to an understanding of suffering, then, is God's omnipotence, and with that go many sufferers' hopes and expectations that God will eradicate suffering and
punish evil once-and-for-all in the here and now.

## "Suffering God" Approach

Secondly, most of the traditional theodicies outlined above con-
ceive of God as impassible, that is, not directly affected by the pain
and suffering of humanity. God, being the immutable source and
ground of all being, is totally separate from creation, all-sufficient
and cannot (and, for some, should not) be affected in God's self
by the suffering of humanity. This position is summarized by
Elizabeth A. Johnson:

> Both theologically and philosophically, language about the
> apathic God, from the Greek *a-patheia* meaning no pathos or
> suffering, seeks to preserve divine freedom from a depend-
> ency on creatures that would in fact render God finite.
> Incapable of being affected by outside influences, the classi-
> cal apathic God acts not out of need or compulsion but from
> serene self-sufficiency. Negating passion and vulnerability as
> divine qualities enables God's universal goodness to operate
> without fear or favor. . . . Independent of the world, God
> can act to save with sheer gratuitous love.[89]

[88]John B. Cobb and David R. Griffin. *Process Theology: An Introductory
Exposition* (Belfast: Christian Journals, 1977) 53, quoted in Surin, 194.

[89]Elizabeth A. Johnson, "Suffering God: Compassion Poured Out," in *She Who
Is: The Mystery of God in Feminist Theological Discourse* (New York: Crossroad,
1992) 247. For an extensive contemporary discussion, see Richard Creel, *Divine
Impassibility: An Essay in Philosophical Theology* (Cambridge, England: Cambridge
University Press, 1986); cf. Michael J. Dodds, "Thomas Aquinas, Human Suffering,
and the Unchanging God of Love," *Theological Studies* 52 (1991) 330–44.

Coupled with this symbol of the impassible God is also the classical attribute of God's omnipotence. Divine power, in this view, is interpreted to mean that nothing occurs apart from divine will and control. Thus, since God can do whatever God wants and since destructive events are not prevented, God must permit them to happen for some purpose. As seen above, this "purpose" can be to punish wrongdoing, to test character, to educate or form personality, or to bring forth a greater good. No matter the extent of personal or global devastation, classical theodicy contends that God's glory is being served.[90]

Furthermore, although classical theism contends that in Jesus God has identified with the depths of human suffering in order to save, it also maintains that Jesus' anguish affects only his finite human nature—thus protecting the image of God as remote and impassible.[91] Even in the eleventh century Anselm of Canterbury recognized the dilemma this engenders when he questions:

> But how art thou compassionate, and at the same time passionless? For if thou art passionless, thou dost not feel sympathy; and if thou dost not feel sympathy, thy heart is not wretched from sympathy with the wretched; but this it is to be compassionate. But if thou art not compassionate, whence cometh so great consolation to the wretched?[92]

In this century religious thinkers from diverse and even opposing viewpoints have proposed a poignant counter to this impassible God—the image and concept of the God who suffers passionately what the world suffers. Such thinkers as Dietrich Bonhoeffer, James Cone, Kazoh Kitamori, Reinhold Niebuhr, Wolfhart Pannenberg, Hans Küng, Jürgen Moltmann, Karl Rahner, William Temple, and Miguel de Unamuno, as well as process, liberation, and feminist theologians generally have been identified with the emergence of the notion that God suffers with us.[93] In this perspective God is an advocate and "fellow sufferer

[90]Ibid., 247–8.

[91]Ibid., 248.

[92]Anselm, *Proslogion,* chapter 8, in *Saint Anselm: Basic Writings,* trans. S. N. Deane (LaSalle, Ill.: Open Court, 1974) 13, quoted in Johnson, 248.

[93]Joanne Carlson Brown and Rebecca Parker, "For God So Loved the World?" in *Christianity, Patriarchy, and Abuse: A Feminist Critique,* ed. Joanne Carlson Brown

who understands," one who is intimately bound up with creation in all its agony and turmoil.[94]

In this "suffering God" perspective, the death of Jesus, the centrality of the cross, and God's identification with human pain and anguish in the person of Jesus are stressed as God's fundamental response to suffering. No longer is suffering simply accepted as ordained or permitted by God, who remains remote, but God's involvement in human anguish affirms the meaningfulness of suffering and sustains hope in the midst of affliction. While this perspective does not resolve all questions of "why" with regard to suffering, it does provide a sense of divine solidarity with actual pain and anguish, which can give comfort, meaning, and hope to the sufferer.[95]

Also, "the suffering-God approach leads us to change our understanding of God's power, and therefore, to qualify our understanding of God's omnipotence."[96] Just as God's loving presence and compassion are emphasized in this approach, so too, must be our response to suffering—one of compassionate care and human solidarity in the ongoing transformation of suffering.[97]

### Liberation Theologies

A third perspective in dialogue with traditional theodicies, liberation theologies actually consist of a varied group of theological perspectives that take seriously the suffering experiences of mar-

---

and Carole R. Bohn (New York: Pilgrim Press, 1989) 14. E.g., see Hans Küng, *The Incarnation of God,* trans. J. R. Stephens (New York: Crossroad, 1987) excursus 2, "Can God Suffer?" 518–25, and Karl Rahner, "On the Theology of the Incarnation," in *Theological Investigations,* vol. 4, trans. Kevin Smyth (Baltimore: Helicon Press, 1966) 105–20. Cf. Marc Steen, "The Theme of the Suffering God: An Exploration," in *God and Human Suffering,* ed. Jan Lambrecht and Raymond Collins (Louvain: Peeters Press, 1990) 69–93, as well as the extensive bibliography in this volume. So widespread is this attempt to integrate suffering into the idea of God, that one author has likened it to the rise of a new orthodoxy; see Ronald Goetz, "The Rise of a New Orthodoxy," *Christian Century* 103/13 (April 16, 1986) 385–9.

[94]See, e.g., Alfred North Whitehead, *Process and Reality: An Essay in Cosmology* (New York: Macmillan, 1929) 532.

[95]Bregman, 1231. Cf. Richard, 125–6.

[96]Richard, 126.

[97]Johnson, 267–8.

ginalized individuals and groups in the world, and locate theology in a praxis-oriented approach. In the words of one author, "liberation theology has accepted as its task the articulation of the pain of the world."[98] For most of these theologies, whether from Africa, Asia, Latin America, or North America and Europe, the context in which the theologian is situated is critical in addressing concrete experiences of suffering. This context is shaped by specific geographic, economic, political, and social realities, as well as a historical reality marked by suffering on a massive scale and of a prolonged duration—all of which must be taken into consideration in any attempts to understand and eradicate suffering.

Consequently, for most liberation theologies, suffering results, in major part, from political, economic, and social exploitation and oppression. Suffering is caused by injustice and poverty, which leads to the destruction of human dignity and solidarity.[99] As noted by Latin American liberation theologian Jon Sobrino, "for liberation theology the major form of suffering in today's world is historical suffering—suffering unjustly inflicted on some by others."[100] An outgrowth of distorted social and personal values, this historical suffering afflicts the majority of people and restricts them from leading lives of purpose and self-direction.

For many liberation theologians, poverty is the main cause of this historical suffering, and poverty can take many guises including hunger, homelessness, unemployment, lack of adequate medical care and access to educational opportunities, as well as "to feel excluded from decisions that affect you, to feel controlled by outside forces, to be unable to deal with problems of daily existence, to be discriminated against."[101] For Peruvian liberation theologian Gustavo Gutiérrez, the poor "irrupt" in history "as a revelation of a contrast situation, a disclosure of contradiction that ruptures history itself,"[102] and challenge long-held beliefs about progress, security, and one's fundamental rights. The poor display for us the

---

[98]Richard, 89.

[99]Ibid., 90.

[100]Ibid., 90, 149.

[101]Peter Henriot, *Opting for the Poor: A Challenge for North Americans* (Washington, D.C.: Center for Concern, 1990) 24–5, quoted in Richard, 91.

[102]Richard, 93. Cf. Rebecca Chopp, *Praxis of Suffering: An Interpretation of Liberation and Political Theologies* (Maryknoll, N.Y.: Orbis Books, 1986).

tenuousness of our existence, and partially because of that, we attempt to distance ourselves from them. This very distancing also increases the suffering for the poor, as noted earlier in this chapter.

As a counterpoint the basic purpose of theology is to liberate the poor from this suffering and to call the faithful to loving and active concern for those caught by forms of structural and systemic oppression. The task of theology is to find a way of speaking about God in the midst of massive public suffering that can involve starvation, discrimination, death, torture, terrorism, and loss of hope and despair. For these theologians, previous theodicies, such as the penal/retribution and the atonement models outlined above, do not take into consideration nor adequately address the unmerited suffering of massive numbers of victims of prolonged discrimination and oppression.

In addition, in contrast to the focus of the generalized psychological/therapeutic approach surveyed above, liberation theologies see acceptance of suffering as capitulation to socio-political forces that are both evil and destructive to most of the world's poor and marginalized. "The ideal human response to this suffering is to struggle against it."[103] Complaint, protest, and resistance are hallmarks of these approaches. As noted by Lucien Richard, in speaking of the language of protest as prophetic language:

> The protest is against the situation and even against God . . .
> it emphasizes the "oughtness" not only of the situation but
> also of God: God himself must be committed to the innocent
> suffering. God cannot be God and accept the situation of suf-
> fering.[104]

Often in conjunction with the "suffering God" approach, God in this view suffers with the poor and is actually known in the midst of suffering. God liberates the poor and oppressed, stands in opposition to totalitarian regimes, racism, class distinctions, and patriarchy, and summons the faithful to envision and establish an entirely different social order. As Richard summarizes:

> Jesus is the model and symbol of opposition to poverty and
> suffering. The salvation brought about by Jesus embraces the

[103]Bregman, 1231.
[104]Richard, 97.

> whole of reality and implies an opposition to whatever is an
> obstacle to full humanity. Jesus liberates us from the very root
> of social injustice. . . . In his liberative and prophetic ac-
> tions, Jesus is a revelation and symbol of God, the compas-
> sionate God. God is a God who saves us not through his
> domination but through his suffering.[105]

In this approach, the cross is both a central symbol of God's solidarity with the poor and oppressed and a revelation of God's love.
On the cross Jesus experienced the suffering of the innocent and its
attendant abandonment. Yet, he also expresses a hope, signified by
the resurrection, in a salvation that liberates one from sin and its
consequences, such as injustice and oppression. In short, "liberation is another word for salvation" in this perspective.[106]

According to Gutiérrez, God has chosen to reveal God's self *to*
the poor and suffering as a God of freedom and gratuitous love.
God also reveals God's self *in* the poor and demands a response
from the faithful characterized by "a fundamental option for the
poor and for the identification of the Christian faith as a journey
of liberating solidarity."[107] God liberates in history, and the faithful are called to solidarity with the poor and oppressed through
involvement in their suffering. Faith, by necessity, leads to action;
and, action, when reflected upon, strengthens and develops faith.
Through this process, one becomes aware that one is an agent of
history, creative and, in part, responsible for one's own destiny and
for the transformation of the world. For the liberation theologian,
faith leads to transformation not only of one's own life, but of the
social and political structures in which one is embedded. In so
doing, the suffering of the poor and marginalized is reduced.

As can be seen in this brief and albeit limited overview of the
contributions of process theology, the "suffering God" approach,
and liberation theologies to the questions raised by suffering, theological responses to human pain need to take into consideration
not only how God acts in history to alleviate anguish and distress,
but also how humans work with God to overcome sin and evil that

---

[105]Ibid.

[106]Gustavo Gutiérrez, "Terrorism, Liberation, and Sexuality," *The Witness*
(April 1977) 10.

[107]Richard, 95.

cause innocent suffering. In these views, God's compassion and loving solidarity with those who suffer is paramount, while God's power is reinterpreted to mean "power-with" rather than "power-over." Therefore, to the traditional theodicy question, God's love and justice are emphasized, whereas God's power is frequently limited or restrained—at times, from the desire to protect human freedom and responsibility.

## CONCLUSION

To return to the question posed earlier in this chapter, what, then, can we say about the mystery of suffering in our times? As the foregoing discussion shows, suffering is a complex, multifaceted experience that is a function of painful experiences and primarily, of the meaning we bring to these experiences. This meaning is affected by such things as physical sensation, emotions, social/political/cultural factors, awareness of the future, anxiety, loss of choice and control, self-hatred and guilt, hope, and a larger context of beliefs within which one places the experience. As Dorothee Sölle concludes:

> . . . "suffering" thus [goes] beyond the scientific diagnosis "pain." The word suffering expresses first the duration and intensity of a pain and then the multi-dimensionality that roots the suffering in the physical and social sphere.[108]

Based on the foregoing discussion, some features to keep in mind when formulating potential theological and spiritual responses to suffering include the fact that suffering is inescapable. Suffering is a fundamental human experience and to attempt to avoid it leads to apathy, trivialization, and an emphasis on the banal, which ultimately destroys our humanity. Further, important to keep in mind is suffering's inexpressibility and unsharability, and its ability to isolate and alienate people from one another. Suffering destroys self-purpose and can lead to individual and collective brokenness, self-hatred, loss of agency and hope, and can culminate in despair. Suffering can dehumanize one to the point of

---

[108]Sölle, *Suffering*, 16.

complicity in one's own affliction and a lack of desire to alleviate one's own or others' suffering. Thus, suffering is also frequently described as a situation of powerlessness and weakness, and of abandonment by others and by God.

However, we experience pain as we interpret it, by the meaning we give to a pain event. This meaning is dependent on a person's own psyche, social and cultural milieu, place in history, and beliefs, and thus makes suffering particular and individual, as well as communal. While being an experience of finitude or of a limit situation, suffering can paradoxically often lead to an encounter with meaning.

Religion has often highlighted this facet of suffering as an encounter with meaning to provide sufferers with solace, comfort, an explanation for their distress, and an impetus for change. However, many of the traditional theological responses fall short in the face of the massive and prolonged suffering witnessed throughout this century. Alternative approaches to traditional questions about how a good, just, and powerful God can allow such horrendous innocent suffering have shifted the emphasis of theological responses to more concrete situations of and pragmatic approaches to suffering. As exemplified by Jürgen Moltmann, this shift in emphasis in the present century has moved theological inquiry more toward finding appropriate responses to the suffering of the innocent:

> The suffering of a single innocent child is an irrefutable rebuttal of the notion of the almighty and kindly God in heaven. For a God who lets the innocent suffer and who permits senseless death is not worthy to be called a God at all. Wherever the suffering of the living in all its manifold forms pierces our consciousness with pain, we lose our childish primal confidence and our trust in God.[109]

With these various contributions and approaches in mind, let us see in the following chapter how the theological responses outlined above resurface in and are challenged by the experiences of women and feminist discussions of those experiences. Are these models reflected by women's writings on suffering? Do women

---

[109]Jürgen Moltmann, *Trinity and Kingdom* (New York: Harper & Row, 1981) 47.

add something else to the discussions? The next chapter will explore the ways women speak of evil and suffering, and investigate how well the traditional theological responses outlined above have addressed the concrete experiences of women in pain.

# 3

# Selected Women's Experiences and Theological Reflections on Suffering

WHEN I FIRST BEGAN THIS STUDY OF WOMEN'S EXPERIENCES OF suffering, I assumed that little was currently available from a religious or faith perspective per se. This assumption turned out to be only partially true.

On the one hand, many North American women novelists, poets, artists, ethicists, biblical scholars, church historians, liturgists, spiritual directors, and popular religious writers do consider suffering in their works. However, most do so from within their broader discipline, say, of history, biblical studies, ethics, pastoral care, art, or literature, and embed their reflections on suffering within a larger discussion (e.g., Phyllis Trible's *Texts of Terror*). Most often, theological reflection on suffering per se is not their primary focus but is interwoven into a broader discussion of women's oppression as reflected in situations of sexism in biblical texts, church history, and societal values and structures.

On the other hand, what I found that confirmed my initial assumption was that only a few contemporary North American feminist theologians have addressed suffering from a specifically theological perspective. While many Asian and African women incorporate suffering directly into their theological discourse,[1] much

---

[1]E.g., see Chung Hyun Kyung, *Struggle to Be the Sun Again: Asian Women's Theology* (Maryknoll, N.Y.: Orbis Books, 1990) and Ursula King, ed., *Feminist Theology from the Third World: A Reader* (Maryknoll, N.Y.: Orbis Books, 1994).

of the North American writing has not addressed suffering specifically from within systematic theology, except as a portion of a larger work on a broader theological theme (e.g., Carter Heyward's dissertation on a theology of mutual relation, Nel Noddings' book on women and evil, or Elizabeth Johnson's recent work on God in feminist discourse). Three very notable exceptions to this are Dorothee Sölle's 1975 study of suffering; the work of womanist theologians such as Delores Williams, who look at suffering through an emphasis on survival; and, more recently, the work of Wendy Farley. It appears, then, that suffering as a viable category for ongoing North American feminist theological discourse has, until quite recently, received little concentrated attention as a major theme for systematic theological reflection.

Why this reticence? I contend that feminist theology has been concerned primarily (and rightly so) with the tasks of retrieval and redefinition, as well as with issues of language and methodology. Without this foundational work, a serious discussion of women's suffering could not be adequately conceived, and now, a new era of theological reflection has begun in which feminists are moving into areas previously left untouched and constructing theologies that take into consideration the suffering of women in a more direct way.

Perhaps a more important factor explaining this lack of serious, open debate on suffering is that previous reflections on evil and suffering have had such deleterious and long-lasting effects on women that many have opted for ignoring or rejecting the category itself for ongoing feminist discussion. Any serious feminist thinker discovers the land mines that await her in a discussion of suffering, including women's long, symbolic association with evil in traditional theism, as well as the consequent admonition to "grin and bear it" because such is the deserved place of women. Rather than further a discussion that has led in the past to a self-defeating passivity and masochism for women in the face of evil and suffering, many writers have concentrated on areas that emphasize more positive means of developing women's place in the world.

Connected with this critical stance is a reluctance to find broad, universalizing answers to profound questions. Many feminists are concerned (again, rightly so) with the penchant in the theological tradition for reducing highly diverse experiences down to broad generalizations about humanity, as well as to extrapolate from particular segments of society broad characteristics intended to apply to humanity in general but really applying to only a few. White feminists, too, have been appropriately criticized for making broad generalizations about women, and so there has been a move away from taking on such topics as suffering from a broad perspective.

I also propose that the lack of theological discussion on suffering per se reflects, in part, the widespread situation of denial, avoidance, and apathy that is so much a part of our contemporary world. Women, too, are affected by the desire to put suffering aside and move on to areas of life where we can see some tangible progress or effects. I would also say that we are, to some degree, afraid of drawing attention to this topic—lest it be, yet again, used against women. In my view suffering has been just too big a topic to take on until this point in the development of feminist discourse.

But, as usual, our literary writers and poets, such as Toni Morrison, Anne Sexton, and Flannery O'Connor have led the way and refused to let suffering get too far from direct view. More and more feminist/womanist theological reflections are using such poetry and fiction as sources for serious theological work,[2] and suffering as an area of focused attention in North American feminist theology is now beginning to take hold.

For the purposes of this study, I have selected a few types of women's recent reflections on suffering that consider suffering from the standpoint of Anselm's adage of "faith seeking understanding," while utilizing the tenets of feminist theology. In some cases, locating this material has been a challenge in itself because, as noted earlier, many of these views of suffering are embedded in larger discussions of related topics. However, my search proved fruitful as these writings represent a wide range of views on suffering—often conflicting with each other in a healthy atmosphere of debate. It is hoped that by bringing these diverse writings together

[2]See Kathleen M. Sands, *Escape from Paradise: Evil and Tragedy in Feminist Theology* (Minneapolis: Fortress Press, 1994) 137–69; Emilie M. Townes, ed., *A Troubling in My Soul: Womanist Perspectives on Evil and Suffering* (Maryknoll, N.Y.: Orbis Books, 1993).

in conversation they can provide the underpinnings for an expanded discussion of a feminist theology of suffering.

## FEMINISM/FEMINIST DEFINED

However, before moving on to identify some key points made by these women's writings, and because many possible definitions, interpretations, and popular assumptions regarding this terminology exist at present, it might be wise to pause a moment to clarify what I mean by "feminism" and "feminist theology." What I mean by "feminism" in this study is based on the definition recently offered by Sandra Schneiders, as

> a comprehensive ideology which is rooted in women's experience of sexual oppression, engages in a critique of patriarchy as an essentially dysfunctional system, embraces an alternative vision for humanity and the earth, and actively seeks to bring this vision to realization.[3]

Noteworthy in this definition is that feminism is a comprehensive theoretical system, grounded in the experience of oppression of women as women, and that such a grounding leads to critical analysis and evaluation of patriarchy's effects on the lives of women in the past and at present.[4] Furthermore, because of their differing life experiences incorporating a wide range of relationships, women provide an alternative perspective that is beneficial not only for themselves but also for men, children, and creation. And finally, such a feminist ideology leads to active efforts to bring this perspective or vision into concrete socio-political situations in order to bring about change and transformation.[5]

Accompanying this view of feminism, "feminist" herein reflects the broad definition provided by Carolyn Osiek as a "concern for

---

[3]Sandra Schneiders, *Beyond Patching: Faith and Feminism in the Catholic Church* (New York/Mahwah, N.J.: Paulist Press, 1991) 15.

[4]Rebecca Chopp also defines feminism in terms of "speaking from the position of marginality." Further, for women of privilege (e.g., white, educated, middle-class), not only do we speak from this position of marginality but also, simultaneously, from a position closer to the "center." See Rebecca Chopp, *The Power to Speak: Feminism, Language, God* (New York: Crossroad, 1991) 16.

[5]Schneiders, 15–31.

the promotion and dignity of women in all aspects of society,"[6] and is further enhanced by Rosemary Ruether's identification of feminist theology's guiding principle in the following:

> The critical principle of feminist theology is the promotion of the full humanity of women. Whatever denies, diminishes, or distorts the full humanity of women is, therefore, appraised as not redemptive.[7]

Thus, the uniqueness of the varied feminist theologies lies in their emphasis on the use of women's experiences as a starting point for doing theological reflection, as well as the centering of their critical norm around the promotion of the dignity and full humanity of women[8]—what I like to call the "flourishing" of women as persons.

Further, the tasks that feminist theologians characteristically set for themselves include (1) a critique of the tradition from feminist perspectives, incorporating the use of secular feminist theories; (2) the recovery of women's contributions in Christian traditions, identifying women not simply as passive victims but as contributing agents in church history and theological reflection; and (3) the development of "constructive theologies," through the work of reshaping the Church's doctrines and teachings, in order to provide a renewed vision of Christianity that incorporates the plurality of women's voices.[9] Thus, generally speaking, the tasks set by feminist theologians are both to deconstruct and construct—to correct or critique traditional theological formulations, but also to reform radically theology's self-understanding, vision, and method

---

[6]Carolyn Osiek, "The Feminist and the Bible," in *Feminist Perspectives on Biblical Scholarship,* ed. Adela Yarbro Collins (Chico, Calif.: Scholars Press, 1985) 97.

[7]Rosemary Ruether, *Sexism and God-Talk: Toward a Feminist Theology* (Boston: Beacon Press, 1983) 18–9.

[8]This "full humanity" of women has been a source of ongoing discussion, and for me, includes not only the "idealized" or positive aspects of being female in the world, but how we negatively impact the world and ourselves. Thus, enhancing this "full humanity" of women for me includes recognizing how we are as total (real) persons, not just idealized symbols for good or ill.

[9]Anne E. Carr, "The New Vision of Feminist Theology: Method," in *Freeing Theology: The Essentials of Theology in Feminist Perspective,* ed. Catherine Mowry LaCugna (San Francisco: HarperSanFrancisco, 1993) 5–29. Cf. Rebecca S. Chopp, "Feminism's Theological Pragmatics: A Social Naturalism of Women's Experience," *Journal of Religion* 67 (1987) 239–56.

for the purpose of what Rebecca Chopp calls "emancipatory transformation."[10]

## A SCHEMA OF WOMEN'S WRITINGS ON SUFFERING

With these basic emphases and tasks of feminist theologies in
mind, let us return to women's writings for a closer look at what
they are saying about suffering. Although these writings, broadly
conceived as theological in nature, can be organized in a variety of
ways, I propose the following schema as a means of sorting out the
various approaches to suffering in the studies I surveyed:[11]

(1) Reconsiderations of evil, or those writings which redefine
evil from the perspective of women. Works by Rosemary Ruether,
Nel Noddings, and Kathleen Sands contribute to this discussion.

(2) Critiques of traditional theodicies and reinterpretations of
the paschal mystery. Included here are those writings that critique
and/or reevaluate the "Augustinian"/punishment-retribution
theodicies, the Irenaean/remedial models, and the redemptive suf-
fering/atonement theodicies, briefly outlined in the previous chapter.[12] In so doing, these writings point out particular limitations and
potential dangers of these theodicies for women. Representative
of this category are works by Carter Heyward, Joanne Carlson
Brown and Rebecca Parker, and Pamela Dickey Young.

(3) Theological reflections that uncover areas not formerly
considered in theology, or those works that highlight hidden or
overlooked areas of suffering that particularly afflict women.
Included in this group are writings by Marie Fortune, Joy Bussert,

---

[10]Chopp, *Power to Speak*, 18–24, 37–47, 59–62, 66–80, 84–95, etc.

[11]These categories are not exhaustive of the material available, but representative and perhaps, helpful in organizing that material. It is also important to note
that this schema is not hard and fast, in that no writer of those discussed stays
tidily within one category only. However, for purposes of discussion, I have placed
writers in each category who speak predominantly to issues of that category.
Furthermore, I am indebted to Flora Keshgegian's survey article on feminist views
of suffering, which provided me with the impetus for this schema. See Flora A.
Keshgegian, "Suffering," in *Dictionary of Feminist Theologies*, ed. Letty M. Russell
and J. Shannon Clarkson (Louisville, Ky.: Westminster/John Knox Press, 1996)
278–80. spirituality

[12]See pp. 38ff.

and Mary Potter Engel that cover issues of abuse and violence against women and between women.[13]

(4) "Wrestling with God" writings, or those works born out of the writer's own direct, lived experiences of suffering. These writings use the daily life experiences of the writer as grist for her reflections on God, humanity, the God-human relation, as well as on relations with other humans and the rest of the created order. Such writers as Melanie May, Pamela Smith, Elizabeth O'Connor, and Jean Blomquist are discussed.

(5) Extensive theological inquiries into suffering that incorporate women's stories and experiences. For several years, the only extensive consideration of suffering from a feminist theologian remained Dorothee Sölle's now classic twenty-year-old work on suffering,[14] but newer voices are being heard, as in the case of Wendy Farley and the womanist anthology edited by Emilie Townes, also considered here.

And finally, (6) those writings pointing toward the development of a feminist theology of suffering, including considerations of methodology, foundational concerns, and trajectories for future study. Patricia Wismer exemplifies this group.

What, then, are some key points that women bring to the study of suffering that parallel what I have presented of the traditional theodicies in the previous chapter? And what do women add to this discussion?

## RECONSIDERATIONS OF EVIL

As noted in the previous section on traditional theodicies, any discussion of suffering is inherently linked to the problem and mystery of evil. For many religious believers, evil (along with sin, ignorance, and death) is what leads to suffering, or suffering is the

[13]Cf. Audre Lorde, "Eye to Eye: Black Women, Hatred, and Anger," in *Sister Outsider: Essays and Speeches* (Trumansburg, N.Y.: Crossing Press, 1984) 145–75.

[14]Although German, Sölle has spent a considerable amount of time in the United States, and her perspective is applicable to our highly industrialized/technological North American milieu. Moreover, her work has influenced many North American authors since its publication, as evidenced by how frequently her work is cited. Therefore, even though she is not strictly "North American," I have included in this schema a discussion of her groundbreaking work on suffering.

result of evil in the world in general and in their lives in particular.[15] Flora Keshgegian reminds us that

> Suffering refers to a condition of pain, sorrow, and/or anguish, which may be experienced physically, emotionally, or spiritually, personally or corporately. It may be the result of . . . natural evil . . . such things as earthquakes and disease, or the result of historical evil or human action . . . such things as war and injustice.[16]

Thus, in the traditional division, moral evil refers to actions of humans whose intent is to harm, whereas natural evil refers to natural occurrences that are considered evil because of their harmful consequences.[17]

## Cultural/Social Evil

While women writing on suffering often utilize the traditional categories of moral and natural evil in their discussions, Nel Noddings, in her book *Women and Evil,* advocates the addition of a third category—that of "cultural" evil. In this category, she speaks of the type of evil generated not "by deliberate acts of an individual agent," but generated by accepted and often "respectable" cultural norms, embedded in the very fabric of a society.[18] While natural evil includes the pain of illness and death and moral evil involves the deliberate infliction of physical or psychic pain by one individual on another (e.g., sexual abuse), cultural evils include such conditions as poverty, racism, war, and sexism.[19] Without ongoing critical evaluation of our cultural practices, we can commit and/or comply with such evil, sometimes unwittingly and devastatingly, with long-term consequences for large groups of people— as in the case of Aristotle's and Kant's denial of the rationality and

---

[15]See results from a reader survey conducted by Karen Sue Smith, "Can You See the Good in Suffering?" *U.S. Catholic* 59 (February 1994) 6–15.

[16]Keshgegian, 279.

[17]Patricia L. Wismer, "Evil," in *New Handbook of Christian Theology,* ed. Donald W. Musser and Joseph L. Price (Nashville: Abingdon Press, 1992) 173.

[18]Nel Noddings, *Women and Evil* (Berkeley: University of California Press, 1989) 104–5.

[19]Ibid., 120–1. Ageism, classism, and discrimination against those with disabilities could also be considered in this category.

autonomy of women; or in the case of white women's oppression of women of color; or in the sense of any woman's complicity in the sexism that keeps herself and other women from their full humanity.

In her landmark systematic critique of Christian theology from a feminist perspective, Rosemary Ruether also recognizes that evil is social and historical, as well as personal, and that the two aspects are different yet tightly interconnected:

> Sin always has a personal as well as a systemic side. But it is never just "individual": there is no evil that is not relational. Sin exists precisely in the distortion of relationality, including relation to oneself. Although there are sins that are committed primarily as personal self-violation or violation of another individual—abuse of one's body by intoxicants, rape, assault, or murder of another—even these very personal acts take place in a systemic, historical, and cultural context.[20]

As Ruether points out in *Sexism and God-Talk,* the Pauline "powers and principalities" exist, not as supernatural, demonic powers beyond humanity or in another realm upon which we can project evil, but as the "heritage of systemic social evil, which conditions our personal choices before we choose and prevents us from fully understanding our own choices and actions."[21]

This addition of a cultural or social category of evil seems particularly important for women, who often experience isolation from the larger society—especially women who are further marginalized in terms of race, class, or socio-economic status, or are removed from the public sector in private child-rearing activities. This condition can lead to a sense that one's suffering is solely personal, and not a part of a larger social heritage and context, further enhancing a sense of isolation and alienation.

Conversely, the moral evil that women can and do inflict on others is also frequently seen in such a privatized light, one that cannot reveal its function within a larger systemic structure that engenders and perpetuates such suffering. As Ruether observes:

---

[20]Ruether, 181.

[21]Ibid., 181–2. Cf. discussions in chapter 2 regarding the importance of cultural context and social connection in the experience of suffering.

> This does not mean that women are historical innocents. They have benefited from other historical oppressions along race and class lines. They also have collaborated with sexism in lateral violence toward themselves and other women. . . .
>
> Women sin by cooperating in their own subjugation, by lateral violence to other women who seek emancipation, and by oppressing groups of people such as children and domestic servants under their control. Women can be racist, classist, self-hating, manipulative toward dominant males, dominating toward children. But these forms of female evil cooperate with and help to perpetuate an overall system of distorted humanity. . . .[22]

Not only is there personal responsibility and accountability for moral choices, but also corporate responsibility to disengage ourselves from the entrapment of our social heritage that does violence to individuals and groups. According to Ruether, it is also imperative to "sort out our *appropriate* responsibility" by recognizing "the difference and interconnection between individual and social evil."[23] Thus, cultural, social, or systemic evil is the creation of humans and is perpetuated by our cooperation with it, but it can also be changed by us. For Ruether, as for most feminists, then:

> . . . in spite of the reality of systemic evil which we inherit, which has already biased us before we can choose, we have not lost our ability to choose good rather than evil, and hence our capacity for responsibility.[24]

This view is in direct opposition to such influential thinkers as Paul, Augustine, and Luther, who contended that through the Fall, humans have lost their fundamental ability and freedom to choose the good.[25] Accordingly, only Christ can restore an alienated humanity back to its own good human potential through his life,

---

[22]Ibid., 165, 180.

[23]Ibid., 181 [my emphasis].

[24]Ibid., 182. Cf. Mary Potter Engel, "Evil, Sin, and Violation of the Vulnerable," in *Lift Every Voice: Constructing Christian Theologies from the Underside,* ed. Susan Brooks Thistlethwaite and Mary Potter Engel (San Francisco: Harper & Row, 1990) 164.

[25]Ibid., 167.

death, and resurrection—an emphasis that some feminist writers such as Ruether believe can lead to a passivity and sense of helplessness in confronting both individual and systemic evil. Rather than taking personal or corporate responsibility for eradicating evil and suffering, one may be led by this view to a belief that such suffering is deserved, or a fatalism that "lets God right the wrongs"—abdicating responsibility and denying potential concrete efforts to change what can be changed for the better. This issue will resurface again in subsequent sections of this schema of women's writings on suffering.

Moreover, for Ruether and for other theologians working from a liberation perspective, part of the danger of systemic evil is that it is not merely the sum total of individual evil, but is "bigger than any of us or all of us *as individuals.* . . . The system transcends us as individuals in space and time. It forms an organizational structure of society and social ideology, which is itself the product of many centuries and generations."[26] In this sense, systemic evil has a life and momentum of its own, inflicting suffering on generations of groups and persons—which often leaves individuals feeling immobilized and unable to change the suffering that occurs as a result of such ingrained evil. Thus, in the face of such social or cultural evil, one significant danger is despair.

Noddings also recognizes the adaptability and resiliency of cultural evils. For her, cultural evils not only are pervasive, resist elimination, and must undergo transformation, but they also "remain potent."[27] This implies that some evils are so resilient and adaptive as to be essentially ineradicable. Thus, we live in a world of natural, personal, and social evils, some of which cannot be completely removed, and some of which we have the potential and responsibility to reduce and eradicate.

### Sexism and the Fall

Most understandably, one area of cultural or systemic evil addressed by feminist writers is the evil of patriarchy and its companion, the sin of sexism. Ruether represents some of the predominant theological concerns of feminist discussions in this area, as she states:

[26]Ibid., 182.
[27]Noddings, 105.

> It is the underlying "error" of patriarchal thinking that the dia-
> lectics of human existence—male/female, body/conscious-
> ness, human/nonhuman nature—are turned into good-evil
> dualisms. Moreover, these dualisms of the polarities of human
> existence scapegoat the "evil" side as "female." Sexism is the
> underlying social foundation of the good-evil ideology.[28]

Many feminist writers identify the influence of Aristotle and Plato,
with their separations of body and spirit, as well as of Augustine's
dualistic mistrust of the body and his rationalistic commitment to
hierarchical order, as underlying this good-evil dualism. Woman,
long associated with materiality, sexuality, and care of basic bodily
needs, has historically been viewed in Christian patriarchal thinking as inferior and evil while the male is viewed as superior and
good.[29]

Rooted in the devaluation of the body and materiality in general, which is, in turn, a bias inherited from the influence of Greek
philosophical thinking, antifemale thinking in Christianity begins
with Paul and the early church Fathers such as Tertullian,
Augustine, and Jerome, continues through the writings of Aquinas,
Luther, and Calvin, up to the present century.[30]

Dangerously, this "good-evil" dichotomy is often conflated
with a second dichotomy, "self-other." Patriarchal thinking relies
"on conceptions of evil residing in the other and on notions that
the other is a more likely agent of evil than oneself."[31] Woman, as
distinctly "other" for most males, has thus become an historical
repository for male projections of evil and, according to these
feminist views, has become symbolically associated with evil both
as the demonic Other and as the rebellious inferior.[32]

This happens, according to Noddings and Ruether, in a combination of projection and exploitation:

---

[28]Ruether, 160.
[29]Sands, 39. Cf. Noddings, 62–3; Joy M. K. Bussert, *Battered Women: From a
Theology of Suffering to an Ethic of Empowerment* (New York: Lutheran Church in
America, Division for Mission in North America, 1986) 5–15.
[30]Bussert, 6–12.
[31]Noddings, 53.
[32]Sands, 5.

> Projection externalizes the sense of inadequacy and negativity
> from the dominant group, making the other the cultural "car-
> rier" of these rejected qualities . . . leads to irrationalities that
> exceed merely the self-interest of the dominant group . . . in
> which the dominant group imagines that by purging society
> of the "other" it can, in some sense, eradicate "evil."[33]

> . . . the authentic, good self is identified with the favored
> center [the male] who dominates the cultural interpretation
> of humanness, and others are described in negative catego-
> ries by contrast. This negative perception of the other is then
> reinforced when the favored group is able to gain power over
> the others, either to annihilate them or reduce them to servile
> status. The two elements are intertwined: The perception of
> the other as inferior, less capable of the good self, rationalizes
> exploitation of them. . . . Thus, we must see two intercon-
> nected but distinguishable aspects to the ideology of the
> "other" as of lesser value: projection and exploitation.[34]

For many, this ideology of male goodness and superiority and female evil and inferiority stifles and suppresses women's autonomy
and sense of self, and becomes the dominant rationale for "keeping women in their place." It is reflected in a variety of secular and
sacred endeavors from "the long tradition that has provided authority for man's speech and woman's silence in the public do-
main,"[35] to the view of women as properties or commodities in
service to the male, to the justification of violence toward women
as a means of "correction" or chastisement.[36]

As Noddings and Ruether show, this conflation of the good-
evil and the self-other dichotomies comes to its most destructive
potency for women in the traditional notion that woman, through
a "grievous lack of moral sensitivity or will," caused the Fall of
Man, which consequently opens humanity up to all sorts of suffering.[37] Frequently noted in women's alternative discussions of
evil, Tertullian's well-known admonition to women as the "Devil's

[33]Ruether, 162–3.
[34]Ibid., 162.
[35]Noddings, 81.
[36]Bussert, 12–5.
[37]Noddings, 51; Ruether, 165–9.

gateway" exhibits this pervasive, sometimes unconscious, theological and popular view:

> Do you not know that each of you is Eve? The sentence of God on this sex of yours lives in this age: the guilt must of necessity live too. *You* are the Devil's gateway. *You* are the unsealer of that forbidden tree. *You* are the first deserter of the divine Law. *You* are she who persuaded him whom the Devil was not valiant enough to attack. *You* destroyed so easily God's image man. On account of your desert, that is death, even the Son of God had to die.[38]

Thus, Eve becomes the cause of the Fall of Adam, and women, as Eve's daughters, share in the guilt, and retain the potential for such radical sin as that to which Eve fell prey. Because of woman's inherent weakness and susceptibility to evil, the origin of evil can be traced back to women and female sexuality—thus justifying the ignorance, negation, or trivialization of all that is identified with the female, as well as justifying punishment and violence toward women, especially those who exhibit a threat to patriarchal values.[39] The consequences of this view for the suffering of women are enormous, as detailed throughout this chapter.

Further, not only is woman responsible for the advent of evil in the world, according to this traditional patriarchal orientation, but this

> male mythology . . . also translates female evil into an ontological principle. The female comes to represent the qualities of materiality, irrationality, carnality, and finitude, which debase the "manly" spirit and drag it down into sin and death.[40]

Such an orientation reinforces the continued subjugation and repression of women, both privately and socially, as "just punishment" for the "primordial sin" of causing man to fall from grace—thus setting in motion a constant struggle between women's seeking to express their autonomy as persons and the coercive ef-

---

[38]Tertullian, *De cultu feminarum,* I.I, trans. Rosemary Ruether, quoted in Noddings, 52. Cf. Ruether, 167.

[39]Ruether, 169–71; Noddings, 35–58.

[40]Ibid., 168–9. Cf. Bussert, 7.

forts of both men and women to keep women from exercising their full humanity. These efforts can range from outright force to contempt, trivialization, and ridicule, and then result in the many forms of suffering women experience as women, from various forms of physical assault to self-hatred and despair.[41]

Furthermore, as a suppressed group, women internalize this false view of humanness and evil which shapes their socialization, thereby becoming complicit in their own self-negation and subsequent suffering. Whereas many think of themselves as superior in a covert way, women are frequently filled with fear and ambiguity about their own humanity.[42] As Joanne Carlson Brown and Rebecca Parker note:

> We come to believe that it is our place to suffer. Breaking silence about the victimization of women and the ways in which we have become anesthetized to our violation is a central theme in women's literature, theology, art, social action, and politics. With every new revelation we confront again the deep and painful secret that sustains us in oppression: We have been convinced that our suffering is justified.[43]

Therefore, as Noddings, Ruether, and other feminist theologians point out, this thinking of woman as evil and inferior is not just an anachronism but contributes to a pervasive misogynist mind-set and undergirds destructive social patterns in our present culture (e.g., male-centered ethics and church doctrines, laws affecting the status of women, or women's cooperation in maintaining the *status quo*). These views are the bricks that build the social, economic, and cultural structures that marginalize women and enhance the notion of woman as "other" and therefore, inferior. Thus, not only do individuals and groups require conversion, but these sexist social structures also require a fundamental turning around (or *metanoia*) to the recognition of women as full and equivalent human persons with men.

[41]Ibid., 169–70.
[42]Ibid., 162. Cf. Dorothee Sölle, *Suffering,* trans. Everett R. Kalin (Philadelphia: Fortress Press, 1975) 12.
[43]Joanne Carlson Brown and Rebecca Parker, "For God So Loved the World?" in *Christianity, Patriarchy, and Abuse: A Feminist Critique,* ed. Joanne Carlson Brown and Carole R. Bohn (New York: Pilgrim Press, 1989) 1.

Evil, then, exists for feminists such as Ruether precisely in this "false naming" of the "other" as evil, in the projection onto another of the rejected qualities of the dominant group, and in the exploitation of another, justified by the ideology of the dominant male group. Consequently, what happens is an elemental distortion of relationship—what feminists often identify as the sin of sexism.

> This very process of false naming and exploitation constitutes the fundamental distortion and corruption of human relationality. Evil comes about precisely by the distortion of the self-other relationship into the good-evil, superior-inferior dualism. The good potential of human nature then is to be sought primarily in conversion to relationality.[44]

For writers such as Noddings and Ruether, the care, development, and enhancement of positive, mutual relations between self and others, as well as with one's own self, is a primary "good," while some of the most significant forms of suffering arise in the corruption and breakdown of this relationality.

As Kathleen Sands observes in *Escape from Paradise:*

> In general, religious feminists make a double move with respect to evil—on the one hand, exorcising the ideologies of evil and inferiority that have been attached to women and nonelite men, and on the other hand reattaching the notions of sin or evil to those same ideologies and the dominative interests they support.[45]

An example of this "double move" is in the work of Mary Potter Engel, who has proposed alternative ways of looking at sin, based on her work with women who have experienced sexual and domestic abuse. She considers the effects of shifting our view of sin—from sin as anger and resistance to sin as moral callousness or "hardening of heart" in the face of violence against women;[46] from sin as disobedience to an authority figure to sin as active betrayal of trust;[47] from sin as pride and self-love to sin as distortion of the

---

[44]Ruether, 163.
[45]Sands, 40.
[46]Engel, 156–7.
[47]Ibid., 157–9.

self's boundaries;[48] from sin as concupiscence to sin as lack of consent to our fragility and vulnerability.[49] In so doing, Engel enables us to see sin from a very different perspective—that of women who experience extreme suffering but who are often "hidden" from the realm of public discourse.

Not only do feminists upend traditional notions of evil and sin, they also transpose the "genres" in which the discussion of evil has traditionally been cast—"from the doctrinal to the symbolic and psychological, from the individual to the social, from the abstractly spiritual to the political." In altering both the genre of the question and the content of the answers, feminist scholars of religion, according to Sands, "have changed theological discourse on evil forever and for the better."[50]

## Disobedience and the Patriarch

Linked to the view of woman as evil and responsible for the Fall is the notion that evil results from humanity's willful disobedience or disregard for God's intended good purposes in creation.[51] Although many traditional theodicies have viewed evil as the activity of a malevolent force separate from God (dualistic theodicies) or as a privation (lack) of the good (Augustine), most prevalent is the view that human sin leads to the evil and suffering experienced by humanity. Through the Fall and original sin, humanity became alienated from its authentic self, was and continues to be unable to rectify the situation on its own, and requires divine redemption to restore that original authenticity.[52]

Christian theology has traditionally spoken of evil, in this sense of sin, as a specifically human capacity in that sin implies a "perversion or corruption of human nature, that is, of one's good or authentic self." Thus, because of the distinctive characteristic of human freedom, humans have a capacity to choose evil over good—a capacity for sin.[53]

[48]Ibid., 159–62.
[49]Ibid., 162–3.
[50]Sands, 40.
[51]See pp. 38–42 above.
[52]Ruether, 159. Cf. Keshgegian, 279.
[53]Ibid., 160.

As Ruether and Sands point out, this is true also from the standpoint of many women writers. For Dorothee Sölle, as an example:

> The concept of sin is a key to helping us understand human suffering in the light of human responsibility. It is misused, though, when seen as punishment for those who suffer. . . . Blaming the victim is the easiest and most superficial way to explain suffering; on the contrary, compassion and cosuffering characterize the way of Christ.[54]

Or, in the case of Ruether:

> Feminism continues, in a new form, the basic Christian perception that sin, as perversion of good potential into evil, is not simply individual but refers to a fallen state of humanity, historically. Feminism's own claim to stand in judgment on patriarchy as evil means it cannot avoid the question of the capacity of humanity for sin.[55]

However, adds Noddings, in traditional views, the human capacity for evil became associated with disobeying "the Father" and his representatives and has been firmly linked not only with sin, but also with guilt, impurity, and fault. One concern of writers such as Noddings is that this way of looking at evil has

> concentrated on the terror induced by disobeying a father, god, or authority, and thereby incurring its wrath . . . (this) turns the protector into a source of new terror and constructs ethics on a foundation of fear.[56]

And further,

> The turn to ethical terror rather than, say, ethical concern already posits a threatening parent or deity who may impose suffering for a mistake, transgression, or even a bit of misfortune. [57]

---

[54]Dorothee Sölle, "Suffering," in *New Handbook of Christian Theology,* ed. Donald W. Muser and Joseph L. Price (Nashville: Abingdon Press, 1992) 465.

[55]Ruether, 161.

[56]Noddings, 9.

[57]Ibid., 10–1.

Here, God becomes more a source of terror and fear, who sends suffering in order to correct and chastise wrongdoing. In this way, suffering becomes a sign of God's disfavor and wrath, and/or the individual's sinful, impure, guilty state. What is problematic is that this can lead to just the concern mentioned earlier by Sölle, that of blaming the sufferer for her/his situation rather than working to alleviate such suffering.

Rather than seeing God as cosufferer (as in the case of the suffering-God viewpoints) or protector/liberator (emphasized in liberation theologies in general), this traditional view distances the sufferer from God and sets up the model of fear-based relations that writers such as Noddings criticize. For Noddings, such a view distorts the relations between God and humans, from loving concern to fear of punishment, and leads to human relationships and actions that imitate such a fear-based relation.

This traditional view of evil as "disobedience to the patriarch" focuses attention on the divine-human relation, especially on appeasing God's wrath and avoiding punishment. Writers such as Noddings stress that, in so doing, the harm that we do to one another is not a primary concern.[58] "Although traditionalists consider that harm, they describe it as evil only when it transgresses the laws of God, state, father, or chief."[59] This sets the investigation of evil off on the wrong track, on a long and perhaps hopeless quest to be justified in God's sight. It distracts from consideration of God as possessing a loving attitude toward sufferers that would relieve and possibly eliminate their suffering:

> Since God, who clearly has the knowledge and power to do otherwise [since traditional theodicies emphasize both God's omniscience and omnipotence], inflicts or allows the greatest of suffering, the infliction of pain cannot be a *primary* ethical abuse. Since God hides himself from us, the neglect of a loving personal relation cannot be a primary evil, and the responsibility for remaining in contact falls to the weak and dependent. Since God presents the world to us in impenetrable mystery, there is precedent for mystification, and the dependent and powerless must learn to trust authority.[60]

[58]Ibid., 15.
[59]Ibid., 90.
[60]Ibid., 20.

Not only, then, does this distort one's image of and relation to the Divine, but it also sets a precedent in dealing with other humans in a way that emphasizes power, mystification, and punishment.

In challenging these views of sin as predominantly disobedience to God the Father and placing primary blame on women for the Fall and original sin, feminist theologies reevaluate evil from women's perspectives. In so doing, not only do writers such as Ruether and Noddings *deconstruct* the traditional views of evil, but they also attempt to *construct* new ways of viewing evil incorporating women's perspectives. Evil from the standpoint of women takes on some different characteristics than the traditional views express, as further demonstrated in the writers that follow.

## Some Additional Views of Evil and Sin from the Perspective of Women

As we have seen, evil for many women writers centers around the distortion and breakdown of relationality, particularly in the form of patriarchy and sexism. What also occurs in patriarchal systems, partially because of the lack of equality, are critical differences between male and female temptations to sin and evil.

An early pioneering article by Valerie Saiving Goldstein, widely debated in feminist circles, notes that women's particular temptations to sin can include "triviality, distractibility, diffuseness; lack of an organized center or focus; dependence on others for one's own self-definition; tolerance at the expense of standards of excellence; inability to respect the boundaries of privacy; sentimentality; and mistrust of reason."[61] More recently, Sandra Schneiders offers a similar list, including "weak submissiveness, fear, self-hatred, jealousy, timidity, self-absorption, small-mindedness, submersion of

[61]Valerie Saiving, "The Human Situation: A Feminine View," *Journal of Religion* 40 (1960)100–12. Reprinted in *Womanspirit Rising: A Feminist Reader in Religion* (San Francisco: Harper & Row, 1979) 25–42. For critiques of this view by other feminists, see Judith Plaskow, *Sex, Sin, And Grace: Women's Experience and the Theologies of Reinhold Niebuhr and Paul Tillich* (Washington, D.C.: University Press of America, 1980) 2–3; Susan Brooks Thistlethwaite, *Sex, Race, and God: Christian Feminism in Black and White* (New York: Crossroad, 1989) 78–9; and Sands, 43. Although the particular traits singled out as tempting to women may be questioned in their universal application, I do think this notion of a marked dif-

personal identity, and manipulation."[62] Whereas male primordial sin may center on pride and self-assertion (and, hence, the emphasis on disobedience), female sin frequently centers around fear of recognizing one's own competence and underdevelopment of the self. Although sin is viewed as a universal condition, it is, according to Sands, "differentially inhibiting to the full development of men and women."[63] The harm done to or by men may not be the same for women; while the resultant suffering can also be quite different along gender lines. As Elizabeth Johnson points out:

> If pride be the primary block on the path to God, then indeed decentering the rapacious self is the work of grace. But the situation is quite different when this language is applied to persons already relegated to the margins of significance and excluded from the exercise of self-definition. For such persons, language of conversion as loss of self, turning from *amor sui,* functions in an ideological way to rob them of power, maintaining them in a subordinate position to the benefit of those who rule. . . . Analysis of women's experience is replete with the realization that within patriarchal systems women's primordial temptation is not to pride and self-assertion but rather to the lack of it.[64]

Thus, situations and activities that induce and augment these conditions for women are considered evil and sinful, and result in further damage to women's full humanity.

A second alternative view of evil and sin occurs in a phenomenological study recently conducted by Nel Noddings. By looking at numerous examples of women's experiences with evil and reactions to ordinary events of life, Noddings discovers that whereas traditional theodicies view evil primarily as disobedience and separation

---

ference between the experience of sin and suffering by males and females in patriarchal systems is very important. In addition, I have found that these traits *do* apply to a large number of women that I have encountered—regardless of ethnic or socio-economic background or sexual orientation or whether they call themselves "feminist" or not.

[62]Sandra M. Schneiders, "The Effects of Women's Experience on their Spirituality," in *Women's Spirituality: Resources for Christian Development,* ed. Joann Wolski Conn (New York/Mahwah, N.J.: Paulist Press, 1986) 39.

[63]Sands, 43.

[64]Johnson, 64.

from God, when one assumes a woman's standpoint, evil often involves a pervasive fear of pain, loss or separation, and helplessness.[65] According to Noddings, when one takes the perspective of
those who, characteristically, have had responsibility for caring,
maintaining, and nurturing, evil is seen as those activities that in-
tend "to inflict or ignore pain, to induce separation or deny relation, to aggravate or ignore helplessness."[66]

Important to highlight in these definitions is that evil involves
the denial and neglect of ordinary *human* relations, in addition to
disruption of the divine-human relation. What Noddings has
found is that women are retrieving the importance of interpersonal relation and the religious significance of "the evil we do to
each other" as primary in their discussions of suffering:

> One of the errors of the Christian tradition, as we have seen,
> is to locate evil in bodily human life and to posit good in a
> spiritual realm vastly separate from ordinary human rela-
> tions. In this tradition the neglect of human relations rarely
> appears as evil because it is so often held to be justified by the
> search for God. Indeed, an undue interest in ordinary life has
> a close association with sin. But from the perspective of
> women's experience we will see that the neglect of relation is
> in fact a basic evil.[67]

Probably because women from every class and ethnic background
have historically fed, nursed, soothed, served, and attempted to relieve suffering in a myriad of relations, activities directed to particular others for their own sakes take precedence in much of this
thinking about evil and suffering.[68] Therefore,

> Real evil—moral evil—occurs when some agent causes . . .
> pain or fails to alleviate it when he or she is clearly in a posi-

---

[65]Noddings, 3, 120. These conditions are not evil in themselves, nor are they
always negative (90–1). E.g., sometimes, pain is "good" in its "biological purpose"
or in the sense of serving as a warning of damage—saving us from greater harm
or even destruction (e.g., to avoid crippling, death, disfigurement). We may use
physical pain to overcome temporarily psychic pain or mental anguish (93). Or,
pain can be good when it is accompanied by hope or happy anticipation, as in the
experience of childbirth.
[66]Ibid., 2, 113.
[67]Ibid., 101. Cf. 96, 100.
[68]Ibid., 108.

> tion to do so. . . . Morality is entirely bound up with how our best reflective experience tells us we should meet and treat each other, and this reflection demands a clear look at evil as that which harms us.[69]

Thus, the harm that individuals inflict on other human beings, whether physical or psychic pain, is of primary concern in many women's discussions of evil, and is seen as preventable through social reform, resistance, and reinterpretation of religious values and social policies.

From the experiences of women, not only pain, but fear of separation and the actual loss induced by real separation are also conditions for evil and suffering, according to Noddings. This separation can take many forms: in the death or desertion of previously close family or friends, in the separation from active engagement in life due to disease or aging; in a fear of being shut out of involvement in life by others; or in any physical separation that induces emotional pain uncompensated by fulfillment, relief, or other positive feelings.[70] It can also include a sense of abandonment or separation from God, as noted by Sölle:

> Suffering is the result of being separated by force or separating oneself from God's life-giving love. . . . It signals a rejection of our connectedness to one another and our separation from the giver of life.[71]

Thus, for many women loss of meaning and therefore, suffering, does not begin in a rejection of or a separation from ideas or principles but from loss of connection with God, other humans, and from ordinary life.[72]

Noddings identifies a third condition, or state of consciousness, associated with evil as experienced by women. Many women experience not only a sense of helplessness but also a mystification that sometimes sustains a "learned helplessness." Feelings of helplessness can run a range from more positive (e.g., when one is relieved of major responsibility and can allow another to take over for a

[69]Ibid., 99.
[70]Ibid., 94–5.
[71]Sölle, ibid.
[72]Noddings, 100.

while) to negative (as in a sense of having no control over one's body, mind, and life).[73] In a woman-centered view of evil within the context of patriarchal cultures, this latter form of helplessness is identified as a major condition for suffering. Anything that "thwarts our emotional sense of being able to or wanting to accomplish something," or "to be helpless when one wants to act, or worse, when one feels that one *must* act—that is an evil."[74] For Dorothee Sölle as well, fundamental to the experience of suffering is the consciousness that one is powerless, or that one's own behavior cannot determine the outcomes of a situation.[75] Such a condition generates anger, frustration, anxiety, and loss of purpose, and is, for the women in Noddings' study, a significant impediment to a sense of well-being, autonomous activity, and wholeness.

Another form of helplessness that can become a serious trap for some women is what Noddings identifies as "learned helplessness." This condition is induced by the conscious or unconscious desire to maintain a sense of dependency or helplessness, and thus, abdicate responsibility for dealing directly with the vicissitudes of life. "We can rest, stay at ease, feel certain that any efforts we might make would be ineffectual anyway and thus wasted."[76] This form of helplessness hinders some women from seeking alternatives to conditions in their lives, from going to the aid of others experiencing personal or social oppression, and sustains their own suffering in situations of neglect, subjugation, and violence.

Finally, women in Noddings' study also identify anxiety over bodily well-being and fear of death, as well as meaninglessness in the face of life's turnings as areas of suffering and conditions for evil.[77] Women fear and suffer from the physical and psychic pain that surrounds illness, torture, and abuse and which precedes death; the separation from loved ones and acquaintances that injury or death entails; and perhaps, most of all, the radical helplessness of conditions of violence and death. Since caring relations are so important to these women's experience of life, the separation

[73]Ibid., 94.

[74]Ibid., 93.

[75]Sölle, on powerlessness, in *Suffering*, 11.

[76]Noddings, 94.

[77]Meaninglessness is also fundamental to Sölle's understanding of suffering. See her *Suffering*, 11–2.

from people and ordinary life, whether through death or injury, can and does lead to a deep sense of anxiety, meaninglessness, and despair.[78]

For the women in Noddings' study, then, evil is "relational and positively real." It is not just the absence of knowledge or "the good," but can even be "the result of trying to do something either genuinely thought to be good or rationalized layer on layer in gross bad faith. Evil and suffering are thus intimately bound up in disputes over goods."[79]

In a third view of sin and evil from the perspective of women, Kathleen Sands heightens this sense that evil is a "something" and not a "nothing." For the traditional rationalist, evil cannot exist because it is a complete lack of goodness, complete unintelligibility, with nothing for its ontological referent. For Sands, on the other hand, evil is

> a negative moral judgment, but it is predicated on a positive ontological judgment. To pronounce something evil is to establish its existence, even while that existence is protested, resisted, refused, or terminated. Evil is not that which destroys itself but the decision to destroy; not that which is unintelligible but that which we may understand and yet refuse; not that which lacks being but the willful destruction or suppression of being.[80]

According to Sands, both ontological judgments and moral judgments are bound to conditions and limitations of consciousness as socially constructed. Moral judgments are always rooted in the interests of real persons and communities, and in a radically plural world, create conflicts of competing goods. Thus, "we cannot be for everything and what we are against has a cost."[81]

> The chaos of the world is therefore much more profound than if it were only a gap between the natural good and the estranged society. There are conflicts among compelling goods, conflicts among standards of goodness, conflicts among methods for achieving goods. The presumed paradise

[78]Noddings, 94.
[79]Ibid., 229.
[80]Sands, 8.
[81]Ibid., 9.

of unrepression, appealing at moments of relative powerlessness, offers little moral wisdom about how to create and destroy in the process of gaining power and wielding it.[82]

For Sands, that which has been called the "mystery of evil" is often
a mystification of ontological and evaluative judgments in their
distinctiveness, in their plurality, and in their interrelations. In her
definition, then, Sands attempts to heighten our awareness of the
ambiguities of evil, and points out that reliance on universal or
transcendent ideals can obscure our understanding of evil in a
postmodern milieu.

### Sands' Typology of Feminist Responses to Evil

Kathleen Sands has also identified three sets of responses to evil by
religious feminists. In her "appreciative critique," she notes that in
each set of responses, feminists (as well as traditional theologians)
demonstrate tendencies toward both dualism and rationalism in
their thinking on evil. Because her typology is helpful in identifying some additional contributions women are making in conversation with traditional views, I have summarized it below:

One pattern of revision, mostly among white feminists including Ruether, attempts to find a positive heritage and future for
women within Christianity and defends the ideal of a transcendent
God. Theologically, these responses vindicate the goodness of bodies and nature along with the goodness of women. In their focus
on preserving the transcendent dimension of God, they also tend,
according to Sands, to reject any unqualified identification of the
divine with the given and immanently real. God, or sometimes
Nature, is seen as an absolutely transcendent and inclusive good,
which grounds a universal intelligibility. Evils, such as male su-
premacy, are distortions or alienations beneath which the faithful
can discern a truth and goodness common to all.[83]

Besides Ruether, religious feminists such as Mary Hunt, Carter
Heyward, Rita Nakashima Brock, and Rebecca Chopp portray the
views of this first set of responses to evil. For Hunt, the problem of
evil became a problem of theological method in that feminist the-

[82]Ibid., 48.
[83]Ibid., 40-1.

ology represents a paradigmatic shift in the question of theodicy—depicting a shift in the genre of the question from doctrinal or speculative to practical and political.[84]

Carter Heyward reevaluates power and its role in evil and suffering. She has argued that "omnipotent or dominating power, far from epitomizing goodness, is the very paradigm of evil in the world."[85] Heyward and others have sought to redeem God with a relational ontology, rather than abandoning God in favor of a purely immanent goodness, and to redefine the divine as "our-power-in-right-relation." Thus, God is seen as a "good" form of power, that empowers the struggle for justice, as well as functions as the source of justice.[86] Power and goodness, redefined, are coupled in the divine, which can serve as a model for human relations.

Rita Nakashima Brock, Carter Heyward, Judith Plaskow, and Patricia Hunter all attempt to retrieve sexuality as a distinct good. Sex, frequently demonized in traditional theologies, is vindicated as an expression of eros—"a good kind of power, rooted in the relational character of created being."[87] The fact that eros has a disruptive, even painful side that cannot be blamed entirely on injustice is not denied, but

> that side too is hallowed among the rhythms of life, in the hope that erotic disruption may ultimately destabilize hierarchical rigidity. The implication, again, is that authentic "nature" can serve as a moral corrective to the inauthenticities of sociality

[84]Ibid., 44. Cf. Mary Hunt, *Feminist Liberation Theology: The Development of Method in Construction* [dissertation] (Berkeley: Graduate Theological Union, 1980) and her contribution to "Roundtable Discussion on Feminist Methodology," *Journal of Feminist Studies in Religion* 1 (Spring 1985) 83–7.

[85]Ibid. Cf. Bussert, who extends this view to the human plane in noting ". . . the fundamental problem undergirding [the] dominance-submission model for the family . . . is the issue of power. Any imbalance of power in a relationship inevitably makes it possible for one person to act abusively toward another . . . to displace hostility, frustration, unresolved anger, or just a bad day at work onto the next ones down in the pecking order—women and children. We need, instead, to begin using the language of mutuality and reciprocity when describing Christian relationships, and to develop new models for the Christian home based on a spirit of mutual regard, affirmation, and mutual understanding." Bussert, 61–2.

[86]Isabel Carter Heyward, *The Redemption of God: A Theology of Mutual Relation* (Washington, D.C.: University Press of America, 1982) 1–2, 6.

[87]Sands, 45.

. . . rape, abuse, and misogynist pornography . . . are instead accounted for as its [eros'] repression or distortion.[88]

Sands also briefly discusses Rebecca Chopp's theology of language, wherein "difference is assumed to be essentially good, while
injustice is thought of as the repression of difference." For writers
like Chopp, speaking openly and freely enhances specificity and
difference among women as well as between men and women,
while difference and even conflict can nurture a solidarity beneficial to all.[89]

For Sands, those who rely on the transcendence of the biblical
God, like the feminist theologians mentioned above, are often alert
to the rationalistic and dualistic patterns in the thought of traditional writers, but not within their own thought. In looking critically at these feminist writings on evil, for example, she notes:

> in Christian thought since Augustine dualistic patterns are
> bound up with rationalistic premises . . . dualism and ratio-
> nalism have been motivated not only by crude misogyny or
> antinaturalism . . . but by laudable intellectual and moral
> aims that religious feminists share. For example, by constru-
> ing the Ideal as transcendent, the feminists just discussed have
> been able to affirm the goodness of women without foreclos-
> ing the possibility of self-critique by and among women.
> Their rationalist belief that all genuine goods are part of a
> transcendent and inclusive Good has shown its advantages as
> well, by mandating a search for the points where apparently
> conflicting interests may become congruent or where various
> liberation movements may form alliances. These and many
> other feminists rely on patterns that I call rationalistic in the
> belief that these ideas support strategies for change that are
> more progressive, more realistic, and less violent than other
> alternatives. Their rationalism, in other words, is not only an
> intellectual but a moral commitment.[90]

However, for Sands the shortcomings of this rationalistic belief
in a transcendent Good, against which all moral actions and judgments are made, include false notions of the alleviation of suffering.

[88]Ibid.
[89]Ibid.
[90]Ibid., 46.

Politically, "an abstract, believed-in Goodness is dangerous because it can easily be made to substitute for real but limited solutions to social evils."[91] Further, by positing that all true goods must find their place within an inclusive and transcendent Good, this belief can lead to what Sands calls an "assumption of a natural congruence of goods" that experience does not bear out (e.g., when liberation of one oppressed group does *not* tend to support the liberation of others). Thus, as Sands warns us, "when ideals are accorded a transcendent reality of their own, they lose their ability either to affirm experience persuasively or to criticize it effectively."[92]

A second pattern of responses to evil by religious feminists, according to Sands, defends an immanent good. White feminists are again predominant here, including Carol Christ, Mary Daly, Charlene Spretnak, and Starhawk, all of whom have rejected Christianity in favor of goddess spiritualities or for what are often termed "postbiblical spiritualities." In this category, the world of patriarchy is unrelievedly evil, and thus, alienated, male-defined rationalities and structures are denied moral authority over women, the earth, and other endangered goods. Nature and women are the grounds of moral authority and immanent ideals.

The language of evil is directed outwardly against patriarchy, and becomes like the language of the "rejected Other" of traditional dualistic theology discussed earlier.[93] For example, writers such as Mary Daly see feminism in a struggle with evil, defined in part as a struggle between being and nonbeing. Patriarchal nonbeing, however, is not a harmless nothingness but "a murderous, systematic opposition to life and specifically to female being. Patriarchy is a reversal of being, a fabrication of lies, that must be seen and rejected in its totality."[94] The most effective way of dealing with this kind of evil, for Daly, is to separate oneself from it. In so doing, according to Sands, "evil guards the borders of a spirituality belonging specifically to women, in which diverse forms of pleasure, beauty, and power can flourish free from moralistic male surveillance."[95]

[91]Ibid., 47.
[92]Ibid.
[93]Ibid., 41–2.
[94]Ibid., 51.
[95]Ibid., 49.

Reinterpretations of evil in postbiblical feminism have also rejected the sense of sex as sinful and have incorporated "eros" as an
immanent ideal. Sexual experience is seen as a channel for the sacred, as in the writings of Starhawk, and sexuality expresses "the
moving force beneath all living forms." "Authentic eros" is contrasted with "sex as power-over," and is seen as a powerful force of
connection that enhances life rather than debases it.[96]

For Sands, these retrievals of the value and positive aspects of
sex and sexuality are both encouraging and limiting to the development of a better way of viewing evil in our lives. While postbiblical feminists like Starhawk illustrate a concrete, passionate
affirmation of life in their work, and their views lead to a prefer-
ence for integration and balance over repression and fragmenta-
tion, they also invite danger, "particularly when good desire is
equated with what is psychologically or socially powerful for us."
Sands (and I would agree here) believes that to judge something
as good ought to require more than to experience it as powerful—
this judgment needs to involve further reflection, for example, on
the ambiguities and consequences of such power.[97]

On the positive side, in postbiblical feminist circles, the mystical and aesthetic dimensions of religion are experiencing profound renewal. This has often fostered, within women-defined
spheres, more integral means of dealing with what has traditionally been viewed as negative, through imaginative and creative
forms of ritual, prayer, and art:

> When aging, decay, anger, and conflict, along with pleasure
> and harmony, are ritually evoked and celebrated, women are
> that much more able to tap into their strongest feelings and
> energies. In those transpersonal depths, many women find
> the wellsprings of the sacred. This has political dimensions,
> too: When we know what we feel . . . we can discern what we
> want and unleash energies to create it.[98]

To their credit, these women-centered spiritualities have not lost
sight of the need to ground their religious reflections in ongoing,
concrete religious experience.

[96]Ibid., 52.
[97]Ibid.
[98]Ibid., 53–4.

Of the shortcomings that Sands notes among this second group of responses by religious feminists, the most important is what she calls the "dualistic bifurcation of good and evil" in these writings. Responses to evil by religious feminists such as Daly often exhibit dualistic tendencies in that they interpret patriarchy as a separate, destructive counterreality. For example, male character is identified as rigidly analytical, manipulative, and dominative; whereas female character is inherently communicative, integrative, and connective.

Where moral language is applied (most often in reference to patriarchy), it "becomes simplistically moral*istic* and where moralism is not applied, there is no adequate vehicle for self-critique."[99] For example, these responses lack an adequate critique of racism and classism among women, as well as a critique of the inherited privileges that white women have benefited from despite patriarchy's negative effects.

And finally, these responses also need, in Sands' words:

> to encounter evil in its authentic mystery. That mystery, in my estimation, is something to be wondered about; it is not the cognitive closure that comes from tracing evil to male nature or any other ontological something. To encounter that mystery is to think about what we are doing in thinking evil, on what authority and at what cost, to other women and other men.[100]

The third and final pattern of responses to evil in Sands' typology is exhibited by Christian scholars of religion who are women of color. They "insist on treating evil as something to be changed rather than something to be understood or explained, so they measure responses to evil in terms of praxis, not in terms of theory alone."[101] Writers such as those represented in the anthology edited by Emilie Townes, entitled *A Troubling in My Soul,* focus on resources and problems specific to their own communities and histories and seek "to affirm the legitimacy of their own, culturally indigenous forms of Christianity."[102] In contrast to the postbiblical

[99]Ibid., 54.
[100]Ibid.
[101]Ibid., 42.
[102]Ibid., 55.

spiritualities, they are less likely to appeal to nature than to justice as the warrant for their ethical claims, and justice is used as a guiding metaphysical first principle and takes on a theological importance close to God.

What these writings by women of color frequently convey is that the evil and suffering that religion reflects and produces for nonelite women is very different than that for whites. For example, they challenge white feminists in their emphasis on abstraction and look for concrete political change. Battles against the suffering experienced by women of color are not just with ideas and symbols, but are also against social, military, and economic forces and therefore, stress the autonomous, systemic features of the oppression faced by women of color and nonelite men. Furthermore, womanists such as Delores Williams contend that "the concept of patriarchy 'leaves out too much,' in particular the responsibility of white women for the oppression of African-American women."[103] The encoding of cultural norms about racial superiority and sexual normality in such gendered symbols as "woman," "body," and "nature" are all considered problematic. Because of its current importance, more on this third response by women of color to situations of evil and suffering will be considered below in a later category of this schema.[104]

## Summary

What can be seen, then, from this overview of women's views of evil and sin is that "feminism represents a fundamental shift in the valuations of good and evil. It makes a fundamental judgment upon some aspects of past descriptions of the nature and etiology of evil as themselves ratifications of evil."[105] These women's discussions on evil emphasize the social and historical dimensions of evil as well as the personal and individual, and redefine evil in terms of distorted or broken relationships not only on the divine-human plane but also with respect to other humans and creation itself.

While often maintaining that sin is a corruption of authentic self, such women-centered discussions move from viewing sin as

[103]Ibid., 56.
[104]See pp. 140–9 below.
[105]Ruether, 160.

primarily disobedience toward God, concupiscence, and impurity, to a variety of forms of sin that lead to suffering for women and others. In these writings, sin is seen as false naming of the "other" as evil and inferior and involves the distortion of the self's boundaries. It can also involve the betrayal of trust, moral callousness, and the inability to accept one's own vulnerability. According to the experiences of the women studied, opportunities for sin and evil which result in suffering are more often associated with the fear of pain and separation, a sense of helplessness, and loss of meaning than with a condition of depravity and guilt.

These writings also move in their reflections on evil and sin from a devaluation of materiality to a reclamation of the goodness and value of the body, sexuality, and ordinary material creation. They reinterpret divine power as empowerment rather than as dominating power, and they identify concrete experiences in which women sense this power, as in eros, sexuality, and pragmatic movements toward justice. Along the way, they seek to unhook traditional views of the Fall from a tendency to scapegoat women as primarily responsible for the origin and continued existence of evil and reevaluate responsibility for changing the conditions of evil that lead to suffering.

In summary, feminist discussions of evil echo those of other liberation theologies in seeing suffering as not only individual but social, with roots in distorted social values and structural sinfulness. They echo process theology in emphasizing the shared responsibility of God and humans for changing situations of personal and systemic evil. They also emphasize the importance of relationality, and remind us that evil often predominantly involves a distortion or breakdown in relations with self, others, and with God. Thus, these writers advocate the primary role that humans, as well as the Divine, have in alleviating situations of personal and systemic evil and thus, in transforming situations of suffering into action and hope.

## CRITIQUES OF TRADITIONAL THEODICIES AND REFLECTIONS ON THE PASCHAL MYSTERY

Closely related to women's reconsiderations of evil are those writings that critique and/or reevaluate the "Augustinian"/punishment-

retribution, the Irenaean/remedial, and the redemptive suffer-
ing/atonement theodicies, and point out particular limitations and
potential dangers of these approaches in light of women's experiences. Although we have already raised some of these concerns,
writers such as Carter Heyward, Pamela Dickey Young, and Joann
Carlson Brown and Rebecca Parker address additional concerns
generated by these traditional theodicies.

### Augustinian/Irenaean Theodicies Critiqued

In *The Redemption of God,* feminist theologian Carter Heyward
returns to the passion of Jesus in order to reclaim for women the
importance of the paschal mystery, as well as to underscore its importance in her theology of mutual relation. Simultaneously, she
also reevaluates both the Irenaean and the Augustinian theodicies
and views these approaches to suffering as misdirecting our attention from the "here and now" and calling into question human
freedom, goodness, and responsibility.[106]

Heyward identifies the divergence between these two traditional views as one of theological emphasis. She views the Irenaean
approach as more "optimistic" in that it stresses that creation is
good and cultivates a theology that centers on humanity, whereas
the Augustinian approach is more "pessimistic" in that the emphasis is on the sin of fallen humanity and on the unbreachable distance between God's omniscience and goodness and humanity's
ignorance of good and evil. Although humanity is not evil in itself,
both theodicies see evil in history stemming from human turning
from God and God's intended purposes, and that Jesus has effected the resolution of the problem of evil in history.[107]

What is valuable in the Irenaean view for Heyward is that it
instructs us to accept the fact of our imperfection and yet to have
hope in the possibility of improvement. What she sees as most
problematic in this approach with regard to suffering is that it
seems to deny direct human responsibility for the evil in history.
Since God is ultimately responsible for humanity's original imperfection, which is at the root of moral evil, then humanity is "naturally imperfect" and "bound to sin on the basis of trial and error in

[106]Heyward, 108.
[107]Ibid., 108–9.

the world."[108] In the Irenaean approach, redemption is humanity's movement from imperfection to perfection, or attainment of the likeness of God, through trial and error. Thus, in Heyward's interpretation of the Irenaean theodicy, moral evil is functionally indispensable to our growth toward perfection; without it, we are not as likely to attain our likeness to God. So, as long as evil is viewed within humanity's movement toward perfection via trial and error

> evil is something we are learning our way out of rather than as a given in human experience; as something we outgrow, rather than as something for which we are *immediately* responsible.[109]

Heyward criticizes this approach as offering too quick a relief from the evil that we do to one another and in creation in the present. In her understanding of the Irenaean approach, what seems most important is not the question of how we make our way from imperfection to perfection, but more a faith in that movement itself. In this theologically optimistic view, all things work together (rather too neatly) toward an ultimate good, which will not be experienced until a far-distant future:

> Our attention is averted from present responsibility for evil in the world to an anticipation of future perfection, which is being effected by God—irrespective, ultimately, of what we do or do not do. In effect, we are being subsumed by divine process. . . . Our voluntary faith in this process is more important than our voluntary participation in it. Religion supersedes ethics.[110]

Such an approach depends on a human capacity to avoid sin and God's ability to bring good out of any evil, which advocates a passive or a submissive stance toward evil and suffering in the world. According to Heyward, "God's justification lies implicitly in humanity's *faith* that all evil remains mysteriously under the subjection of God's providential creativity and foreknowledge, and is functionally vital to humanity's moral growth."[111] God might even

[108]Ibid., 126.
[109]Ibid., 127.
[110]Ibid.
[111]Ibid., 116.

permit or ordain evil and suffering in this view, so that good can be more fully experienced in contrast to evil, thereby clarifying for us the distinction.

But, for Heyward the question becomes, what, then, does it take for God to intervene, given the legacy of historical violence? When will God act, and under what conditions, to save people from senseless suffering—only "in some future arena of human and divine life?"

> This understanding of redemption presupposes the ultimacy of an essentially ahistorical deity and the penultimacy of human life in the world. It presumes a scale of higher and lower values: God is more valuable than humanity; heaven, more valuable than earth; the future realm of God, more valuable than present relation. To understand redemption eschatologically is to attribute penultimate value to ourselves and to what we experience as real in the present world. There is always something more, something better, than our life together on earth. Even such a moral outrage as the Holocaust cannot be taken with *ultimate* seriousness, for, in the end, God will redeem the world, including . . . victims of humanity's injustice to humanity.[112]

In this way humans are ultimately relieved from responsibility for what happens in history, and this can lead to the infliction of untold atrocities on others and an unwillingness to see what we can change in terms of suffering.[113]

For Heyward this process transcends our individual and collective choices to sin or not sin, or even to proceed as a part of this divine process of soul-making or not. Thus, it not only removes our responsibility, but also overshadows any individual experience of relation to God that we can choose to accept or reject. "In short, we do not need *relation* to God. We are *in* God. . . . God has been perfect all along . . . and hence is completely unaffected by our choices and acts."[114] Thus, in her critique Heyward joins many other women writers in underscoring the negative effects this ap-

[112]Ibid., 131.
[113]Ibid., 130.
[114]Ibid., 127.

proach has on both ethics (person-to-person relations) and on
faith (person-to-God relations).

While Irenaeus can be faulted for his failure to acknowledge
our immediate responsibility to come to terms with our own evil
effects and questioned for suggesting that God permits evil and
suffering merely to provide a contrast between good and evil,
"Augustine can be cited as having failed to acknowledge emphati-
cally our immediate responsibility to know and do what is good in
the world." Whereas Irenaeus denies the radicality of evil and the
role of human choice in doing good and evil, Augustine, the other
side of the coin from Irenaeus, emphasizes the self as "universally,
unavoidably, and irresponsibly corrupt," caught in a thoroughly
evil condition and bound to make harmful choices.[115]

For Heyward both solutions to the problem of evil and suffering "fall short of helping us understand ourselves as agents of both
moral good (justice) and moral evil (injustice) in the world."[116]
One looks forward to an eschatological resolution (Irenaean) and
the other looks backward at a lost, primordial state of innocence
(Augustinian).[117] Both can lead to a passive acceptance and resignation in the face of present suffering, and thus, can lead to little
change or amelioration of unjust situations. This leaves the faithful waiting for God to change things, whereas Heyward believes
we should claim the responsibility we do have for making changes
toward a just and less tormented world. For Heyward, then, redemption does not come in a heaven above the world, or in some
end time of history, but in what she calls an "immediate redemption," a "liberation of human beings from unjust relation in the
present world," which seeks "to make right relation between and
among ourselves here and now."[118]

## Redemptive/Atonement Theodicies Critiqued

Another area of theological debate among feminists regarding suffering is that of the redemptive suffering of Jesus and theodicies

---

[115]Ibid., 128. Cf. lengthy discussion above in the previous section on evil for
more on problems raised by the Augustinian approach.

[116]Ibid.

[117]Ibid., 131.

[118]Ibid., 132.

that utilize this as an explanation and model for human suffering. As Flora Keshgegian states, throughout Christian doctrine and devotional practice,

> the remedy for suffering is . . . found in the salvation offered through the life, death, and resurrection of Jesus Christ. Especially in Western Christianity, the passion and cross of Christ have been regarded as the locus of God's action for salvation. As a result, Christianity developed the notion of redemptive suffering: suffering as a good or necessary condition for salvation and as imitative of Jesus Christ's saving act.[119]

Feminists and many others from groups experiencing oppression and violence find just this point difficult—how can suffering be seen as a means to salvation?

More specifically, how can Jesus' death be seen as salvific? For many women, a tradition that elevates the death of a son wherein the father silently stands by, condones, or wills this death appears as a form of "divine child abuse," and portrays a God who advocates cruelty and violence, even to one's own beloved.[120] Joanne Carlson Brown and Rebecca Parker, two of the most vocal critics of atonement theodicies, note that this can have consequences beyond the theological and religious, in that

> the image of God the father demanding and carrying out the suffering and death of his own son has sustained a culture of abuse and led to the abandonment of victims of abuse and oppression. Until this image is shattered it will be almost impossible to create a just society.[121]

For many critics, such a response to suffering raises serious questions. How can one be reconciled to God through such a death? And why would one even *want* to be reconciled to such a God?

Further, as Pamela Dickey Young points out, if the suffering of Jesus is the necessary condition for God's forgiveness and for reconciliation, even if it is not seen as one person of the Trinity "punishing" another, "it still runs the risk of glorifying suffering in the

[119]Keshgegian, 279.
[120]Rita Nakashima Brock, *Journeys by Heart: A Christology of Erotic Power* (New York: Crossroad, 1988) 53–70. Cf. Brown and Parker, 2, 26.
[121]Brown and Parker, 9.

name of forgiveness. Wherein is the *necessity* of the suffering of God in the incarnate Jesus Christ, unless imposed by God on Godself as a condition of restoration of relationship?"[122] In traditional approaches, the belief that Jesus must necessarily suffer and die *as a human* in order for salvation and reconciliation to be effected appears to be for the sake of formulaic or contractual agreements, focusing on God's honor above God's value and love for humanity.[123] As Brown and Parker contend, "it may be that this fundamental tenet of Christianity—Christ's suffering and dying *for us*—upholds actions and attitudes that accept, glorify, and even encourage [our] suffering."[124]

What is more, contend critics of the redemptive/atonement theodicy, if Jesus, the paradigmatic human, suffered, then suffering becomes an example "to be lauded, sought, or imposed on others to aid human-to-human relationship."[125] Due to the fact that such a view has been disproportionately applied to women, as we have seen and will see in further sections of this schema, feminists point out that this suffering of Jesus is used uncritically as an example to be imitated by the faithful. Since women are most often assigned the role of suffering servant in Church and society, some believe it encourages martyrdom and the continued victimization of women.[126]

For example, Brown and Parker's discussion of the moral influence form of traditional theodicy (originating with Abelard and continuing today in varied forms of both traditional and liberation theologies) notes that such theodicies are often

> founded on the belief that an innocent, suffering victim and only an innocent, suffering victim for whose suffering we are in some way responsible has the power to confront us with our guilt and move us to a new decision. This belief has subtle and terrifying connections as to how victims of violence can be viewed. . . . Sometimes this amounts to using the victims for someone else's edification.[127]

[122]Pamela Dickey Young, "Beyond Moral Influence to an Atoning Life," *Theology Today* 52 (1995) 348.
[123]Ibid. Cf. Brown and Parker, 4, 7–11.
[124]Brown and Parker, 4.
[125]Young, 349. Cf. Brown and Parker, 2.
[126]Brown and Parker, 3, 12–3.
[127]Ibid., 12.

The problem with this, for Brown and Parker, is that it asks the innocent and powerless to suffer in order to bring the evildoer to repentance and change. It elevates concern for the evildoer above that for the sufferer, and "makes victims the servants of the evildoers' salvation."[128] In so doing not only does it perpetuate the view that suffering is part of a divinely-ordained process of personal and social transformation, but it also ignores the responsibility and choice of the evildoer to change.

Thus, as Young also points out, "to place suffering at the center of the Christian tradition does not affect everyone equally."[129] Some are expected to follow the example of this suffering Jesus more than others, due to the very social, political, and religious systems that need changing. Such a theology "can lead to extended pain . . . to destruction of the human spirit through the death of a person's sense of power, worth, dignity, or creativity . . . it can lead to actual death."[130] According to these critics, such a theology can result in the continuation of much of the suffering women experience that *can* be alleviated. With these concerns in mind, how, then, can we understand and reinterpret "a tradition that would seem to glorify suffering by portraying it as central to redemption?"[131]

As a starting point, it is important to note that, for writers such as Young, a focus on the physical suffering of Jesus on the cross misplaces the emphasis of reconciliation. For Young, the moment of reconciliation is not in the physical suffering in and of itself, but in the moment of forgiveness, in the offer of renewed relationship, in ". . . that continuous offer of grace, of integrity, of fellowship restored . . . experienced by followers throughout Jesus' life and in his resurrection, not solely, or even necessarily, in his suffering."[132]

What has happened in the traditional views is that the restoration of broken relationships through Jesus' encounters with those he met *throughout* his ministry has been downplayed, while salvific emphasis has been placed on Jesus' death over and above his life and ministry.[133] As Young points out, if, however, atonement is in-

---

[128]Ibid., 20.
[129]Young, 345.
[130]Brown and Parker, 7.
[131]Young, 344.
[132]Ibid., 349.
[133]Ibid.

tegrally linked to incarnation, then the whole event of Jesus Christ, rather than only or primarily his death and resurrection, can be seen as God's gracious overcoming of the powers of sin, death, and evil.[134] Seen in this way, suffering, though part of the process of reconciliation, is not the *necessary condition* for restoration of wholeness and relationship. Thus, suffering is not something that necessarily should be actively sought in order to restore or mend a broken world.

For Young, in this movement beyond the traditional views of Jesus' death as *the* saving or atoning act par excellence, Jesus' death is but one embodiment of the suffering of God, which is "part of the process but not the whole of the act of reconciliation."[135] What is significant in Jesus' suffering is that God bears ("suffers")[136] in God's very self the evils that humans do to one another and to God, and still offers reconciliation—not as a one-time past event but as a continuous offer. As Young sees it, "the powers of evil are neither set aside nor conquered but *taken up into God* who, in spite of them, offers the grace that enables us to resist and to mend."[137]

What is also important to note here, I believe, is that it is God who takes up and bears this type of suffering, and not humans. In this view, Jesus' human suffering and death is not a necessary condition for reconciliation, but God's suffering in Jesus is "the result of creaturely actions against God and one another. The crucifixion makes clear the pain that creatures have caused for God,"[138] but it also makes clear, for me, that it is God and not us who ultimately bears this kind and level of suffering and effects the process of reconciliation.[139] For me, in Jesus' suffering and resurrection is a message that it is God who disempowers the sin of the world so that it no longer allows the suffering or affliction to be "our lord" and we its "slaves," as Simone Weil would say. Lou Ann Trost makes a similar point in that

[134]Cf. Lou Ann Trost, "On Suffering, Violence, and Power," *Currents in Theology and Mission* 21 (1994) 38–9.
[135]Young, 352.
[136]See Helen Luke, n. 26 in chapter 2.
[137]Young, 351 [my emphasis].
[138]Ibid., 352.
[139]Cf. Patricia Wilson-Kastner, *Faith, Feminism, and the Christ* (Philadelphia: Fortress Press, 1983) 99–100, 105–6.

Atonement theory must be held together with justification by grace through faith. . . . The grace is that we do not have to, we cannot, save self or others. Here the Reformation principle of justification by faith can guard against faulty interpretation. If it is God who "justifies," who "makes righteous," who forgives and heals, then Jesus' suffering, death, and resurrection mean God identifies with us in suffering. The power of God to confront death and give new life empowers victims with the courage to confront perpetrators of violence in the confidence that God has ultimate power of life and death.[140]

Not only does God bear such suffering, but also moves beyond that to an offer of grace and restored relationship for all involved—evildoer and victim.

This does not mean, however, that the powerless should be sacrificial instruments for the reconciliation of others. It does not mean

that God courts or wishes suffering, either for Godself or for God's creatures. Suffering that could have been prevented is an evil to be resisted. That grace is possible despite suffering is a testimony to God's love not an argument for more suffering.[141]

According to Young and others, this means that Jesus' death should not be viewed as a glorification of suffering, but should be seen as the product of human evil, not divine will. What is important in Jesus' life and worthy of imitation is his resistance to evil and his refusal to compromise with that which destroys life, rather than what has often been viewed as his passive acceptance of suffering and death.[142]

That in Jesus' death we can see a resistance to human evil does not make the death salvific. That in death we recognize the full humanity of Jesus and know that all must die does not make violent death a matter to be lauded. It must itself be resisted as evil.[143]

[140]Trost, 38.
[141]Young, 354–5.
[142]Cf. Brown and Parker, 18.
[143]Young, 353.

Writers, such as Brown and Parker, also critique some of the contemporary reevaluations of the traditional theodicies, including the suffering-God approach with its emphasis on patient endurance of suffering for a greater good and liberation approaches which highlight the necessity of suffering in the historical process of struggle for liberation. For example, they raise a number of issues with regard to the suffering-God approach, including the following concern:

> By confusing "suffering with" with action that does something about evil instead of asserting that testifying for life is what sustains justice, the Suffering God theologies continue in a new form the traditional piety that sanctions suffering as imitation of the holy one. Because God suffers and God is good, we are good if we suffer. If we are not suffering, we are not good. To be like God is to take on the pain of all.[144]

Thus, the suffering-God approach suggests that the more one suffers, the closer one approaches God, and yet the more one legitimates violence done by people resistant to grace and abundant life. The main problem with this theodicy, according to Brown and Parker, is that it suggests that suffering and pain are tantamount to love and form the foundation of social action.[145]

Moreover, in rethinking these traditional interpretations of the suffering and death of Jesus, one needs to reconsider not only the concept of atonement or reconciliation, but also to reevaluate such theological categories as original sin and anthropology (what it means to be human) in light of our contemporary postmodern context. For Young, as an example, interpretations of the saving work of Jesus must be seen within a context where the human predicament (that which we need to be saved from) involves "a lack of integrity, a lack of wholeness in relation."[146] Suffering, in

---

[144]Brown and Parker, 19.

[145]Ibid. Moreover, cf. Wismer's question "Exactly how . . . does God's suffering with us actually help eliminate, or at least, mitigate, our suffering?" in Patricia L. Wismer, "For Women in Pain," in *In the Embrace of God: Feminist Approaches to Theological Anthropology,* ed. Ann O'Hara Graff (Maryknoll, N.Y.: Orbis Books, 1995) 142.

[146]Young, 346.

her view, is the result of the breakdown of integrity, but it also destroys integrity.

Further, we are born into a world or a condition "where living human life to its fullest and bringing out the fullness of life in others (human and nonhuman) is not the norm but the exception."[147] We come into an already-given world of "original sin," characterized by alienation, broken relationships, and lack of integrity, and often experience this condition on an intellectual level as a "lack of meaning or a search for meaning."[148] Thus, for writers such as Young, the violent suffering and death of Jesus does not speak so much of salvation or redemption, but of this condition of human evil, brokenness, failure, and lack of integrity. Stated in a slightly different way, Jesus' suffering epitomizes what happens to humans in the midst of a world characterized by such sin. In this way, it leads us to the knowledge of our need for salvation from such evil, as noted by Carter Heyward in the following:

> The experience of suffering—actual endurance of pain—is foundational to an authentic understanding of the *need* for redemption. It is not that we should "seek suffering" as a spiritual path. Rather, we cannot avoid it if we are living fully, human, passionate lives in solidarity with one another and other creatures.[149]

Also, since the powers of evil and sin continue to exist in the face of a God who, in the traditional view, is thought to have definitively conquered them in the atoning death of Jesus, for many writers God's goodness is frequently called into question when suffering continues, especially of the magnitude witnessed in this century. In a search to retain God's goodness as a primary divine attribute, writers like Young call for a reconsideration of God's power or omnipotence in light of the continuing existence of suffering.

> If our view of God's power is not a view of the coercive power of one who can unilaterally bring about an end to sin, death, and evil but is a view of a relational power that wills the over-

[147]Ibid.
[148]Ibid.
[149]Isabel Carter Heyward, "Suffering, Redemption, and Christ: Shifting the Grounds of Feminist Christology," *Christianity and Crisis* 49 (December 11, 1989) 381 [my emphasis].

> coming of sin, death, and evil and yet, in God's freedom, can-
> not override the freedoms of creatures, then we need to find a
> different way to talk about what God does in Jesus Christ . . .
> a view of God's power as relational rather than as coercive
> gives a way to understand the goodness of God and the sal-
> vific will of God in the face of the continuance of evil.[150]

In her view, if one sees God's power as relational, then one's expectations of what God and humans do are somewhat different
than the traditional approaches might advocate. Rather than expect God to override human freedom, or rather than blame God
for the freedoms exercised by others,

> what one does do . . . is affirm that God offers to the world
> the best possible range of choices in the exercise of freedom
> and responds to the exercise of creaturely freedoms in ways
> that seek to elicit the best possible creaturely responses.[151]

Young, along with other theologians from liberation and
process perspectives, hope to retain the goodness of God and reinterpret the meaning of God's power in the face of ongoing suffering. God's power, for many of these writers, is not omnipotent and
almighty. By modifying this view of God's power, they shift the
focus on what God does alone to alleviate suffering to include what
humans can and should do in the present to help eradicate the evil
and suffering that is within our control.

Thus, in reconsidering the redemptive/atonement theodicies,
writers such as Young, Brown, and Parker highlight the way such
theodicies often dismiss the actual suffering people experience, as
well as how such viewpoints particularly affect women. They also
reevaluate aspects of God, such as God's omnipotence and control
over every facet of life, while attempting to retain God's goodness
toward humanity and creation. In so doing, some writers hope for
a theology of the cross that does not glorify suffering, but retains
the centrality of the cross for Christian life.[152]

[150]Young, 350.

[151]Ibid. Cf. Wismer's discussion of "power-over" vs. "power-with," in "For
Women in Pain," 142.

[152]Wismer, "For Women in Pain," 143. Cf. Sharon Garred Thornton, *Pastoral
Care and the Reality of Suffering: Pastoral Theology from the Perspective of a
Theology of the Cross* (Berkeley: Graduate Theological Union, 1991).

In all these instances that critique both the traditional and the more contemporary theodicies, many of the feminist writings that I surveyed challenge how any form of suffering can ultimately be helpful or redemptive. Rather than propose that we merely endure suffering, even for a greater good in some cases, they advocate a focus on a commitment to life and vehemently oppose uncritical acceptance of the "suffering servant" model. In the words of Brown and Parker, "suffering is never redemptive and suffering cannot be redeemed."[153]

> It is not acceptance of suffering that gives life; it is commitment to life that gives life. The question, moreover, is not, Am I willing to suffer? but Do I desire fully to live? This distinction . . . makes a great difference in how people interpret and respond to suffering.[154]

While this point is well-taken, another voice offers a contrasting view to that of Brown and Parker, in particular, and the re-evaluations of atonement theodicy, in general. Lou Ann Trost notes that christological interpretations like that of Brown and Parker make Jesus into merely a model for us, and she agrees that such an exemplary model can be and is easily abused as a justification for victimizing the powerless and condoning ongoing suffering.[155] As a corrective, what she calls for is the incorporation of a trinitarian/incarnational model that emphasizes the work of God in Jesus and the Holy Spirit. For her:

> atonement must be held within the context of the doctrine of incarnation, of belief in the trinitarian God whose creative love is ever healing and restoring the world, who in Jesus frees all from the powers of evil, whose ultimate life-giving is in Jesus' resurrection and sending of the Holy Spirit.[156]

In Trost's view we are not called upon to repeat the saving event of Jesus, but to face suffering and support resistance against evil in all its forms. The example of Jesus and other martyrs should

---

[153]Brown and Parker, 27.
[154]Ibid., 18.
[155]Trost, 38.
[156]Ibid.

not be used to keep the powerless in a place of suffering or to accept needless suffering or death, but neither should it be jettisoned, since it provides a means of courage and hope for many sufferers in desperate situations. In contrast to Brown and Parker, Trost believes that using those who have suffered before as figures of hope and examples of a life of courage and resistance can enliven the struggles many people have in dealing with their own experiences of suffering. It is thus their lives, and not their suffering and deaths, that give hope to the anguished and oppressed.[157]

Trost also aids us in seeing Brown and Parker's claim that suffering is never redemptive in a slightly different light. She portrays a more nuanced view than they: for her, it is not the suffering that is redeemable but the "person's *life* which is redeemed *from* suffering, bondage, sin, and death. It is in the light of such redemption, seen as healing, that that which someone *has* suffered can be interpreted in such a way that it is not determinative for the rest of her or his days."[158] In this view, suffering itself is not being elevated as something to be imitated, but is recognized as a real condition from which most people need ongoing healing and release. Therefore, the suffering itself is not redemptive, but it is God in Christ and the Holy Spirit, in the gospel (the "good news") which carries the freeing power of God, that can redeem persons and lives from bondage to sin and suffering.

## THEOLOGICAL REFLECTIONS THAT UNCOVER AREAS NOT FORMERLY CONSIDERED IN THEOLOGY

Centrally connected to these concerns over the traditional theodicies, some feminist writings also raise critical awareness of women's suffering that results from particular situations of violence against women, initiated by men but also by other women. This third category of writings by women highlights concrete, often

---

[157]Trost, 39. Cf. section on womanist views of suffering, pp. 140–9 below.
[158]Ibid., 40. Cf. Pamela A. Smith, "Chronic Pain and Creative Possibility: A Psychological Phenomenon Confronts Theologies of Suffering," in *Broken and Whole: Essays on Religion and the Body,* ed. Maureen Tilley and Susan Ross (Latham, N.Y.: University Press of America, 1995) 179: "Suffering, it seems, is that which one ought to hope to be redeemed or liberated from, not redeemed or liberated by."

hidden or overlooked areas of suffering that afflict women in particular. These works may deal with a wide range of concerns such as domestic abuse, sexual assault, and homophobia,[159] and identify traditional religious beliefs and practices that have contributed to such suffering. I shall cover some key points made in the abuse literature in particular, because abuse affects so many women across ethnic and socio-economic boundaries and because this literature exemplifies the work currently being done regarding women's experiences of suffering.

One area that has been neglected by previous theological discussions that is now receiving greater attention by women writers is how traditional views of God, atonement, suffering, and women have affected those who have experienced physical and sexual abuse or assault.[160] Based on her work as the director of the Center for Prevention of Sexual and Domestic Violence in Seattle, Marie Fortune notes that women who have been raped, battered, and/or sexually abused as children often attempt to understand their suffering in light of their religious beliefs. They repeatedly raise the now-familiar questions of their suffering: Why do I suffer in this way? Where is God in my suffering? and Why is there suffering at all? Such questions entail not only the cause and source, but also the meaning or purpose of their suffering.[161]

---

[159]Due to limitations of space, I have not delved into the emerging literature on homophobia and theology. See, as starting points for an investigation into this area of suffering for women, "Misogyny and Homophobia: The Unexplored Connections," in Beverly Wildung Harrison, *Making the Connections: Essays in Feminist Social Ethics,* ed. Carol S. Robb (Boston: Beacon Press, 1985) 135–51; and "Sexuality and Social Policy," 105–8.

[160]Some startling statistics indicate the prevalence of abuse toward women and the importance of including the experience of these women in a discussion of suffering: one out of five women in the United States is battered; one out of seven married women is sexually abused by her husband; almost one out of two women will become a victim of completed or attempted rape in her lifetime. Domestic violence is *the* major cause of injury to women. Cited in Engel, 152. Cf. R. Emerson Dobash and Russell Dobash, *Violence Against Wives: A Case Against the Patriarchy* (New York: Macmillan, 1979) 72–4: "The fact is that for most people and especially for women and children, the family is the most violent group to which they are likely to belong. Despite fears to the contrary, it is not a stranger, but a so-called loved one who is most likely to assault, rape, or murder us," quoted in Bussert, 21.

[161]Marie F. Fortune, "The Transformation of Suffering: A Biblical and Theological Perspective," in *Christianity, Patriarchy, and Abuse: A Feminist*

What Fortune and others have also found, though, is that the traditional theological responses to suffering are highly unsatisfactory and even deadly for women who are afflicted by pervasive and prolonged physical and sexual abuse. That God "permits" evil and suffering and "chooses" not to intervene in order to preserve humanity's free will is a highly untenable resolution to the violence these women experience repeatedly to their person or that the children in their care experience. Rather than provide these women with understanding and resolution to their situation, the incorporation of traditional views of the meaning of suffering has often led many women to further and more pronounced trauma.

For instance, in seeking answers to their questions surrounding suffering, women who are victims of physical and sexual abuse, like most sufferers, look for someone responsible or reasons for the assault or abuse they experience. Due in part to the traditional theological viewpoints discussed earlier in this chapter on women, sexuality, and sin, that search most often results in blaming God or themselves, rather than the actual assailant. "She understands the situation to reflect God's acting to bring about her suffering for a justifiable reason; she blames herself and accepts her battering as God's will for her."[162] The battered woman, rather than seeing God as a liberator from such a situation, sees God as the ultimate instigator of her trauma because of her own lack or fault. Rather than seeing that she could resist such violence and utilizing time-honored traditional approaches to suffering, her religious beliefs and community often counsel passivity, guilt, and acceptance in the face of such violence:

> The purpose of suffering is then the lesson it teaches, and the result should be a stronger faith in God. Purposefulness somehow softens the pain of suffering. If some greater good is salvaged, then perhaps the suffering was worth it.[163]

---

*Critique,* ed. Joanne Carlson Brown and Carole R. Bohn (New York: Pilgrim Press, 1989) 139. I am grateful to Jane Grovijahn for her referrals to this and other works in the abuse literature, as well as her insistence on the importance of seeing the theological implications of these materials for my discussions of suffering. Cf. Bussert, 69.

[162]Ibid., 140. Cf. Engel, 155.

[163]Fortune, 141.

We should wonder, though, whether it is truly worth it at such a
high cost to the woman, her husband, and her children.[164]

Fortune has also repeatedly found that battered women often
believe their current rape, beatings, and/or devaluation are due to
some previous "sin" or act on their part, and that God is punishing
them in the present as a form of judgment for an act of the (often
distant) past.[165] As Joy M. K. Bussert also finds:

> Particularly if she grew up in a religious tradition that honors
> the inherent value of each individual person, that all persons
> are created in the image of God and are deserving of respect
> and consideration—and yet that has not been her experience
> in her own life—she will begin to turn inward and try to lo-
> cate the source of the problem within herself. As women
> begin to ask "Why?" and there doesn't seem to be any appar-
> ent reason for the abuse, they can only conclude that "there
> must be something wrong with me. I must have done some-
> thing to deserve this. I must be no good." Many women spend
> hours recalling the little wrongs they committed as children,
> wondering if God is punishing them for past "sins."[166]

Although this is seen in a pronounced way in work with women
who have experienced sexual and physical abuse, I would also add
that this is a common habit for many women, in general, who experience suffering—to look for fault in themselves first and foremost—due, in part, to the way women have often been viewed and
socialized within Christian tradition and society as a whole.

In this way the traditional sensibility of guilt, which may be
helpful in a situation in which a person has actually committed a
grievous act, is, in the situation of sexual assault and violence,
twisted and inverted in a way destructive to these women. Guilt, in
this case, functions to continue the violence, oppressiveness, and
suffering—not to turn it around or alleviate it. Evil, in this case, becomes an obfuscation of the truth and a misuse of a valid sensibility (guilt) for destructive ends.

According to Fortune and Bussert, this happens in part because victims of domestic violence rarely identify their actual

[164]See, e.g., "A Batterer's Perspective," in Bussert, 87–90. Cf. Bussert, 41–53.
[165]Fortune, 140.
[166]Bussert, 70–1.

abuser as responsible for the violent acts that destroy their physical, emotional, and social well-being.[167] Although blaming herself or God allows the woman to explain what is happening to her and to gain some control over her seemingly senseless situation, this displacement of her anger and blame on God and herself can deflect her attention from questioning, confronting, resisting, and protesting the actual perpetrator of her suffering. By blaming God or herself, the abused woman does not even question the abuse or violence, which produces little motivation to seek justice or resolution for herself and for others, such as her children, that may be affected or involved.[168] Her anger inverts itself as blame toward herself as the cause or at God as the source for her being singled out for such suffering. This further drives her from potential sources of healing, separates her from the love of God that could enable and empower her to seek change for this situation, and often leaves her with a sense of powerlessness and abandonment.

As an alternative, Fortune suggests that a reinterpretation of God as "righteous anger" at the actual persons and circumstances causing the suffering in cases of domestic violence and sexual assault, and as a "source of compassion" in the midst of acts of violence might prove more healthy and life-enhancing than seeing God as the author of the violence (for whatever "good" reason) that afflicts these women.[169] Carter Heyward also advocates such a stance, and grounds her view with a discussion of Jesus' anger as depicted in the Gospel of Mark. She sees Jesus' most characteristic expressions of pain as irony, indignation, and rage as alternatives to self-doubt, depression, and impotence, and links this anger with his prophetic courage and love of humanity:[170]

> Jesus' anger [except in Mark 15:34] was not at God, or "reality," or "life," or "the world," or "the way things are." The anger was not diffuse or unfocused. Jesus' anger had a specific target: non-relation, broken relation, violated relation, the destruction of

---

[167]Fortune, 140. Cf. Bussert, 30.

[168]Ibid., 143. Wismer also notes that women often move too quickly to forgiveness before experiencing their own anger, which leads to repression and denial—a form of "short-circuiting" the pain, "For Women in Pain," 144.

[169]Ibid., 141. Cf. Engel, 156.

[170]Heyward, 55.

God in the world: injustice, misuse, and abuse of humanity
by humanity.[171]

In seeking other ways of dealing with the suffering of abused
women, writers such as Bussert, Fortune, and Mary Potter Engel
who work in direct ministries with these women also look to the
roots of Christian tradition for some of the underpinnings of violent behavior by males toward females. They all vehemently critique the tradition within Christianity that glorifies self-sacrifice
and obedience for women, that emphasizes the mind-body dualism
inherited from Greek philosophy, and that views women as inherently evil and inferior to men.[172] Kathleen Sands also more point-
edly notes that "the violence and exploitation that women suffer
as women are not simply due to social structures in the abstract,
but to the entrenched and familiar privileges of maleness."[173]

For example, Bussert notes that the views of Tertullian and
Augustine have been used to justify woman's subordinate status to
man, which has led to a domination-submission dynamic often expected or taken for granted between males and females. ". . . since
femaleness was equated with the inferior body, it followed that
woman must naturally live in submission to man in hierarchical
fashion, even as the body must be subject to the spirit, in the right
ordering of the Christian life."[174] She points out that the writings of
theologians such as Luther are used to buttress the view that, because of the Fall, woman must accept her assigned subordinate role
in life, as it is commanded by God, and obey her husband absolutely:

> The woman bears subordination just as unwillingly as she
> bears those pains and inconveniences that have been placed
> upon her flesh. The rule remains with the husband and the
> wife is compelled to obey him by God's command. He rules
> the home and the state. . . . The woman, on the other hand,
> is like a nail driven into the wall. She sits at home and for this
> reason Paul . . . calls her a domestic.[175]

[171]Ibid., 56.
[172]For example, see Bussert, 6–8.
[173]Sands, 53.
[174]Bussert, 9.
[175]Martin Luther, *Luther's Works,* ed. Jaroslav Pelikan (St. Louis: Concordia
Publishing House, 1955) vol. 1, *Lectures on Genesis,* 68–9, quoted in Bussert, 11.

This insistence on the absolute obedience of the woman to her husband has been one of the repeated justifications for domestic abuse—inflicting physical punishment to "correct" disobedient wives or demanding sexual attention as a wifely duty.[176] Writers such as Bussert highlight this link between religious doctrine and women's suffering in order to show that doctrines that are developed without the involvement and consideration of women's experiences can have violent consequences, such as the suffering incurred through physical and sexual abuse:

> Men today who come into the treatment programs for violent partners are men who suffer from this culturally imposed mind-body split within themselves and who choose to project it outward onto women through physical violence. They are products of the verbal violence contained in the writings of the religious thinkers of our inherited past. This verbal violence, as we have seen, is rooted in a profound sense of alienation from self, God, and others and continues to foster hatred toward women and provide the theological ammunition for violence against them.[177]

Another contribution that Fortune and others have made to the discussion of suffering from the perspective of women who experience physical and sexual abuse is to remind us to distinguish among types of suffering. In order to understand or find meaning in experiences of trauma and anguish, Fortune suggests that one must clearly distinguish between voluntary and involuntary suffering when making religious claims regarding value and meaning. Voluntary suffering occurs when the individual or group *chooses* the painful experience in order to accomplish a greater good, whereas involuntary suffering never serves the greater good because it is *inflicted* by one on another, against one's will.[178] In the former case, one chooses to suffer the consequences of one's commitments even in the face of oppressive authority that threatens one's life, while in the latter, suffering comes from the infliction of power over another human being. Therefore, choice in suffering can make all the difference in how the suffering is incorporated

[176]Bussert, 12.
[177]Ibid., 15.
[178]Fortune, 141–2.

into one's life and/or resisted or protested, and how such suffering leads to a greater fullness of being or a destruction of one's person.

Another major theological problem that arises for writers such as Fortune and Bussert is the habit of condoning or accepting abuse by using Christ as a model of suffering and self-sacrifice to be imitated, in particular, by women. As noted previously, mainline contemporary theologians frequently utilize the "suffering servant" theme as a visible reminder of God's identification with those who suffer, in order to offer solace and hope. The "suffering-God" approach has been used to comfort battered women, but, for writers such as Bussert, this perspective does not "carry the biblical message far enough":

> I find in working with battered women that all too often the direct application of this theological perspective to a woman's life-experience actually serves to glorify suffering and reinforces her belief that it is "Christ-like" to remain in a violent relationship. We need, instead, to begin articulating a faith that will provide women with resources for strength rather than resources for endurance.[179]

Fortune also debates the "suffering servant" interpretation of the paschal mystery with the point that Jesus' crucifixion was "a witness to his love, not his suffering," and does not advocate a love of sacrifice, but is to be seen as an "act for right relation."[180] For her, the view that Jesus' suffering was moved by love and not by a preoccupation with sacrifice is more in keeping with the overall Christian proclamation of the "good news."[181]

Fortune also uses the example of Jesus' encounter with the man born blind (John 9:1-12) to suggest a different response toward suffering to imitate. In her view Jesus *heals* the man's blindness; he does not spend time finding someone to blame for the man's condition but restates the search for meaning in terms of concrete, pragmatic action. Rather than discussing its cause, Jesus acts to relieve suffering and provides us with a model of action,

---

[179]Bussert, 65.

[180]Fortune, 142.

[181]Cf. Lucien Richard's discussion of Edward Schillebeeckx, *What Are They Saying about the Theology of Suffering?* (New York/Mahwah, N.J.: Paulist Press, 1992) 4, 7, 34.

rather than blame-finding, in the face of suffering.[182] So should we act to heal ourselves rather than simply and passively sacrificing ourselves. For Fortune, as well as for many feminists, the real question is not "why" suffering occurs, but what do we *do* with the very real suffering that exists?[183]

Fortune distinguishes another set of potential responses to suffering: that of endurance vs. transformation. Underlying the endurance approach is the view that holds God ultimately responsible for suffering and includes the twin beliefs that God is both omniscient and omnipotent. Because God is all-knowing and all-powerful, the cause and meaning of suffering lie in God's control. Thus, endurance becomes a viable means of dealing with suffering within this framework because the suffering must be deserved as punishment or endured as a moral example, or otherwise God would alleviate it. This can lead to what Fortune calls a "doormat theology" wherein it is "God's will" that people suffer and our only recourse is to endure and passively submit to suffering when it occurs. Consequently, "this understanding of the meaning of suffering comforts the comfortable and afflicts the afflicted but ignores the demands of a God who seeks justice and promises abundance of life."[184]

For Fortune and others, there is no virtue to endurance if no greater good for all is at stake. For example, endurance does not usually help the abuser (although a desire to help the abuser is one reason women commonly voice for remaining in the abusive situation) for it does not bring him to repentance or redemption.

Rather than endurance, Fortune contends that the paschal mystery points to another interpretation of suffering. This interpretation does not sanction or sanctify suffering, but points to the possibility of new life coming forth from the pain of suffering—the paschal mystery points to transformation. For her, as for Bussert, the key lies in seeing the suffering of Jesus on the cross in light of the resurrection and subsequent events:

> The resurrection and subsequent events were the surprising realization that in the midst of profound suffering, God is

[182]Fortune, 143.
[183]Ibid., 146.
[184]Ibid., 144.

> present and new life is possible. . . . It is not a model of how
> suffering should be borne but a witness to God's desire that
> no one should have to suffer such violence again.[185]

The paschal mystery is not a witness to the suffering that God
sends to appease a wrongdoing, to chastise disobedience, or even
to provide an occasion for transformation, but a witness to the
love through which God counters suffering with life. It is a witness
to "the faith that the way things are is not the way things have to
be."[186]

According to Fortune, women who experience personal violence can rely on the message of Jesus' suffering and resurrection:
that God is present in the midst of their pain but also in their
movement away from the situation of violence, as they utilize
whatever means available within themselves and from others to do
so. In so doing, the sufferer moves from a powerless, passive position of victim (who waits for God or someone else to help her) to
a more mature, confident position of caring for herself with the
help of God and others. Bussert identifies this as a movement from
a "theology of suffering" to an "ethic of empowerment which
would enable her to begin reconstructing a new life for herself and
her children."[187] Thus, for Fortune and others, "endurance means
remaining a victim; transformation means becoming a survivor,"
with God's help.[188] In this way the passive, self-sacrificing victim
can become an agent for her own transformation.

What this literature on abuse and assault adds to our understanding of suffering for women is multifaceted and is similar to
what the work of Latin American liberation theologians has done
for the conditions of poverty and political oppression. These writers show how traditional theological responses have failed many
women in their struggles to understand their experiences of suffering and, as in the case of domestic abuse, have actually com-
pounded women's suffering. Thus, this literature highlights the
importance of selectively and critically using traditional sources,
perspectives, and categories (such as sin, guilt, self-sacrifice, and

---

[185]Ibid., 145. Cf. Bussert, 66.
[186]Ibid., 146.
[187]Bussert, 66.
[188]Fortune, ibid.

obedience) in understanding and discussing suffering generated from such situations as domestic abuse and rape.

These writings also reevaluate behaviors previously believed to be sinful (such as anger) and retrieve their positive use in actually assisting people in finding healing and resolution for their suffering. These contributions by women to discussions of suffering also emphasize the critical role that women sufferers themselves need to take in alleviating situations of abuse and oppression. This entails choosing to take a different stance toward the suffering in their lives that focuses on what one *can* do, rather than assuming that nothing will change, that the problems are too large and insurmountable, and that God somehow ordains this suffering. In so doing, healing and hope are possible in situations that are otherwise destructive to the flourishing of women's full humanity.

## "WRESTLING WITH GOD" WRITINGS

A fourth category in this schema of women's writings on suffering receives its title from the recurring phrase or metaphor found in most of these works. Born out of the writer's own experiences, these works take the writer's daily life experiences of pain and limitation as grist for her reflections on God, humanity, and God-human relations. These works, unlike many of the writings surveyed thus far in this schema, speak of an encounter with God's presence in the midst of pain and suffering, a restored sense of hope, and an opening up of possibilities not seen prior to the experience of suffering. Pamela Smith, Melanie May, Elizabeth O'Connor, and Jean Blomquist exemplify the writings in this category.

### Pamela Smith

In a paper presented at an annual meeting of the College Theology Society, Pamela Smith discusses what she calls "the uncanny psychic kinship between pain and imagination." Based on her own life-long experiences with chronic illnesses, as well as on those of many others whose lives have been marked by both substantial limitation and "resolute creative activity," she observes that the experience of pain does not inevitably produce "psychic and emotional paralysis." On the contrary, such pain and limitation often lead, quite unexpectedly, to a connection between chronic pain and "creative possibility."[189]

For instance, according to Smith's study, many who are afflicted by chronic illness and disabilities perceive their physical limits as actually helping them to structure their creative projects. Their physical limits, isolation, and marginalization serve to give them considerable freedom from outside demands. Moreover, many experience and exhibit unusual "energy boosts" and remarkable abilities for concentration, which they specifically relate to their imposed limitations and which, for a time, even mitigate the manifestations of their illness.[190] In these cases, such illnesses or conditions are not imagined by the sufferers to be totally debilitating or crippling, and thus are not perceived as overruling everything else in their worlds.[191] For them, what is frequently more important than their illness or suffering is the creative project at hand.

What seems significant here is that at times, the person's sense of purpose and drive to create can overshadow the effects of the condition or illness. In some cases, reports Smith, the need to create is so great in an individual as to actually "*generate* an illness which provides the person with both the limits and the freedom he or she must have to be able to create."[192] Thus, the drive to create is served by an illness or condition "which is not excruciating but is bothersome, does require attention, imposes some limits, and demands a mitigation of certain types of activities."[193]

Also noted by Smith are individuals who imagine their condition as serving a greater purpose and who incorporate humor in dealing with the negative effects of their illness. Many, she reports, who sense a greater purpose for their lives and work beyond the pain that they experience and who use humor to confront the daily

---

[189]Smith, 159. Cf. Elaine Scarry, *The Body in Pain: The Making and Unmaking of the World* (New York: Oxford University Press, 1985) 205, 218. Smith's study includes a wide range of sources besides her own experience, such as her work with children, teenagers, young adults, mid-lifers, and seniors, as well as selected written sources that serve as case studies of the link between pain and creativity.

[190]Ibid., 162. Cf. Janet K. Ruffing, "Physical Illness: A Mystically Transformative Element in the Life of Elizabeth Leseur," *Spiritual Life* 40 (1994) 220–9.

[191]Ibid., 164.

[192]Ibid., 163 [my emphasis].

[193]Ibid.

limits imposed by their condition experience a temporary suspension of the debilitating effects of their ailments. This, she believes, is corroborated by recent biomedical thinking that links "positive and negative stress to multiple endocrine effects [e.g., endorphin production] and significant changes in the total sense of well-being in a human."[194] Even in those with significant disabilities, the creative work and the sense of purpose surrounding it provide, in many cases, extended moments of relief, of "self-forgetfulness and pain-release."

Juxtaposed with some of the findings by Eric Cassell and David Morris discussed earlier in this work, it is interesting to consider that suffering, in some cases, can be used to serve creative purposes, to enhance creative focus and direction, and can even keep adverse effects of an illness at bay, particularly in the most intense phases of the creative process.[195] The suffering experienced in these cases is not a completely debilitating event, but is used to further the interests and goals of the creative chronically ill.

Smith, echoing the insights of Elaine Scarry, also contends that the creative process itself is a means for the re-creation or redefinition (the "remaking") of the self. As Scarry notes, the artifact, or thing made from the creative process, is not the only product of the creative activity. "The object is . . . a fulcrum or lever across which the force of creation moves back onto the human site and remakes the maker."[196] For Smith, too, creative action alters the very reality of the one who undertakes it, and part of its purpose is to "remake" the creative person as well. As she states:

> The work of the chronically ill, chronically pained person, can be understood as restructuring a world, a life, and a personal identity fractured or impaired by disability. Such reality-alteration can truly be a lifeline: an assurance that the whole of reality is far better and far more manageable than the grim moments of suffering imply. The creative process itself is the route to the realization of a vision. It is also a means to the re-definition of the self.[197]

[194]Ibid. Cf. Cassell's discussion on the ability to alter the experience of suffering in chapter 2, pp. 25–30 above.

[195]Ibid., 164.

[196]Scarry, 307.

[197]Smith, 166.

The pain, vulnerability, and marginalization that the chronically ill and disabled do experience in much of their lives are, in these moments, relegated to the periphery of their lives, and, at least for a time, the self is experienced as "skilled, accomplished, and powerful." For Smith, then, through the process of creation, some chronically ill or disabled people experience an "embodied transformation" or "remaking" of the self.[198]

According to Smith and Scarry, this transformation involves a refashioning of "pain to pleasure," as these sufferers "somehow believe that the world, life, and they themselves are transformed by what they dream and do. Meanwhile, they have enjoyed the pleasure of being consumed in their work, wedded to it, made fruitful."[199] Because they are able to be engaged and productive, the creative chronically ill often risk exhaustion and subsequent major physical setbacks to create their artifacts, but also to experience this "emergence of a new self beyond the self."

While Smith recognizes the potential hazards of endorsing an uncritical view of such suffering,[200] as cautioned also in previous sections of this chapter, she also concludes that "the creative chronically ill both relieve their pain and reshape their lives by their creative production." In so doing she and Scarry believe not only does the pain inflicted by unremitting disease, oppression, war, battering, and physical injuries render people isolated and immobilized, it can also lead to a situation wherein the person's world is actually reconstructed or remade—what Scarry calls an "act of imagining" or "belief" that can transcend and transform the body's pain.[201]

What this implies, then, is that through some types of suffering (perhaps, that which is determined ineradicable by changes in human conduct, or that which is categorized as natural evil), some individuals are led to a transformation of that very affliction, but also of the self that is so afflicted. If one agrees with Smith, how one perceives and creatively uses adversity and suffering, then, can lead to the degree to which one is debilitated by it or not—thus influencing the impact of the suffering. For Smith, then, physical and

---

[198]Ibid., 166–7.
[199]Ibid., 167.
[200]Ibid., 170–5.
[201]Ibid., 159. Scarry, 205.

psychological suffering can be, although not always is, an occasion for transformation.

## Melanie May

In a moving depiction of her own personal "wrestlings" with God in three painful bodily experiences of suffering, feminist theologian Melanie May relates that in and through such wrestling, she has become a "believer."[202] Through her own struggles with pain and suffering, which have demanded she confront her own finitude and lack of control, May has experienced revelations of divine presence and human connectedness.

For example, at the height of excruciating physical pain from a spinal cord inflammation, when "even the vibration of footfalls on the floor was virtually unbearable," a paradoxical will to live surged through her like a "roaring inside."[203] Very close to death and in response to this roaring, what she "knew" she needed at that moment was "connection," and quickly contacted a close friend. Through the vigil and prayers of that friend, May subsequently experienced "a rush of presence pervading the room."[204] According to her friend, the room was filled with "a great, glowing light," and May experienced what she portrays as "a resurrection reversal. Death indeed not an ending but a new beginning."[205]

According to May, through such intense suffering experiences, she has learned a number of crucial things about being a woman who suffers. First, that she is not merely finite and in possession of a body, but that, to a great extent, she *is* her body.[206] In contrast to the traditional notion that one must transcend one's body in order to attain spiritual knowledge and release from suffering, May encounters a revelation of "an ever-faithful Presence" *via* her body, *in the midst of her bodily existence* of pain and limitation, at the point where she was most vulnerable and most lacking her own control

---

[202]Melanie May, *A Body Knows: A Theopoetics of Death and Resurrection* (New York: Continuum, 1995) 14. As Elizabeth O'Connor notes, "It is when all is lost that we ask from the center of being the questions on which life hangs," "Creative Suffering," in *Our Many Selves* (New York: Harper & Row, 1971) 95.

[203]Ibid., 24.
[204]Ibid., 29.
[205]Ibid., 30.
[206]Ibid., 18.

over what was happening.[207] As Elizabeth O'Connor has also said about suffering's ability to bring us to an encounter with something beyond our own understanding:

> Suffering has the possibility of stabbing us awake. It shakes us out of accustomed ways so that we see ourselves as we are, powerless to change, yet needing change. . . . Suffering can drive us deep into ourselves where, not on the surface of our lives, but at the center of being . . . [we] stand in the way of receiving an answer. Suffering has the possibility of showing us the One that we have heard of.[208]

Through these experiences, May thus learned that "what our bodies know is a life-giving source of . . . knowledge of God."[209] And, what her body "knew" and "articulated" was "the truth that to be alive is to be connected," with oneself, with others, and with God.[210]

Such experiences of suffering also prepare us, according to May and others, to be persons of authority, an authority which derives not from belief in certain teachings or external sources, but from a presence that can be directly experienced within the self:[211]

> I begin to believe authority is bearing witness in one's body— word and deed—to the Good News so people can see and come to seek promised life abundant . . . bearing witness is revelatory, not regulatory.[212]

As O'Connor also echoes, "that is the witness of faith. It does not come from outside oneself. It grows up inside, cradled in the griefs of a hundred nights. If we live, we discover that our suffering was also the seedbed of our faith."[213]

Moreover, as a counterpoint to passive submissiveness and resignation in the face of suffering, May has also found in her experiences of anguish that

[207]Ibid., 69.
[208]O'Connor, 99.
[209]May, 23.
[210]Ibid., 40.
[211]Cf. O'Connor, 100.
[212]May, 73.
[213]O'Connor, 95.

presence heals hopelessness, heals hopelessness that resigns
and reckons reality is fated and so sets up barriers against our
selves, one another, and God. To speak of presence, then, is
also to speak of communion . . . that is anticipated in hope
wherever the struggle for survival and life abundant still goes
on. The promise of presence is, in this sense, what Paul
Ricoeur has spoken about as an "affirmation . . . [of] the
restoration of [human] positivity," as an "upsurging of the
possible," on the other side of ennui, exile, and evil.[214]

By reflecting on her own experiences of pain, human limitation,
and vulnerability, May identifies a changed perspective in herself—
one that testifies

not to apathy or bitterness or cynicism or despair in the face
of human impotence or life's tragedy. I did not conclude we
were best counseled to resign ourselves to an inexorable momentum by which the world and we with it would inevitably
be swept along or away. My changed perspective was a gesture
of grace in the face of life's mystery, the mystery that grief and
ecstasy, as dying and rising, are always mingled moments.[215]

For her, then, embodied life has to do with mystery, ambiguity, and paradox. It has to do with vulnerability and limitation,
and that without an awareness of our limits, we are imprisoned in
an untruth.[216] Embodied life is life in which we become aware that
we cannot "do it all" ourselves, alone, and that we are not in control. "For to tell the truth is to be possessed . . . by a message that
comes to us to upset the safety and security we would preserve
and protect."[217]

But, embodied life also has to do with bearing witness to the
truth of God's presence, in the here-and-now, even or especially in
the midst of such human impotence and tragedy:

We who would be possessed prepare ourselves by being present
to ourselves, to one another, and to God—by recognizing the
promise of revelatory presence. . . . The promise of revelatory

[214]May, 69.
[215]Ibid., 17–8.
[216]Ibid., 18.
[217]Ibid., 88.

presence is realized when we lay our bodies bare, ready and
willing to become the flesh of our words.[218]

What I think she means, partially, by this is that when we do really
let go and allow ourselves to suffer and be in pain, to stop running
from the pain, and recognize that we are not always able to control
it or our lives, then we can come to an encounter with meaning
and with God's healing presence.[219] When we have exhausted all
our own efforts marshaled against the suffering, we can encounter
a presence that is life-giving, survival-making, and hope-produc-
ing. This is similar to what O'Connor speaks of in an "acceptance"
of suffering:

> There is a suffering which we overcome by struggling with it,
> and there is a suffering which we overcome by acceptance.
> . . . If we are *willing to experience* our suffering, which is
> what is meant by acceptance, it will in turn allow us to go on
> to the claims of new feelings that belong to different hours.[220]

Anticipating that some may take this as an admonition to suffer senselessly, May also emphasizes that this "witnessing" through
one's bodily experiences of pain and vulnerability must always involve choice and assent. She insists, "I speak of laying my body bare,
not of *being* laid bare, not of violation. I speak of a choice, a choice
made after counting the cost of doing so in our violent society."[221]
Consequently, such experiences of suffering, as May depicts,
have also led her "to explore new and life-giving forms of human
connection, in relation to [her] family and community, but especially what it means to be the church today."[222] Thus, not only were
these encounters with God transforming for herself individually,
but also suffering experiences that led to enhanced relationships
with others.[223]

[218]Ibid.
[219]Ibid., 100. Cf. Jean Blomquist, *Wrestling till Dawn: Awakening to Life in
Times of Struggle* (Nashville: Upper Room Books, 1994) 13.
[220]O'Connor, 94 [my emphasis].
[221]May, 88.
[222]Ibid., 20–1.
[223]Cf. Blomquist, 122–3.

## Jean Blomquist

In *Wrestling till Dawn,* Jean Blomquist exemplifies the type of writing by numerous women of faith who tell their life stories of "personal challenge and loss, of confusion and pain, of wrestling to see the face of God, [and] of striving to live in faithfulness." Here, she represents those women who seek to find understanding in the midst of doubt, disease, guilt, worthlessness, and a sense of failure—who "wrestle in fear with the power of the unknown" and "recognize the rawness, roughness, and reality of struggle."[224] In the course of reflecting on such common experiences as her divorce, the death of her mother, ill health, depression, and financial problems, Blomquist adds to our understanding of suffering through the lens of women's experiences in three ways.

First, she portrays that through some of her experiences of vulnerability and pain, she became paradoxically "less rigid, more accepting, more cognizant of others' pain." Her own pain gradually "opened" her heart and "broadened" her faith, and helped her to accept others as they were, complete with feelings and reactions that adversely affected her.[225] For example, rather than severely judging or blaming herself and closing inward on her pain, Blomquist notes that she became able (in the case of the breakdown of her marriage) to be more compassionate through confronting her pain. By accepting or confronting her loss, guilt, and vulnerability, she began to be more receptive to God's presence with and compassion toward herself, which consequently, enabled her to become more compassionate with others.[226]

Such acceptance of suffering, for Blomquist as well as for O'Connor and May, is not a passive endeavor, but is "an active, dynamic process," in which acceptance is "lived into" or "wrestled into."[227] Thus, ironically, the more she embraced her vulnerability, the stronger and more open she became—the more her horizons and boundaries of self expanded.[228] As she notes:

[224]Ibid., 14–5.
[225]Ibid., 26.
[226]Ibid., 47–9, 52.
[227]Ibid., 39.
[228]Ibid., 25.

Persevering through hard times . . . can mean that we will
develop an added depth as persons, a greater resiliency in life,
a greater capacity for love and compassion, a truer sense of
who we really are and of how to care for ourselves and others. Our struggles, instead of defeating us, can help us move
more fully and faithfully into life.[229]

A second contribution that Blomquist's writing provides is an
alternative view of the action of surrender in suffering. For most
feminists the term "surrender" is very loaded, highly suspect, and
potentially deadly for women who have experienced prolonged
marginalization and oppression. However, for Blomquist, surrender takes on new meaning in the context of her own experiences of
suffering, particularly as she addresses the limitations imposed by
her lupus condition:

In many ways, surrender is at the heart of my pursuit of healing. . . . Surrender is not an abandonment of ourselves in
the face of difficulty, nor is surrender synonymous with submission. We yield ourselves to God freely, not under coercion.
Surrender is not resignation. It is an invitation into something
greater, fuller than ourselves. It is also an invitation to be ourselves more fully.[230]

Important to note here is that this yielding is voluntary, and such
yielding is not to the suffering or to an abuser imposing the suffering, but is the giving of our suffering to God, like an offering.
For her, then,

Surrender is not so much a giving up as it is an *opening* up. It
is a dynamic living and striving in the face of the unknown.
When we surrender in faith, we enter into the power of God,
into the realm of all possibility. We open ourselves to new
perspectives, thoughts, and dimensions of life and living yet
to be explored. We do not give ourselves up in the sense of ex-
tinguishing ourselves, but instead the little lick of light we are
joins with the holy flaming that is God. We are brought more
fully into ourselves and at the same time brought into that
fullness which is greater than all that is. . . . My surrendering

[229]Ibid., 14.
[230]Ibid., 67.

> to the power of God involves a reaching, a yearning for what
> is beyond. . . .[231]

Thus, in this type of surrender as an offering, one does not abolish oneself in the suffering but moves into a new dimension wherein the self is enhanced by a power beyond oneself.

A third contribution that Blomquist makes to our understanding of suffering is that even though we move through and beyond certain experiences of suffering, the mystery of suffering remains. She highlights that the movement beyond experiences of loss, separation, death, and failure does not automatically answer all the questions we have regarding suffering in our lives—such as, how does such suffering bring us to a truer sense of self? Nor does it answer whether or not we have to suffer in such a way in order to gain such knowledge. For her, even as suffering subsides, such questions remain.[232] What she has learned, though, is to live more with and into the questions, and to see that, at times, the greatest joy can rise from the deepest pain.[233]

In summary, then, I propose that the "wrestling with God" writings represented in this section most closely relate to and build upon the final traditional theodicy discussed in the previous chapter—the faith category. It seems that for many women, the faith response, which includes resistance and protest as well as surrender and trust, still provides a viable perspective for some women in pain. As Elizabeth O'Connor speaks of the writers of the Hebrew Bible and the New Testament, so do her words apply to the women writers represented in this section:

> They find suffering integral to life. They resist it, petition God
> to remove it, question it, endure it, rebel against it, accept it.
> As they wrestle with their suffering, they find they wrestle
> with their [God]. Something happens to them—something as
> radical as new birth. The burden of their message does not be-
> come suffering but change—transformation.[234]

---

[231]Ibid.
[232]Ibid., 27. Cf. Sidney Callahan, "A Mother's Death: Is This What God Demands?" *Commonweal* 123 (May 17, 1996) 7–8.
[233]Blomquist, 27, 114. Cf. Wismer, "For Women in Pain," 149.
[234]O'Connor, 99.

What these writings speak of, then, is that the way of life is arduous and risky, ambiguous and unexpected; but also, fruitful, involving encounters with meaning, renewed possibility and hope, and with a faithful presence—both divine and human.

Oddly, it seems to me, few feminist evaluations of suffering address this category except in the negative consequences that a faith stance has effected on women. As an alternative, these writings, represented by Smith, May, O'Connor, and Blomquist, are thus a much-needed voice in a phenomenology of women's suffering since they speak not only of substantial distress and limitation, but also of an intimate encounter with God and with new meaning in the very midst of suffering. In the following chapters I shall use this category of writings as a cornerstone for hope in constructing a theological/spiritual response to the suffering of women.

## EXTENSIVE THEOLOGICAL INQUIRIES INTO SUFFERING THAT INCORPORATE WOMEN'S STORIES AND EXPERIENCES

### Dorothee Sölle's Study of Suffering

In a now-classic work on suffering published more than twenty years ago, Dorothee Sölle delineated one of the few comprehensive views of suffering by a woman theologian. Although her study is not focused solely on the experiences of women, women's stories of suffering help to ground her theological viewpoints in the concrete and particular, and thus, her study can serve as a viable framework for discussion here. In addition, since her views have significantly affected many of the writers included in this chapter, I believe her work is of prime importance to the development of North American feminist theologies of suffering.[235]

One of the most useful aspects of Sölle's study for women's experiences of suffering is the critical link she makes between lan-

[235]Rather than go through her study point-by-point, it seems more helpful here to highlight some important factors in her understanding of suffering from a theological perspective. Moreover, because her work is pivotal for the development of my own "mystical/political" spirituality in response to suffering, I shall forego an extensive discussion of all her views here, but shall incorporate some of her contributions in the following chapters. Please also note that her work has been used to augment the views expressed elsewhere in this work.

guage and suffering. As shown earlier in the discussions of the work of Elaine Scarry, Eric Cassell, David Morris, and Simone Weil, two of the most difficult aspects of suffering are its inexpressibility and the personal and social isolation that ensues from such experiences. Sölle concurs with them, in that for her

> . . . one of the fundamental experiences about suffering is precisely the lack of communication, the dissolution of meaningful and productive ties. . . . To stand under the burden of suffering always means to become more and more isolated.[236]

In order to move through and out of situations of suffering, the sufferer must therefore find a way, according to Sölle, to identify, express, and share her situation. Although some may speak for others in cases of extreme suffering, it is essential that the sufferer herself participate in the articulation of her own pain in order to find healing and change.

In advocating the importance of language and expression for confronting and overcoming suffering, Sölle identifies three phases that provide movement out of the destructive effects of suffering, using experiences as widespread as debilitating factory conditions to the consequences of war, from repressive domestic roles to excruciating physical and psychological torture to guide her observations. As she finds, the process of pain begins with a state of numbness (what she calls Phase One), wherein one is unable to speak, think, or act on her own behalf or for others. This phase includes a sense of pronounced helplessness, generated by the weight of affliction, and a sense of powerlessness to change the situation (comparable to the findings of Cassell depicted in chapter 2). Hallmarks of this stage of suffering include muteness and isolation, a turning-in on the pain which is frequently characterized by chronic submissiveness and resignation. The level at which one may communicate one's experience is in "animal-like" wailings and moaning, but most often is found in silence. The sufferer's behavior is reactive and defensive, and she has no apparent productive way to express her pain or to extricate herself from the situation.[237]

[236]Sölle, *Suffering,* 75.
[237]Ibid., 69–70.

For some, though, who seek to confront their suffering, a desire to find a language that expresses what the suffering is like moves them into Phase Two of Sölle's process through suffering. This stage involves attempts at establishing communication with others, and is characterized by lament and a crying out against the situation creating the suffering. Petitioning and prayer occur, with particular emphasis on one's own innocence. For Sölle, prayer, especially, can be essential in resisting suffering in our contemporary society. As she notes:

> in industrial society prayer is "in itself a subversive act—an act of 'shameless' self-assertion over against this world." It is an act by which people dare to put their desires into words and thereby handle their suffering differently from the way society recommends to them. Prayer is an all-encompassing act by which people transcend the mute God of an apathetically endured reality and go over to the speaking God of a reality experienced with feeling in pain and happiness.[238]

In this second phase, through prayer and other forms of expression, the sufferer utilizes both rationality to analyze the condition of suffering but also emotion to articulate what is actually happening, in a language akin to the psalms.[239] As Sölle emphasizes:

> I consider the stage of lament, of articulation . . . to be an indispensable step on the way to the third stage, in which liberation and help for the unfortunate can be organized. The way leads out of isolated suffering through communication (by lament) to the solidarity in which change occurs. . . . By giving voice to lament one can intercept and work on [her] suffering within the framework of communication. The hopelessness of certain forms of suffering . . . can be endured where the pain can still be articulated.[240]

Moreover, becoming more sensitized to and descriptive of one's suffering also allows for a certain distance or autonomy to develop with regard to the situation. As echoed by bioethicist Eric Cassell, this "ability to remain autonomous requires that things

[238]Ibid., 78.
[239]Ibid., 71–2.
[240]Ibid., 74.

over which one has no control do not remove all of one's choices or the ability to choose."[241] Through this distancing, the sufferer is able to see her situation from alternative perspectives, and, in so doing, makes a way for some articulation of hope for change.

For many women who have been counseled to remain silent in their suffering, this second phase of articulation seems particularly significant. If one agrees with Sölle, and it seems reasonable to do so, expression in the form of petition, prayer, and protest can therefore help move some sufferers from despair and potential death to the beginnings of hope and new life. As she states, and my own experiences support:

> If people cannot speak about their affliction they will be de-
> stroyed by it, or swallowed up by apathy. It is not important
> where they find the language or what form it takes. But
> people's lives depend on being able to put their situation into
> words, or rather, learning to express themselves, which in-
> cludes the nonverbal possibilities of expression. Without the
> capacity to communicate with others there can be no change.
> To become speechless, to be totally without any relationship,
> that is death.[242]

Phase Two, then, not only helps the sufferer to depict and share with others the situation as it really is for her, but also "presses beyond itself" to another stage in which solidarity with other sufferers moves into action for change.[243]

In Phase Three, the suffering is intensified, to a certain degree, in that the sufferer begins to see the situation in such a way that she can no longer camouflage the painful aspects of her situation from herself and others. This produces new conflicts, both internal and external, which can subsequently provide an impetus for change. On the more positive side, solidarity with other sufferers develops through the expression and identification of one's pain with others', and together, new questions and options for changing the situation

---

[241]Cassell, 1902.

[242]Sölle, *Suffering*, 76. Cf. Dana Crowley Jack, *Silencing the Self: Women and Depression* (New York: Harper Perennial, 1993) and Ann Wilson Schaef, *Women's Reality: An Emerging Female System in a White Male Society* (San Francisco: Harper & Row, 1985).

[243]Ibid., 72.

arise. This phase is also characterized by the increased use of rational language to combat conditions that produce suffering, and more active (versus reactive) behavior occurs in organizing for liberation from suffering. Thus, in this phase, some forms of suffering (e.g., that which society produces) are recognized as eradicable, and efforts are made communally to overcome such suffering.[244]

It is notable in her development of a language for suffering that Sölle refrains from discussing the first phase of the pain process in depth, ostensibly because she does not want to advocate the common stance of "suffering in silence" as an adequate response to suffering. However, I believe this phase is particularly important for the subsequent movement toward change of the sufferer's condition. For instance, while the sufferer in this phase is "caught" in silence and helplessness, what is it that moves her to an attitude in which she can begin to speak or cry out about her pain (in Phase Two)? I propose that a closer look at what might happen here at this stage to help move the sufferer into the next phase is needed, in order to enhance the significance of Sölle's contribution to theologies of suffering.

For here, in the mute numbness, I believe, is where one's unexpected encounter with God often occurs. Such an encounter can provide the impetus to move the sufferer out of her anguish long enough to discover that a change in the way she looks at her suffering might be possible. Aspects of this encounter with the presence of God and a movement toward creative possibility, as well as a subsequent development of solidarity with others, have already been noted by Smith, May, and Blomquist in the previous section of this study; more discussion on this encounter will follow. At present, what is notable is that it is unclear what actually motivates the sufferer to move from Phase One to Phase Two, wherein one begins to work on her suffering. In this early work of Sölle's thinking on suffering, it is unclear how the attitude in which change is even seen as an option develops.

One hint of how we might look at the impetus that moves one from mute suffering to lament does come later in Sölle's book and demonstrates a further contribution she makes in her theological study of suffering. Perhaps her elaboration on the theme of ac-

[244]Ibid., 72–4.

ceptance of suffering within the Christian tradition, wherein she enhances our understanding of the distinction between submission and acceptance, can help us better understand the experience and motivation that moves the sufferer from Phase One to Two.

In speaking of the tradition of acceptance of suffering in Christianity and retrieving the insights of the medieval mystics on suffering, Sölle identifies how a type of acceptance of suffering can be seen as positive:

> The strength of this position is its relationship to reality, even to wretched conditions. Every acceptance of suffering is an acceptance of that which exists. The denial of every form of suffering can result in a flight from reality in which contact with reality becomes ever thinner, ever more fragmentary. It is impossible to remove oneself totally from suffering, unless one removes oneself from life itself, no longer enters into relationships, makes oneself invulnerable. Contrary to what one might wish, pain, losses, amputations are part of even the smoothest life one can imagine. . . . The more strongly we affirm reality, the more we are immersed in it, the more deeply we are touched by these processes of dying which surround us and press in upon us.[245]

For her, then, suffering that is consciously experienced and unreservedly affirmed is not a denial of reality, or of the real evil that produces the suffering. On the contrary, it is more a removal of the fatalism and paralysis that surrounds such suffering and an affirmation of the totality of one's experience as a human, including its ambiguities and harshness. In this kind of acceptance of suffering, "the person goes far beyond merely enduring conditions as they are—[s]he lives love for reality, [s]he affirms the totality of [her] present experience, even its painful segments."[246] Suffering that is accepted and affirmed in this way is able, according to Sölle, to show its transforming power.

This coming to love reality as it presents itself to us also supersedes the traditional questions of theodicy. The point in this experience of acceptance of suffering reality is no longer why God caused this or that, neither is it a confirmation that God sends suffering

[245]Ibid., 88.
[246]Ibid., 91.

to teach or punish us. It is more about loving life in its fullness and ambiguity. This understanding of the acceptance of suffering in Christianity is "an attempt to see life as a whole as meaningful and to shape it as happiness."[247] Herein, God is seen as a "lover of life" who does not desire the suffering of people for any reason, but instead, their happiness.

As Sölle further notes, the "traditional symbol for this affirmed and loved totality is 'God,'" so that loving this totality also involves loving God unconditionally.[248] Therefore, rather than fixating on what God gives, denies, or permits, or on justifying a good and powerful God in the midst of suffering, the emphasis is more on "love *toward God,* toward one who certainly is not over us like a perfect being but one who is in the process of becoming, as is everything we love."[249] Through affirmation and love of our lives as they are, even in the painful aspects, our relationship to reality, to God, changes:

> The prerequisite for acceptance is a deeper love for reality, a love that avoids placing conditions on reality. Only when we stop making conditions that a person has to satisfy before we yield ourselves to him, only then do we love him. . . . The same thing is true of the relationship to reality, that is, of love for God. It cannot be made dependent on the fulfillment of certain conditions.[250]

What this means, I believe, is that in truly confronting our suffering we have an opportunity to love God for God's Self and not as a projection of our own needs and desires (no matter how valid they are). In our reflections on suffering, we can come to understand God as a reality that neither barricades us against the pain of our existence nor admonishes us to remain in a place of passive suffering. God no longer becomes the source or cause of our suffering, nor the One who keeps us from all suffering. God discloses our reality to us as composed both of joy and sorrow, suffers with us in the pain, and helps us move from a place of passive suffering and resignation. In experiencing and accepting our suffering in

[247]Ibid., 108.
[248]Ibid.
[249]Ibid., 92.
[250]Ibid.

this way, we learn to love the One who exists, partially, as the Incomprehensible, the Paradoxical, the Holy Mystery, and we learn to act out of a changed perspective that does not expect God to "save" us in a particular way. In so doing, we also come to share in the transformation of our own suffering.

Most importantly, according to Sölle, this unconditional love of reality does not defuse desires to change reality, but "can allow itself the most absurd desires—it can pray for them and it can work for them, precisely because it does not make the existence of God depend on the fulfillment of these desires."[251] In this understanding of suffering, then, people work at accepting reality as it presents itself, but also, because they become free of the fear of suffering, work at transforming it. Suffering, in this view, is understood as something that produces change, as a "yes of faith, even against all experience."[252]

Of course, this stance of acceptance is problematic and involves several dangers and distortions when taken to an extreme—the greatest of which is the potential for masochism (for the individual) and for maintenance of existing conditions or the *status quo* (in society). It can become what Sölle calls a "false reconciliation, a naive identification with that which 'is,' though it is in no sense very good," or merely a veiled form of pious submission that is used to justify injustice and oppression.[253]

Rather than seeing this radical acceptance as a passion for masochistic suffering or as a means for maintaining unjust situations, the affirmation of suffering, when it is not forced from a person, has what Sölle calls a "mystical core": that a love for God "can be stronger than every form of affliction."[254] What this means is something very different than blind submission and passive resignation in the face of suffering: it is placing one's affliction as secondary to a love for God so that the suffering itself does not become all-encompassing, or in religious terms, idolatrous.

For Sölle, the "mystics' question remains how people can come to accept grief as joy. Thus, it is not the theodicy question, whether

[251]Ibid., 94.
[252]Ibid., 93.
[253]Ibid., 103.
[254]Ibid., 93.

God wants to punish the sufferers or whether he has forgotten them or whether he loves them in spite of their suffering—or precisely because of it." It is more the question of how one can put her "love for God into practice . . . the question is whether the 'love-power,' the will, can lead people to such a transforming kind of suffering."[255]

In this view suffering can bring us to a detachment from our bondage to any thing, person, or situation that takes away our freedom, and can enhance our receptiveness to the action of God in our lives:

> The Christian understanding of suffering, as it expresses itself in the mysticism of the cross, is different from this [the ideal of a stoical tranquility]. Here the stance over against suffering is not that of averting or avoiding it. . . . The mystical way points in the opposite direction: the soul is open to suffering, abandons itself to suffering, holds back nothing. It does not make itself small and untouchable, distant and insensitive; it is affected by suffering in the fullest possible way.[256]

Through such action, we learn to let go of our attachments to things, persons, ideas, and situations that keep us bound in mute suffering and paralysis. We learn to let go of the fear that keeps us so attached. In such a way we can become more attuned to the presence and action of God, which engenders a calm strength that involves freedom to choose alternative paths. By giving oneself over to suffering reality, as May expressed in the previous "wrestling with God" section, we come to a new perspective and a new strength. As Sölle contends:

> This "proneness to suffering," that is, the suffering that a person has experienced as well as the capacity to suffer, is what makes [her] stronger than anything that comes [her] way . . . what is decisive for Christian mysticism is first of all the knowledge that the one who suffers wrong is also stronger (not just morally better) than the one who does wrong. That "God is always with the one who is suffering" entails not only consolation but also strengthening: a rejection of every ide-

[255]Ibid., 95.
[256]Ibid., 101–2.

ology of punishment, which [is] so useful for the cementing of privileges and for oppression.[257]

What is important here is that, at times, one "takes on" suffering, fully comes to know it, but in a way that disempowers it. By consciously taking on suffering one is changed and the suffering's hold on us is changed through the conscious assenting. This is very different than an imposed martyrdom:

> The Christian idea of the acceptance of suffering means something more than and different from what is expressed in the words "put up with, tolerate, bear." With these words, the object, the suffering itself, remains unchanged. It is borne . . . as an injustice; it is tolerated, although intolerable; borne, although unbearable. "Put up with" and "tolerate" point to stoic tranquility rather than to Christian acceptance. The word "take," also in its combination with "on, up, over," means that the person doing the accepting is [herself] changed. What I "take" belongs to me in a different sense from something I only bear. . . . I say yes, I consent, I assent. . . .[258]

In a type of mystical defiance, one is newly empowered through the action of God's presence, and thus chooses to do battle with doubt and agony, meaninglessness and despair. Mysticism's treatment of suffering, then, is not "its irrationality, which miraculously transforms suffering into a desired good. *What is decisive is much more the taking away of power from the one who causes the suffering,*"[259] and returning power to the sufferer.

Thus, the sufferer, through her willingness to experience ("to take on") the suffering, can overcome the fear, despair, and sense of powerlessness that keeps her locked into the mute suffering of Phase One of Sölle's schema. She can choose to approach her suffering in a way which transforms herself and the suffering itself. By so doing she is empowered to work constructively toward dealing with her situation, leading her to share her pain with others, and together, efforts are made to alleviate continued suffering. For Sölle, then, Christianity's affirmation of suffering is "only part of

[257]Ibid., 102.
[258]Ibid., 103.
[259]Ibid., 93 [my emphasis].

the great love for life as a whole that Christians express with the word 'believe.' To be able to believe means to say yes to this life, to this finitude, to work on it and hold it open for the promised future."[260]

Sölle also takes a different path than most women writers on suffering in the way she distinguishes types of suffering. Rather than divide suffering by its causes (natural, moral, or social evil), or distinguish between suffering that can and cannot be alleviated, she advocates a division into "meaningful" and "meaningless" suffering. The former is *any* suffering which "impels one to act and thereby produces change," regardless of the source or cause, or even the belief that it can be alleviated or not; the latter is suffering "on which people can no longer work, since it has destroyed all their essential powers."[261]

Meaningful suffering arises, for Sölle, from conscious experiencing and vivid remembering of the suffering one has encountered, which fuels a cry of rebellion on behalf of self and others. Especially, those who "learn" from suffering, "who do not blunt or forget the pain,"[262] are capable of transforming the act of suffering into purposeful activity. This is because

> . . . all suffering that does not destroy them teaches them to
> love life all the more; it teaches a greater readiness to act for
> change. [This] suffering makes one more sensitive to the pain
> in the world. It can teach us to put forth a greater love for
> everything that exists.[263]

In this type of suffering, then, expression and action are powerful counters to depression and despair, and act as tools in moving out of suffering that debilitates and silences.

Meaningless or senseless suffering, on the other hand, "deprives us of the activity of living. It merely destroys, it does not alter."[264] In such suffering those affected by it no longer perceive that they have any possibility, which leads to the abandonment of

[260]Ibid., 107.
[261]Ibid.
[262]Ibid., 135.
[263]Ibid., 125.
[264]Ibid., 126.

all hope for oneself and to apathy. The person so afflicted, as noted also by Weil, cannot care about anyone else but herself, empathy dies, and alienation increasingly separates the person from others. She becomes pre-occupied with her suffering to the exclusion of everything else. As a result, death, the cessation of all activity, becomes increasingly attractive as a resolution to suffering.[265] Such suffering often imposes silence as a response, which further alienates the sufferer from others, and "turns a person in on [herself] completely; it destroys [her] ability to communicate."[266]

For Sölle, such a distinction into meaningful and meaningless suffering is valid since it is a closer depiction of our reality than other distinctions of types of suffering. More importantly, it also keeps us from creating a hierarchy of suffering—such as determining that some suffering is more significant than others, or that some suffering is "right" and others, "wrong"—which can destroy our capacity for perceiving suffering at all. For Sölle:

> there is no wrong suffering. There is imaginary, sham, feigned, simulated, pretended suffering. But the assertion that someone suffers for the right or wrong reason presupposes a divine, all-penetrating judgment able to distinguish historically obsolete forms of suffering from those in our time, instead of leaving this decision to the sufferers themselves.[267]

This final point also seems extremely important in suffering for women: that it is up to the sufferer herself to determine what is meaningful and meaningless suffering in her circumstances. Through her own discernment, she must come to an understanding of her suffering and to her own decisions whether her suffering is for a greater purpose or whether it is merely passive martyrdom.

Another area of Sölle's work that I wish to highlight at this point is her discussion of innocent suffering. Perceptively, Sölle explores the experience of extreme, unmerited suffering wherein God can often appear to be more of a tyrant and avenger of God's honor than One who loves, accompanies, and protects one in the midst of severe suffering. In using Job as emblematic of innocent

[265]Ibid., 68–9.
[266]Ibid., 69.
[267]Ibid., 106–7.

suffering, she guides us through the images of God that one often
utilizes in the midst of such extreme suffering.

In the story of Job, she notes three primary interpretations of
God that many women sufferers also hold in the midst of unmerited suffering. The first image of God that often arises is the
"tyrant-tester" God. This is the One who devises absurd and often
gruesome tests of righteousness that involve severe suffering, and
that are increasingly impossible for any human to fulfill.[268] As with
Job, the senselessness of these tests for the innocent sufferer soon
becomes clear. They serve no purpose other than to demonstrate
the strength and capriciousness of this God so imaged.

What one must do in the face of such a God, if she follows Job's
example, is to stand against, complain, and do battle with this
image of God that obscures the knowledge of her innocence and
the goodness of God. As Job learns not to have anything to do with
this tyrant-tester God, so too, it seems, Sölle suggests that the innocent sufferer must refuse "to allow [herself] to be made the object of testing" by such a God.[269] In relinquishing this image of God
as tyrant-tester, the sufferer becomes stronger, can insist on her
rights, and demand justice in her suffering. In so doing, her image
of God no longer hinders her from seeking improvement of her
situation.

Further, according to Sölle, the second possible God depicted
in the story of Job and often held by innocent sufferers, is the One
who punishes, who "avenges people's offenses relentlessly."[270] This
is the view that suffering can always be traced to human sin and
punishment for guilt, since a righteous God would never reject a
blameless one. Therefore, anyone suffering to extreme must be
guilty and deserving of such punishment.

Just as Job insisted on the truth of his innocence as well as the
reality of his suffering, so too, implies Sölle, must the innocent
sufferer do similarly, and learn to call into question the God image
whose essence is "power" to punish and not "justice."[271] In seeking
an understanding of why the innocent suffer, one must dispense,

---

[268]Ibid., 110–1.
[269]Ibid., 112.
[270]Ibid., 113.
[271]Ibid., 114.

then, with "an understanding of God that combines justice and omnipotence."[272]

A third interpretation of God, as depicted in the book of Job, that needs to be relinquished by innocent sufferers is that of the almighty creator God, who calls one to submission and obedience in the face of human suffering.[273] This is the One who exemplifies the ultimate power and awesomeness of the creator of all that is, while emphasizing the total insignificance of humans in relation to such a God. The human sufferer in light of this image of God has no rights whatsoever. God's justice and concern for humans are thus overpowered by God's distance, purity, self-righteousness, and might.[274]

By using an interpretation of the suffering of Job, Sölle implies that what innocent suffering often can do (positively) is compel one to abandon or relinquish destructive images of God in the midst of suffering. One can move away from the arbitrary tester-God, the avenging-God, and the almighty creator-God, to a fourth interpretation—a God who takes seriously the sufferer's protest and rebellion, One who is a witness to her innocence and rescues her from debilitating guilt, and One who becomes a true advocate and redeemer, a true helper and companion.[275] For Sölle, such a God is One who has suffered and knows such unmerited, extreme suffering in God's very Self.[276] For the Christian, then, in abandoning these destructive images of God, one can come closer to the God depicted in the "good news."

This brief discussion of Sölle's significant study of suffering does not exhaust the many insights she provides for developing responses to women's suffering. Nonetheless, her insights into the importance of language and expression to the movement through suffering to change; her understanding of acceptance and affirmation in Christian responses to suffering; and her distinctions of suffering into meaningless and meaningful, as well as her admonition to dispense with destructive images of God in innocent suffering, all seem particularly useful in constructing viable theological and

[272]Ibid., 116.
[273]Ibid., 117.
[274]Ibid., 118.
[275]Ibid.
[276]Ibid., 118–9.

spiritual responses to women's experiences of suffering. Her views will resurface in subsequent chapters.

## Wendy Farley's Tragic Suffering

In a more recent work on the theology of suffering, Wendy Farley focuses even more intensively on the theme of extreme and meaningless suffering that Sölle distinguishes. In her *Tragic Vision and Divine Compassion,* Farley concentrates on the perennial question of why the good or the most vulnerable and innocent must suffer, and are so often destroyed by that which is beyond their control. As she notes:

> Once human suffering is possible, nothing restricts its range so that the kindest, or the weakest, or the most admirable people will be magically protected from it. Nothing limits suffering, in its intensity, from driving people to despair through grief, pain, or cruelty. Once suffering is posited as an essential component of human existence, radical suffering threatens every person. No one is protected from suffering that is so terrible that it breaks the spirit.[277]

Farley's concerns lie with this suffering that she labels "radical" or "tragic," in which the virtuous and innocent are the most vulnerable to suffering and destruction, and with the inadequacy of the responses that traditional theodicies have posited in addressing such suffering.[278] In her view, in the face of radical suffering, traditional theodicies are limited in their ability "to exorcise the demons that whisper that life is futile, suffering meaningless, and the cosmos an empty and evil void."[279] Farley looks for an alternative conceptual framework in which radical suffering can be addressed more effectively.

Farley begins by defining such radical or tragic suffering as that form of suffering "that has the power to dehumanize and degrade human beings . . . and that cannot be traced to punishment or

---

[277]Wendy Farley, *Tragic Vision and Divine Compassion: A Contemporary Theodicy* (Louisville, Ky.: Westminster/John Knox Press, 1990) 34.

[278]In this chapter, I shall briefly describe Farley's views of radical suffering, but shall give her accounts of tragedy and divine compassion more attention in subsequent chapters, as they lend inspiration and support to many of my own views.

[279]Ibid., 22.

desert."[280] This form of suffering arises out of the sense that one is suffering not because one has done something wrong, but because something is wrong with the very way one's life is conditioned or structured. It involves a sense of radical contingency and vulnerability—a sense that one is at the mercy of something or someone that seeks to destroy life and all that one defines as good and true. No matter what one does, how well one behaves, or how well one justifies the suffering that occurs, she is still vulnerable to a destruction that may not only take her life, but may also destroy her very humanity and dignity along the way.

Farley also recognizes that this radical suffering is both concrete and contextual, and arises out of a particular set of cultural, economic, social, and personal circumstances. It is experienced immediately and personally. Thus, it is not "your" or "their" suffering; it is "my" or "our" suffering. Partially because of these unique particularities, this innocent or unmerited suffering robs one of both her humanity and her dignity—primarily because it cannot be understood as something deserved or purposeful.[281] Despite the uniqueness of these individual experiences of radical suffering, what remains consistent, however, is that radical suffering is destructive and unjust:[282]

> Radical suffering is present when the negativity of a situation is experienced as an assault on one's personhood *as such*. . . . Radical suffering assaults and degrades that about a person which makes her or him most human. This assault reduces the capacity of the sufferer to exercise freedom, to feel affection, to hope, to love God. Radical suffering pinches the spirit of the sufferer, numbing it and diminishing its range. The distinctiveness of radical suffering does not lie in its intensity or its injustice but in its power over the sufferer.[283]

Perhaps, as Sölle has pointed out in her discussion of a mystical acceptance of suffering, it takes a strength engendered by God to break this kind of power over one.

---

[280]Ibid., 12.
[281]Ibid., 21.
[282]Ibid., 55–6.
[283]Ibid., 53–4.

This "power over the sufferer" involves not only physical consequences, but also emotional and spiritual, as was noted previously by Weil's discussion of affliction and in Sölle's discussion of meaningless and innocent suffering. One's basic human dignity is assaulted to the point of self-loathing and despair, and the sufferer and her self-image become crippled by her condition:

> Radical suffering defines the human being as a victim or sufferer, so she (or he) becomes a deformed creature whose *habitus* is suffering. All experience is absorbed into suffering and the sufferer is impaled upon her pain. The past is gone and the future a miserable repetition of the present. . . . Radical suffering is the incurable wound of despair that annihilates the future, severs relationships, and withholds from suffering any possible meaning.[284]

Due to such abasement, and particularly if the suffering is prolonged, the radical sufferer may no longer even realize that she has been wronged, and she becomes crippled to defend herself effectively. Thus, such suffering "can create a soul incapable of self-defense because the spark of self-respect or dignity has been snuffed out by humiliation and pain."[285] In so doing such tragic or radical suffering does not make the sufferer stronger, wiser, more courageous, or more compassionate; it does not serve some greater purpose for the individual but actually damages and destroys its victims.[286]

In addressing such suffering and as an alternative response to those posited by the traditional theodicies outlined in the previous chapter, Farley proposes a theodicy that incorporates a tragic vision of reality, as well as a phenomenology of divine compassion. In developing her alternative theodicy, she identifies three ways that she breaks with traditional theodicies.

First, she places suffering, not sin, at the center of the problem of evil since she finds suffering a more compelling anomaly and challenge to Christian faith.[287] Second, the conceptual framework

[284]Ibid., 58–9.
[285]Ibid., 55.
[286]Ibid., 22.
[287]Ibid., 12.

of her reflections is governed by tragedy rather than by a notion of the Fall. She is drawn to tragedy

> in order to find categories for evil that do not justify or explain suffering. Tragedy is . . . rooted in a deep sense of value of creation, . . . driven by a desire for justice, but it does not find this desire satisfied in history. Nor does . . . [it] consider speculations about a Fall or eschatological harmony adequate substitutes for historical justice and compassion.[288]

And, third, she repudiates the assumption that the appropriate model for divine power is the power to dominate. For her, the concept of omnipotence does little to illuminate our understanding of a God radically other, yet good, and so she seeks a different metaphor of divine power in the midst of radical suffering—one modeled on love and expressed in compassion, rather than on domination.[289]

Significant for her study, and important for the discussion at present is her second deviation from the focus of traditional theodicies—that of finding an alternative conceptual framework for addressing experiences of radical suffering. For Farley, through the incorporation of a concept of tragedy rather than an emphasis on the Fall, radical suffering in a world ordered by a gracious and loving God is not "explained away" or justified but is recognized and affirmed in its powerful destructiveness.

Classical tragedy, as does our everyday existence, attests to a reality in which "the suffering is raw, unmediated by justice or utility; it witnesses to the power of absurdity or malice or sheer force to bring down what is noble and good."[290] In her view, such suffering, especially on a massive scale such as that inflicted by Pol Pot or in El Salvador, the "troubles" in Northern Ireland or the Middle East conflicts, cannot be resolved by explanations relying on the Fall, or which appeal to suffering as a necessity for penal retribution, purgation, vindication, pedagogy, or redemption. The horrific cruelty of radical human suffering defies such attempts to justify it.[291] As

[288]Ibid., 13.
[289]Ibid.
[290]Ibid., 24.
[291]Ibid., 19.

an alternative framework for confronting such suffering, and "unlike traditional theodicies, tragedy does not attempt to penetrate the opacity of evil by providing justifications of suffering. It recognizes that certain kinds of suffering are unredeemably unjust," and such suffering should be an essential component of theological reflection.[292]

In Farley's view tragedy provides a viable framework for confronting such suffering in that it "presses upon us a dark vision of reality," but it also presupposes a moral order which transcends this dark vision by "the apprehension of ultimate goodness." In tragedy the emphasis remains the problem of "the *injustice* of certain events and sufferings rather than the *justice* of punishing sinners. Justice is restored not so much when [the sufferer] is punished, but when . . . [she] is vindicated and relieved of persecution."[293] Thus, driven by a desire for justice, tragedy, as an alternative for Farley, "retains the sharp edge of anger at the unfairness and destructiveness of suffering," while retaining a sense of a broader ethical order in which our suffering occurs. For her, a study of tragedy may, therefore, assist theology in viewing the problem of evil in a new way, while taking actual, concrete experiences of suffering more seriously.[294]

For instance, radical suffering confronts theology with a problem that cannot be addressed within the context of the Fall since a theology governed by guilt is not equipped to recognize and respond to the existence of such unjust and destructive suffering.[295] In dealing with such suffering, tragedy, on the other hand, recognizes and exhibits that the threat and reality of radical suffering is embedded in the very conditions of our embodied human existence. It

> places evil within a context that is more inclusive than human fault. This is not to say that sin, guilt, cruelty, and indifference have no role in evil. But all human action occurs in an environment that is not entirely shaped by human decision or desire.[296]

[292]Ibid., 22.
[293]Ibid., 29.
[294]Ibid., 13, 19.
[295]Ibid., 29.
[296]Ibid., 31.

Tragedy allows theology to see that creation is good, creatures and relationships are good, but are, nonetheless, conditioned by a finite existence which includes conflict, ignorance, deception, fragility, and limitation. This "tragic structure," as she identifies it, is not evil in itself, but makes suffering "both possible and inevitable prior to any human action."[297]

Tragedy, then, provides an alternative to the traditional paradigm based on the Fall and guilt in that

> tragic vision locates the possibility of suffering in the conditions of existence and in the fragility of human freedom. The very structures that make human existence possible make us subject to the destructive power of suffering. Since guilt is not the primary problem, atonement and forgiveness cannot help transcend tragedy. Tragic suffering cannot be atoned for; it must be defied. Compassion is that power which survives to resist tragic suffering.[298]

Thus, the suffering that is of concern for tragedy is that which is undeserved and yet has the power to damage and destroy the sufferer. Such radical suffering involves an evil so powerful that it destroys possibility—of change, harmony, or even hope. For Farley, what can restore such possibility is a combination of resistance and compassion. "If suffering and destruction cannot be overcome, they can be resisted. It is in the resistance itself, in this refusal to give up the passion for justice, that tragedy is transcended."[299] Compassion is the power that resists and defies such tragic suffering with a resilience of a passion for justice and hope. According to Farley, then:

> A tragic vision is branded by suffering, but the mark of tragedy is defiance rather than despair. The beginning of a tragic vision is anger and sorrow in the face of suffering. The horror of suffering provokes resistance. As such, it is an ethical (and ultimately theological) response to suffering: it begins and ends in compassion.[300]

[297]Ibid., 31–2.
[298]Ibid., 29.
[299]Ibid., 27.
[300]Ibid., 37.

More on Farley's views on tragedy and divine compassion will be discussed in the following chapters, whereas the theme of resistance to suffering and tragedy is given even more attention in the theological writings of women of color. I shall now turn to one anthology of such writings, by African-American theologians, to complete this section of my schema of women's works on evil and suffering.

## Womanist Contributions

Women of color have long spoken of resistance and acts of defiance in the face of their sufferings, as testified in a recent anthology of womanist writings on evil and suffering, entitled *A Troubling in My Soul* and edited by Emilie M. Townes.[301] In this eclectic compilation of essays by a variety of womanist scholars and practitioners, these writers utilize the experiences of historical and contemporary African-American women to formulate praxis-oriented approaches for confronting evil and suffering in their communities. As Kathleen Sands notes, womanists here are less concerned about theorizing about suffering or "reconceptualizing God than with uncovering the resources for combatting injustices in African-American women's lives."[302] One such fundamental resource identified repeatedly in these writings is resistance.

For example, in her essay that begins formulating a theology of suffering from a womanist perspective, M. Shawn Copeland identifies resistance as a characteristic feature of slave narratives by African-American women who "wade through their sorrows, managing their suffering, rather than being managed by it."[303] When these women are given their own voice, when they relate and

---

[301]*A Troubling in My Soul: Womanist Perspectives on Evil and Suffering,* ed. Emilie M. Townes (Maryknoll, N.Y.: Orbis Books, 1993). As Townes notes, womanist theologians critique the limitations of white feminist theology for ignoring race and class issues and Black theology for disregarding gender and class issues. They are committed to an integrated analysis of race, gender, and class as these affect theological discourse. Given space considerations, I have selected but a few essays from this anthology to devote my attention; I believe these are fairly representative of the concerns discussed by all, but refer the reader to the richness of the anthology itself.

[302]Sands, 56.

[303]M. Shawn Copeland, "Wading through Many Sorrows: Toward a Theology of Suffering in Womanist Perspective," in *Troubling,* 118.

interpret their experiences on their own terms, they disclose their active roles as agents of resistance rather than passive subjects of oppression.[304] From these writings Copeland culls various forms of resistance that enabled these women to survive the brutalities of slavery, "make meaning" of their suffering, and call others to help change the conditions under which they lived.

Resistance for these slave women included verbal self-defense and defiance.[305] "Sass" or "back talk" was often used to confront and cope with situations in which the sufferer was physically, psychologically, and socially abused. As Copeland notes:

> Enslaved Black women use sass to guard, regain, and secure self-esteem; to obtain and hold psychological distance; to speak truth; to challenge "the atmosphere of moral ambiguity that surrounds them"; and sometimes, to protect against sexual assault.[306]

Similar to Sölle's important link between the articulation of suffering and the movement out of suffering, language was a crucial form of resistance for these women, as well as bold, audacious behavior. Wit, cunning, and moral courage were used to gain a measure of psychological freedom from unjust and cruel slave owners.[307] Sometimes, despite the potential deadly repercussions, actual physical flight from the situation was also used. Overall, these women resisted their imposed suffering through a refusal to be conquered psychologically or defiled physically.[308]

According to Copeland's reading of these slave narratives, another fundamental resource that these women used to counter their suffering was their religious consciousness. Shaping "Christian practices, rituals, and values to their own particular experiences, religio-cultural expectations, and personal needs," these women formed a distinctive image of themselves and "fashioned an inner world, a scale of values and fixed points of vantage from which to judge the world around them and themselves."[309]

[304]Ibid., 110.
[305]Ibid., 113.
[306]Ibid., 121.
[307]Ibid., 116, 121.
[308]Ibid., 114–5.
[309]Ibid., 119.

Utilizing Christian biblical material, they also mediated their pain through comparisons with biblical events of God's liberation of oppressed peoples, and expressed their pain and hope for freedom in their spirituals. These stories and songs told of God's mercy, testified to the ways in which enslaved people met God in the midst of their suffering and struggles, and depicted how God suffered alongside them, as symbolized by the cross of Jesus.[310] The spirituals also functioned as a resource of resistance to suffering by also serving as coded messages, signifying the movement of slaves on the Underground Railway.

Not only is resistance a characteristic feature of these slave narratives by African-American women; it is also a key element in Copeland's emerging theology of suffering in womanist perspective. She stresses that Black women can learn resistance from their foremothers, in order to define themselves and dismantle the images that have been used to control and demean them.[311] One way to do this is in reevaluating cardinal Christian virtues in light of Black women's experiences. Along with other writers in this anthology, Copeland calls for a critical reevaluation and reinterpretation of such virtues as patience, love, servanthood, faith, hope, and forebearance in order to distance oneself from any form of masochism.[312] More generally, she calls for Black women to critically evaluate all Christian tenets against their experience, and encourages ". . . the dialectic between oppression, conscious reflection on the experience of that oppression, and activism to resist and change it." In so doing, as shown in the slave narratives that she analyzes, what is hopeful is that "the matrix of domination is responsive to human agency; the struggle of Black women suggests that there is choice and power to act—and to do so mindfully, artfully."[313]

Further, as with Sölle, another component of her theology of suffering is the essential role of memory in responding to situations of suffering:

[310]Ibid., 120.

[311]Ibid., 124. Cf. Frances E. Wood, "Take My Yoke upon You: The Role of the Church in the Oppression of African-American Women," in *Troubling*, 37–46.

[312]Ibid. Cf. Jacquelyn Grant, "The Sin of Servanthood and the Deliverance of Discipleship," in *Troubling*, 199–216; Cheryl Gilkes, "The 'Loves' and 'Troubles' of African-American Women's Bodies," in *Troubling*, 240.

[313]Ibid., 123.

> For the enslaved community, memory was a vital and empowering act. Remembering gave the slaves access to "naming, placing, and signifying," and thus, the recovery, the reconstitution of identity, culture, and self. Memory, then, was an essential source of resistance.[314]

In remembering and retelling the lives and sufferings of those who "made it through," one not only honors those who have suffered before, but also strengthens herself in her own struggles by imitating the strategies adopted by others in handling their own suffering.[315] Through remembering, solidarity is also heightened.

And finally, Copeland's theology of suffering stresses the need to repel "every tendency toward any *ersatz* spiritualization of evil and suffering, of pain and oppression."[316] Along with other writers in this anthology, she is concerned that any viable theology of suffering for African-American women steers clear of condoning suffering per se, and retains a sense of outrage regarding any further social suffering and degradation of Black women. For her, the emphasis in a theology of suffering needs to remain on understanding and clarifying "the liberating Word and deed of God in Jesus of Nazareth for all . . . who strive against the principalities and structures, the powers and forces of evil."[317] Black women are encouraged to "invite God to partner them in the redemption of Black people," and that their suffering be used not as a justification for further victimization, but for purposes of emancipation.[318] As the women slaves of the narratives she analyzes model, Copeland encourages Black women who suffer to become "living witnesses to the power of divine grace, not merely to sustain men and women through such evil, but to enable them to turn victimization into Christian triumph."[319]

Clarice Martin, another womanist writer in Townes' anthology, echoes this partnership with God as a means for combating

---

[314]Ibid., 121. Cf. Clarice J. Martin, "Biblical Theodicy and Black Women's Spiritual Autobiography: 'The Miry Bog, the Desolate Pit, a New Song in My Mouth,'" in *Troubling*, 28.

[315]Ibid., 124–5.

[316]Ibid., 123.

[317]Ibid.

[318]Ibid., 124.

[319]Ibid., 119.

evil that assails African-American women. Basing her considerations on a study of nineteenth-century political thinker Maria Stewart, Martin identifies in Stewart's writings what she calls "a praxis of active, oppositional engagement against racial suffering and evil," and notes that Stewart believed that resistance was the highest form of obedience to God.[320] In Stewart's spiritual autobiography, this "praxis of oppositional engagement" is delineated as the stance that actively confronts and resists the causes and effects of suffering and evil, and is lauded as an appropriate and effective response to individual and institutional racism.[321]

Martin also finds, in her study of Stewart's writings, not a standard justification of God in the midst of heinous racial oppression, but a concern with how "God is near to and acts on behalf of the powerless and the disenfranchised in the interests of divine justice."[322] Through the use of biblical traditions, Stewart affirms and promulgates in her writings a God who is involved in history, fights against the oppressive evils of life, and advances social, economic, and political justice for the poor and unwanted in society. Through the use of polemical and pragmatic comparisons between biblical stories and present racial suffering, Stewart arrives at a fundamental tenet of African-American religious faith: that God is a God of liberation and freedom, and became man in Jesus Christ so that God's kingdom would make freedom a reality for all. As Martin states, for Stewart and many other African-Americans, "the Bible witnesses . . . to God as one who maintains and works out forcefully and creatively freedom and the formation of community for the alien and the alienated."[323]

Not only is this God creatively and forcefully working out freedom and a life for the oppressed, but also the sufferer works in partnership with God to effect divine justice in history. Martin stresses:

> Liberation from suffering, evil, and oppression was thus perceived to represent only the beginning of a journey wherein one acts *with* God to exemplify the realities of freedom and justice and community formation within the sociopolitical

[320]Martin, 22.
[321]Ibid., 25.
[322]Ibid., 23.
[323]Ibid., 24, 26.

and religious institutions of a society. It is the combination of "the mighty acts of God" . . . and "human response" that reverses the suffering and evil of oppression that thwarts the purposes of God. . . . "It is not simply by divine fiat, but by conflict, struggle, and overt human choice that men [sic] are liberated and community is formed . . . the freedom sought and effected is both political and spiritual, the fellowship created is both social and religious."[324]

Thus, according to Martin, through a partnership with God that actively resists manifestations of evil, the Black sufferer avoids paralysis and passive submissiveness in the face of destructive evil and suffering, and can begin securing a truly human life and personhood in the African-American community.[325]

In addition to uncovering resources for combatting injustices against the African-American community, writers in Townes' anthology also redefine the concepts of sin and suffering from a womanist perspective, as exemplified in the essays by Delores Williams and Townes herself. Utilizing both Black female and Black male sources, Delores Williams redefines the notion of sin from a womanist perspective and places guilt on the side of society at large, as well as within the African-American community itself.

As she explores the variety of ways African-Americans have historically spoken of sin in slave songs, autobiographical statements of ex-slaves, and Black theology, Williams identifies the development of a distinctively Black female consciousness about sin as involving social conditions that instill personal unworthiness and perpetuate bodily defilement of African-American women.

As an example, she shows how, in Black women's full-length, autobiographical narratives from the nineteenth and early-twentieth centuries, the development of a female consciousness of sin "often proceeds from feelings of personal unworthiness to a sense of somebodiness bestowed by an encounter with Jesus. Reaching the level of 'somebodiness' amounts to what they see as liberation."[326] Rather than identify specific individual sins, these autobiographies indicate that the sense of personal unworthiness seems to stem from

---

[324]Ibid., 24, quoting Stewart.
[325]Ibid., 32.
[326]Delores S. Williams, "A Womanist Perspective on Sin," in *Troubling*, 140.

a type of sin that is frequently understood as "an ontological sense whereby the flaw or fault is in existence itself."[327] Rather than trace sin to specific acts of disobedience or wrongdoing, these writers seem to be saying that there is something corrupt in the very nature of human existence and in their daily human relations.

Williams links this development of a female consciousness of sin with James Cone's method of identifying sin as society's way of taking away people's humanity. Using Cone's and the Black community's belief in social sin, womanist theologians, according to Williams, "claim that society's way of devaluing Black womanhood is also sin. For Black women's womanhood is their humanity. To devalue Black women's womanhood is to take away their humanity."[328] Thus, in constructing a womanist notion of sin informed by Black theology's belief in social sin, Williams redefines sin as the devaluation of Black womanhood and the defilement of their bodies, through such situations as overwork, lynching, and rape, "as the social sin American patriarchy and demonarchy have committed against Black women and their children."[329]

Williams also notes four distinctive features of her womanist notion of sin. (1) It takes the human body and its sexual resources very seriously such that "the abuse and depletion of these resources amount to defilement, which constitutes sin."[330] (2) To devalue the womanhood and sexuality (regardless of sexual orientation) of Black women is sin since Black women's womanhood and sexual being are in the image of God, as is that of humanity in general. (3) The womanist notion of sin that she identifies in this essay also takes seriously Black women's depleted self-esteem, and thus, notions of salvation for the African-American community must include elevating and healing Black women's self-esteem. (4) She also suggests a parallel between the defilement of Black women's bodies and the defilement of nature, and calls for an alleviation of the various forms of sin as devaluation and defilement through ongoing communal work.[331]

[327]Ibid.
[328]Ibid., 145.
[329]Ibid., 144.
[330]Ibid., 146.
[331]Ibid., 146–7. For another reinterpretation of sin from a feminist perspective, see Farley, 42–51.

Before leaving Williams' concept of sin, it is also significant to note, in my view, that the movement from the suffering incurred by this social sin of devaluation and defilement, from a sense of unworthiness to "somebodiness," has come through an encounter with God or Jesus for many of the Black women depicted in Williams' essay. For example, she notes that "it is through a personal encounter with Jesus that they are empowered not only to believe that one can gain victory over this flaw in existence called sin." This encounter also empowers "some to preach and believe that preaching is a proper vocation for a woman."[332] Liberation from the effects of social sin often occurs for these women amid mystical or visionary experiences "apparently precipitated by mental depression or even inclinations toward suicide associated with these feelings of unworthiness."[333] Thus, in the very midst of a situation of life-threatening suffering, these women testify to an encounter with God or Jesus that transforms their lives thereafter.

Besides sin, another redefinition from a womanist perspective comes with regard to suffering itself. Drawing on the writings of Audre Lorde,[334] suffering, for Townes, is defined as "unscrutinized and unmetabolized pain," a passive reaction to the given in one's life. She distinguishes pain from suffering in the following:

> Suffering is the inescapable cycle of reliving pain over and over again when it is triggered by events or people. It is a static process which usually ends in oppression. Pain is an experience that is recognized, named, and then used for transformation. It is a dynamic process pointing toward transformation.[335]

In her view, suffering is a "failure to use freedom for the purposes of liberation," a way of being that prevents effective action and subverts the individual and the community from saying a firm "no" to their oppression. Suffering, by this definition, is sinful because the sufferer does not exercise her intrinsic freedom to choose, on her own behalf, to move from suffering to justice. Thus,

[332]Ibid., 142.
[333]Ibid., 140.
[334]Lorde, 171–2.
[335]Emilie M. Townes, "Living in the New Jerusalem: The Rhetoric and Movement of Liberation in the House of Evil," in *Troubling*, 84.

the challenge for the African-American community in dealing
with suffering, as Townes sees it, is to work "in partnership with
the intention of moving from suffering to pain, individually and
communally."[336]

But, this is not done by humans alone. Townes' views are also
based on a resurrection faith, in that she believes in the nonfinal-
ity of suffering due to God's expression of God's Self in the death
and resurrection of Jesus. For her, if one takes the resurrection
event seriously,

> true suffering has been removed through the redemptive
> event of the resurrection. Through the Suffering Servant, God
> has spoken against evil and injustice. The empty cross and
> tomb are symbols of the victory. The oppressed are set free to
> struggle against injustice, not out of their suffering, but out of
> their pain that can be recognized and named as injustice and
> brokenness. The resurrection moves humanity past suffering
> to pain and struggle. The resurrection is God's breaking into
> history to transform suffering into wholeness—to move the
> person from victim to change agent. The gospel message calls
> for transformation.[337]

Townes also further emphasizes that a ". . . womanist ethical
reflection rejects suffering as God's will" and, echoing Farley's concerns, "believes that it is an outrage that there is suffering at all."[338]
In her understanding a womanist ethic seeks to change the suffering situation, partially by vociferously challenging the inevitability and desirability of suffering.[339] Given her definitions as noted
above, Townes warns that "suffering, and any discussion that accepts suffering as good, is susceptible to being shaped into a tool
of oppression."[340]

As can be seen in these brief excerpts from the chorus of voices
in Townes' anthology, these womanist writings on suffering and
evil more often than not depict a confidence in the ultimacy of
justice upheld by God. Faith in God is the abiding background for

[336]Ibid.
[337]Ibid., 84.
[338]Ibid., 78, 83–4.
[339]Ibid., 84.
[340]Ibid., 85.

many of these writers, but this faith is not meant to foster passivity or substitute believed-in answers for real ones. Similar to the writers on abuse in a previous section of this schema, these womanist writers represented in Townes' anthology challenge the historical misuse of Christian sources to support the oppression of Black women and advocate a selective and critical use of inherited traditional sources. They call for a substantial revision of eurocentric doctrines (e.g., atonement doctrines, in which salvation comes through the defilement and death of an innocent victim) which do not prove salvific for African-American women.[341] In so doing, they call individuals and groups within their communities to work toward alleviating conditions of suffering.

Yet, many of these writers also speak of a God of liberation in the midst of suffering, who may not serve as a guarantor of liberation, but who ignites human initiative and struggle and works alongside and with the sufferer to gain freedom. As Kathleen Sands notes, behind these liberation hopes is a transcendent faith.[342] In the words of Delores Williams:

> The greatest truth of black women's survival and quality-of-life struggle is that they have worked without hesitation and with all the energy they could muster. . . . They depended upon their strength and upon each other. But in the final analysis the message is clear: they trusted the end to God. Every important event in the stories of . . . black women turns on this trust.[343]

## WRITINGS POINTING TOWARD THE DEVELOPMENT OF A FEMINIST THEOLOGY OF SUFFERING

As can be seen by the foregoing discussions, the writings of women on suffering are diverse and yet capable of being loosely categorized into the schema proposed above. Another useful way of looking at these writings has been proposed by Patricia Wismer, wherein she identifies two major voices in writings which respond

[341]Sands, 57–8.
[342]Ibid., 58.
[343]Delores S. Williams, *Sisters in the Wilderness: The Challenge of Womanist God-Talk* (Maryknoll, N.Y.: Orbis Books, 1993) 238–9.

theologically and pastorally to the suffering of women. Because Wismer's view expresses clearly some of my own observations after looking at this material, I include it here.

The first major voice is most typified by such writers as Brown and Parker, who focus on the type of suffering caused by human agents, and whose goal is to expose and criticize any rationalization or legitimization of the suffering of women. This voice, with its tone of righteous indignation and firm refusal to accept any suffering as redemptive, contends that such ideals as self-sacrifice and obedience have kept women locked in their suffering and should be repudiated. For them, commitment to life is key and suffering should never be directly chosen since it is never, or rarely, redemptive.[344]

A second major voice, typified by some of the "wrestling with God" writers, addresses the suffering caused by natural processes (rather than moral agency) and advocates a kind of acceptance and confrontation of suffering. For these writers life and suffering or death are not opposed but interrelated; for them, "being committed to life includes accepting death."[345] They advocate living fully with the situations that are presented to one, even finding some meaning in death.

In Wismer's view, and I agree, both voices must be included in any viable feminist theology of suffering. The first reminds us never to minimize the actual suffering of women or settle for suffering that could be eliminated. The second reminds us to discover meaning in suffering (especially that which cannot be eliminated), and concentrates on ways we can encounter, accept, and grow through it. For her, both voices need to be held in tension or harmony:

> A feminist theology of suffering, then, should state both that suffering can never be justified *and* that suffering must be accepted as part of life. It should state both that suffering can never be redeemed *and* that meaning can be found in suffering.[346]

Before her own recent death, Wismer also used these "voices" to sketch an outline of factors to be considered in a feminist the-

---

[344]Wismer, "For Women in Pain," 146.
[345]Ibid., 146–7.
[346]Ibid., 148.

ology of suffering. Drawing upon her concern that any adequate Christian theology of suffering must have "experiential relevance" and thus must speak to the real-life experiences of women in pain, she delineated these factors in the form of four questions, as follows:[347]

(1) What are the causes of my suffering and how can they be eliminated? This question affirms the critique generated by the first voice and addresses the tendency to be masochistic and seek a passive martyrdom in suffering.

(2) How can I find meaning in my suffering and grow through it? This incorporates the second voice and addresses the need to integrate unavoidable suffering into one's life.

(3) When and how should I take on suffering I could avoid? This question recognizes both the problematic character of and the necessity (e.g., for the sake of love and justice) for becoming involved in situations that increase personal suffering.

(4) Why am I suffering, and who suffers with me? The first question here is, for Wismer as well as most of the writers I studied, essentially unanswerable, and yet, for her and for me, must be voiced. In her words, "we must resist closing the question because we cannot know the ultimate reason for our suffering," and, as with Blomquist, advocates living with the question.[348] Such a stance leads, not to trivializing one's suffering or making God into a type of sadist, but can gradually lead to the second question in this set. "Who suffers with me" *is* answerable and can lead to healing through the revelation of support and meaning, as specifically shown in Sölle's work on suffering. Such a combination of these questions, then, creates a needed integration of both voices which can assist in the development of feminist theologies of suffering.[349]

## SUMMARY

Overall, as can be seen by the foregoing discussions by women writers, these women are struggling to find a new theological language regarding suffering that takes into account the diverse experiences

[347]Ibid., 149.
[348]Ibid.
[349]Ibid.

of women. While paralleling a variety of views about suffering in traditional approaches (e.g., sin as the breakdown of authentic being), feminist theologies critique a number of generally accepted beliefs regarding religious views of suffering.

For instance, they challenge both that suffering is the result of the Fall and therefore, women's particular fault, and that suffering can be good or redemptive.[350] Many feminist theologies also contend that the theological tradition which has spawned the various theodicies summarized in the previous chapter has nurtured and reinforced abuse and fostered women's passive compliance with suffering (similar to Simone Weil's view of the sufferer's complicity in the continuance of her own suffering). For many feminist writers, as noted in the foregoing, these traditional theological responses to the questions of suffering can actually contribute to the suffering of the powerless and oppressed rather than aid their understanding of and bring resolution for their situations.[351]

## General Trends

In the writings surveyed for this chapter, I see at least five general trends in women's writings on suffering that differ from traditional approaches to the questions raised by suffering. *First, a shift from the abstract theodicy question to more practical, concrete discussions of evil and suffering.* This trend includes a shift from focusing on God as source of our suffering to focusing on what God is doing to alleviate suffering, as well as what we need to do to change suffering situations.

Many women writers I surveyed are not seeking to resolve the theodicy question per se (mainly, because it remains for them rationally and sensibly irresolvable), but to concentrate theological and pastoral attention on what can be done to ameliorate or alleviate actual, lived situations of suffering. In this praxis-oriented approach, the fundamental question in these writings often shifts from "why does a good, just, and omnipotent God allow evil and suffering to occur?" to "why do we, created in the image of God, permit such evil and suffering to continue?"[352] Stated slightly dif-

---

[350]Keshgegian, 279.
[351]Ibid. Cf. Wismer, "For Women in Pain," 140.
[352]Fortune, 143, and Sölle, "Suffering," 466.

ferently, the orientation for many feminist writers shifts to how can we allow certain types of suffering to go unchallenged, rather than how God can allow such suffering to occur in the first place. Thus, these writings seek less to justify a good and omnipotent God but more to identify or underscore a good humanity, worthy of God's attention and care to the level of sharing in our suffering, as well as in the resolutions of our suffering.

Further, in these writings by women, the focus frequently shifts from blaming God as the author of our suffering, to determining how God suffers with the afflicted and intimately knows the depths of that suffering. As discussed in the previous chapter, this suffering-God approach emphasizes the compassionate and empowering presence of God in the midst of distress rather than a distant, impassible God who is unaffected by humanity's turmoil.

Not only does the focus shift from blaming God as the source of suffering, but it also shifts from blaming the one who suffers as such a cause. For many of these writers what is of major concern is that the suffering exists, and the source of it may not always be concretely identified. What is more important than, say, the standard questions of theodicy is determining what actual responsibilities one has for relieving one's own and others' suffering. The focus thus shifts from a more abstract consideration (can we justify God in the midst of such suffering?) to more pragmatic considerations of care, nurture, and justice.

For many of these writers, ascribing blame either to God or to oneself frequently leads only to a debilitating helplessness and immobilizing passivity or resignation—a particularly dangerous form of evil for women that frequently only generates more suffering. In addition, many feminist thinkers believe that too much concentration on "causes" for suffering in God or oneself can be a dead end, because such causes or origins are ultimately unknowable and potentially damaging to one's image of God, as well as one's own self-concept.

Moreover, such a focus can often lead to deflecting responsibility for suffering from an actual perpetrator (such as a rapist, an abusive domestic partner, or systemic sexism within an organization or tradition) to a distant divine being or one's self, who may already be in a relatively powerless position. In so doing, motivation to act, seek justice, resolve, or eliminate that suffering which can be alleviated is diminished or thwarted, and often leads to just the sort of "sin" that Valerie Saiving Goldstein warned against that can be women's particular temptation and danger—underdevelopment or negation of the self. Thus, ascribing divine or personal blame for suffering is often viewed as misguided and dangerous, leading to further suffering and further devaluation of women by others and themselves. Rather than seeking someone or something to blame, then, many writers advocate ways of finding appropriate responsibility and accountability for the suffering that occurs.

Overall, then, women's writings on suffering reflect points made more generally by Patricia Wismer in a discussion on recent approaches to evil and suffering. As she notes, these writings

> often having a liberation emphasis, focus on what God is doing to combat evil (e.g., suffering with, sparking resistance, and bringing resurrection out of death); what people should be doing to combat evil (e.g., making the option for the poor, struggling against structural injustice, eschewing masochism, and being with those who suffer); and how humanity can relate to God in the meantime (e.g., expressing anger at God in the manner of the Hebrew psalms of lament, practicing contemplation, and celebrating liturgy and sacraments with others in the community of faith).[353]

A second trend that I see is that these *women's writings bear witness to another shift, that from looking at sin, evil, and suffering as one, monolithic experience to differentiating among various types of suffering.* Together, these writings attempt to look at the complexity and diversity of suffering, including suffering that is intrinsic to the human condition with its limits and contingencies, the suffering that one inflicts on another, as well as that which a society perpetuates in its very structures and policies. Along with other liberation theologies, the various feminist approaches surveyed also tend to be concerned with the suffering that violence, abuse, and systemic injustice and oppression generate—that is, with particular, concrete forms of suffering rather than "suffering in general." Many are concerned with situations of suffering traced to the effects of everything from poverty to patriarchy, engendered

[353]Wismer, "Evil," 175.

as a result of distorted social, political, and religious values. Distinctions are made as to how social location, ethnic and cultural parameters, and one's historical milieu affect the questions asked and the resolutions sought in the experience of suffering.

Overall, distinctions are also made among (1) suffering which can be alleviated, (2) that which cannot, and (3) that which might be taken on in order to bring about some greater good (e.g., to right or change a situation of social injustice, to recover from a life-threatening addiction, to challenge one to make needed changes in one's life).[354] Nonetheless, it is my observation that the suffering that cannot be eradicated by changes in social, political, and religious systems is given less attention, at present, in this literature. Little so far is said about how one might actually come to terms with what Wendy Farley identifies as "tragic" or "radical" suffering.

Moreover, this focus on the importance of distinguishing types of suffering is critical for many women writers since the specific type of suffering may lead to very different theological and spiritual approaches in dealing with that situation. No single approach is considered adequate for all instances of suffering. An approach may be viable in some circumstances and, literally, deadly in others.

A third general trend that can be identified in these writings involves *a shift in the focus of the meaning and significance of relationality in one's faith journey.* Whereas many of the traditional theological approaches to suffering have dealt primarily with the man-God (literally, in many cases) relation, emphasis in women's writing on evil and suffering has centered around the preservation and enhancement of a greater variety of relationships—be they with God, one's self, other humans, or the created order. Because God is relational for many of these writers, we are relational, and our suffering exists in the midst of or because of broken and deteriorating relations. Evil, itself, in many cases is a condition of the deterioration or destruction of relationships.

A fourth general trend in feminist discussions of suffering deals with *which part of the traditional theodicy question—God's justice, goodness, or power—is most often relinquished or rejected in women's depictions of evil and suffering.* In most of the literature surveyed, and as is common with liberation and process theologies

[354]Keshgegian, 279.

in general, divine omnipotence is most often set aside, limited, or reinterpreted. As Pamela Smith notes:

> The question of whether or not the God who is encountered in suffering ought to be thought of as omnipotent or non-omnipotent is a central issue for all sufferers.[355]

While in the received interpretations of traditional theodicies, God's power is most often associated with strength, domination, and coercion, feminist interpretations, following the general liberation approach, reorient an understanding of God's power as "enabling, as empowering, as compassionate."[356] Again, as noted by Smith:

> God should not be expected to heal all ills or even to be able to. God instead should be expected to be a continuing life-force and freedom at work within, and sometimes in spite of, everything. . . . God is encountered in impulses to altruism and liberation.[357]

Accordingly, divine omnipotence is quite often reinterpreted in these writings to mean that which "empowers persevering hope and compassionate, humanitarian response."[358]

While most attempt to retain the view of the goodness and compassion of God toward those who suffer, some writings also call into question God's goodness. This occurs particularly in the critiques of atonement theodicies wherein women question the rationale and compassion of a God who demands the death of a beloved son to achieve reconciliation with humanity, or the imitation of the suffering-servant model as a way of responding to human suffering.

On the human side, a fifth general trend that is disclosed by women's writings on suffering involves *the development of different ways of viewing the human person that are intended to be more helpful to women who suffer*. As deftly outlined by Patricia Wismer,[359] many thinkers are developing a feminist theological anthropology that reevaluates such areas as the body, relationality, virtues, sin,

[355]Smith, 175.
[356]Wismer, "Evil," 174.
[357]Smith, 178.
[358]Ibid., 177.
[359]Wismer, "For Women in Pain," 150–7.

and grace. For example, many explore the necessity for a more holistic understanding of the human person, in which we see ourselves as "embodied" beings, with feelings as well as minds. For most of these writers, it is critical to have an accurate picture of the basic goodness and worth of bodies and feelings, and to understand that, to a great extent, "we are our bodies."[360] Such a view also seeks to incorporate the ambiguity that is part of bodily experience, including both the goodness and the tragedy of living in a body that can suffer.

Further, as noted by Wismer in discussing women's writings on suffering, God is related to our bodies more positively than traditional theology often gives credence. In many of these women's writings, the emphasis is on God's delight in our embodied existence (as, for example, in our sexuality), and that God is expressed through our bodies in the world (e.g., Heyward's and Brock's work on the erotic).

Connected to this valuing of embodiment is another foundational principle for feminist theological anthropology which deals with relationality. As noted in the third general trend above, for most of these writers relationship is key to an understanding of what it is to be human. The "self is ontologically constituted by its relationships" as well as by its physicality.[361] In these women's writings on suffering, as Wismer points out, a trend appears that removes the connection between autonomy and identity, and emphasizes the importance of the self-in-relation with others. Many contend that a great deal of the human-generated suffering could be reduced by the recognition and positive development of one's relations within oneself and between self and others—especially with those who seem distinctly "other."[362]

Another aspect of this feminist theological anthropology is the need for revision of many traditional "virtues" that are "toxic" to women—such as obedience at all costs, self-negation and self-sacrifice, or the suppression or denial of feelings in order to attain a higher spiritual plane.[363] For example, a retrieval of the critical

[360]Ibid., 150. Cf. May, 18.
[361]Ibid., 151.
[362]Ibid., 152.
[363]E.g., Blomquist, 48.

importance of acknowledging one's feelings in suffering situations is highlighted. As Wismer notes, "as long as one's own pain is repressed, one cannot acknowledge anyone else's pain."[364] Many of these writers on suffering (such as Fortune) seek, in particular, to recover anger as a viable Christian virtue for women, and follow Beverly Wildung Harrison in seeing anger as a "mode of connectedness to others" and a "vivid form of caring." It signifies, at times, a form of resistance and protest to the quality of the social and political relations in which women are immersed.[365] Furthermore, hidden or unexpressed anger can lead to an atrophy of one's power to love, act, and deepen relation in the world.[366]

A fourth area being revised in feminist theological anthropologies, according to Wismer, and that I found in the women's writings surveyed, is sin. Critiques of the traditional views of evil and sin note a deep-seated gender bias, and the desire to punish sin rather than heal it.[367] Some women's writings go so far as to say that "the basic sin of women should be viewed as self-loss, self-denial, self-destruction, or, . . . masochism,"[368] while others alter even this view by incorporating concerns from the perspectives of women of color. Rather than see sin, for example, as disobedience, many women identify basic human sinfulness as anything which breaks down or damages our relationships with self and others— including acts, attitudes, entrenched social biases, distorted values, and the like.

A fifth area of reevaluation by feminist theologians is in the area of grace. For many of these writers, grace is what Wismer calls "radically immanent" in that it is viewed as a powerful life force which enhances connectedness and our capacity for intimacy. This grace profoundly integrates our body, spirit, reason, and passion, and helps us to fulfill our basic human desire to give and receive love.[369] Grace is always present and available within and between

---

[364]Wismer, "For Women in Pain," 153. Cf. Blomquist, who says the same of anger and forgiveness, 24.

[365]Cf. Beverly Wildung Harrison, "The Power of Anger in the Work of Love," in *Making the Connections,* 3–21.

[366]Wismer, "For Women in Pain," 153–4.

[367]Ibid., 154–5.

[368]Ibid., 155.

[369]Ibid., 155–6.

humans, and especially in situations of suffering, and yet may manifest itself in unexpected and paradoxical ways. For many of these writers, then, grace heals our sinfulness in such a way that our relations with one another and with God are restored.

## Any Value to Suffering?

In addition to these five general trends in women's writings on suffering, there appears to be no general consensus about the value of suffering. Some ascribe value to suffering as effective for healing and redemption; others see suffering as never intrinsically good, but inevitable and problematic; while others oppose seeing any redemptive value whatsoever in suffering.[370] Some see the value as survival—living through the suffering, and living well, beyond it.[371]

> Even those who argue for the redemptive value of the cross, however, are careful not to suggest that suffering is good in and of itself. Rather, suffering for the sake of justice and compassion, healing and liberation may be effective toward redemption.[372]

Nonetheless, juxtaposed with those that flatly state that suffering is never redemptive are such writings as those from the "wrestling with God" category. Writers such as Blomquist, May, and Smith give expression to a certain value in suffering—that of moving us beyond our rational categories of trying to "understand" or control suffering to an encounter with new meaning in the very midst of suffering. I shall pursue this in greater detail in the following chapters because I believe this is a significant area that needs further development in feminist theological responses to suffering.

## Areas That Are Troubling or Missing from These Discussions

In the broadly "theological" writings I surveyed, relatively little discussion occurs of evil specifically generated by women toward other

---

[370]Keshgegian, 280.
[371]Engel, 152.
[372]Keshgegian, ibid.

women, or toward others in general. The two obvious exceptions to this statement are those writings which speak of women's maintenance of patriarchal values and structures, and womanist writings, wherein not only incidents of sexism but also racism and classism rear their heads. It is my view that more theological discussion in this area is also needed, particularly as women gain ground in the public sphere and as our access to power in the public and academic spheres develops. For example, betrayal of women by other women in the workplace—often out of fear of losing personal gains made—is frequently an issue with those whom I am in contact with, but is rarely addressed in the theological literature.

Another area left unaddressed by these writings is regarding experiences of evil as an actual palpable, malevolent force. These writings do not yet deal with experiences that many women anecdotally report of an actual presence that is sensed as malevolent and destructive to life, that appears to mimic God but in actuality leads to more suffering. Future discussions in this area might be helpful in that these experiences concretely ground the view that evil is not a "nothing" but a "something." These discussions might also enhance our understanding of the suffering that cannot necessarily be dealt with through changes in social and political values and structures, but might best be addressed on a psychological or spiritual plane.

Finally, the experience of radical suffering, as defined by Wendy Farley, has also not been fully addressed by most theological writers, except as a part of a larger discussion regarding the political and social underpinnings of today's suffering for women. However, this area of radical suffering is just the area that I am most interested in, and that I believe gives many women the most consternation while raising the most questions about God. Because of this, the final chapter of this work will look more closely at the experience of radical suffering, and at a proposed theological/spiritual response to such suffering. Beforehand, however, one element that has not yet been considered in depth that may prove fruitful for the task of the final chapter is to look more closely at recent work that incorporates a tragic vision into Christian discussions of suffering.

# 4

# Tragic Vision and Suffering

IT HAS BEEN OVER TWENTY YEARS SINCE THE WORDS "TRAGEDY" AND "tragic" entered my life in a very pointed way with the abrupt and unanticipated deaths of both my parents within a twenty-four-hour period. Upon hearing of their deaths from a particularly virulent strain of viral pneumonia, many of their friends and our relatives referred to these events as "tragic" to express their horror, pity, and inability to comprehend such a startling event in all our lives. My own initial response was a mixture of terror, disbelief, anger, and guilt—terror at making literal life-and-death decisions affecting my own parents, numb disbelief that this could happen as all my efforts to do the "right thing" ended in their deaths, anger with doctors who acted as if they were gods but were only human after all, and guilt that I had failed somehow to know enough or to pray hard enough to stem this outcome.

Numbed by these events, I myself did not consciously ascribe these terms "tragedy" or "tragic" to what was happening. But, what I have subsequently discovered is that out of this life-changing experience, these terms lodged in my unconscious to such a degree that I pursued (somewhat unwittingly) their meanings in courses taken both in my undergraduate and graduate studies, as well as in the kinds of literature I have tended to read since then. Intertwined with additional life experiences that have underscored the limitations of our individual and collective efforts to avoid and deal effectively with profound suffering, these informal studies of the various forms of tragedy in classical Greek literature, through the medieval and Renaissance periods, into the modern and postmodern

exposed for me the profound tenuousness and vulnerability of the lives we lead. Something in these writings "grabbed" me, spoke to my own experiences, and demanded to be incorporated into my faith as a Christian. What I came later to understand was that this "something" involves tragedy's concern with unmerited suffering, choice, and the limits of human understanding and control over the outcomes of our actions. Tragedy, as interpreted by Larry Bouchard, speaks of endurance in the face of extreme suffering, unwelcome choices that demand to be made, self-defeating psychic and physical forces, and of situations that can baffle one's capacities to understand, control, and restore the situation to a better level.[1]

Besides this desire to incorporate such a tragic sensibility into my own Christian faith, what I also found in my studies was a love-hate relationship between Christianity and tragedy. Whereas much Christian literature, art, and music have used the tragic as an aspect, if not the focus, of their subject matter, much Christian theological and philosophical thought has discounted or neglected its value for the development of theological responses to suffering. As noted by Bouchard, Christian views have tended to interpret tragedy "in terms of the destructive effects of sin or to reject tragedy as a fatalistic denial of human responsibility for evil."[2] With a few exceptions, such as Max Scheler's essay on the tragic,[3] only until quite recently has there been an interest in the tragic per se in theological circles.[4] Perhaps this antipathy is due to a concentration on particular definitions or works that exhibit the tragic in a way that seems antithetical to Christian doctrine and faith or, perhaps, to misconceptions of tragedy. Nonetheless, can tragedy provide Christian faith with a valuable way of looking at some forms of evil

---

[1] Larry D. Bouchard, "Tragedy," in *Encyclopedia of Bioethics*, vol. 5, ed. Warren Thomas Reich, rev. ed. (New York: Macmillan Library Reference USA/Simon & Schuster Macmillan, 1995) 2491.

[2] Ibid., 2493.

[3] Max Scheler, "On the Tragic," *Cross Currents* 4 (1954) 178–91. Cf. Karl Jaspers, *Tragedy Is Not Enough,* trans. Harald A. T. Reiche, Harry T. Moore, Karl W. Deutsch (Boston: Beacon Press, 1952. Reprint, Hamden, Conn.: Shoe String Press, Archon Books, 1969).

[4] For more recent studies, see Hauerwas, Ruprecht, Ricoeur, Miller, Halliwell, Quinn, Farley, Sands, etc.

and suffering, and thus provide a foundation for developing viable responses to such suffering?

In this chapter I hope to explore how an incorporation of a tragic vision of reality, through which one comes face-to-face with human finitude, might enhance theological considerations on evil and radical suffering for women. Due to limitations of space and my lack of knowledge of the entire corpus of tragic literature and its secondary discussions, I do not cover every aspect of tragedy nor assume an expert's understanding. With the help of insights gained from writers such as Larry Bouchard, Paul Ricoeur, Wendy Farley, Kathleen Sands, and Tiina Allik, I merely wish to consider formally how a tragic vision might help those seeking viable theological responses to suffering. In so doing, this chapter will concentrate on (1) themes that regularly emerge in tragic stories, (2) how they speak of a tragic structure of reality, (3) a way of looking at the story of Job as an example of tragic suffering, and (4) why these might be important to a discussion on the value of suffering for women. I hope to cover such areas as human fallibility or fragility, freedom, and openness within a context of larger sources of significance, and to advocate the use of this tragic vision in such a way as to empower one to move through suffering to hope, resistance, and compassion.

## THEMES

As with many of the areas already previously discussed, including feminism, evil, and suffering itself, there are many views of tragedy and no one, all-encompassing theory.[5] The term can refer both to human experience (as in reference to my family's experience) and to a literary tradition spawned by early Greek dramatists such as Aeschylus, Sophocles, and Euripides, and further developed by a variety of philosophers and literary authors from Aristotle to Hegel, Schopenhauer, and Nietzsche; from Shakespeare, Boccacio, and Racine to such contemporary writers as Arthur Miller, Shusaku Endo, and Toni Morrison. Traces of a tragic sensibility can also be found in biblical narratives such as Job, Lamentations,

---

[5]See Morris Weitz, "Tragedy," in *Encyclopedia of Philosophy*, vol. 8, ed. Paul Edwards (New York: Macmillan Co. and The Free Press, 1967) 160–1.

and the story of Saul, as well as the lament Psalms, as noted by Wendy Farley.[6] Significantly, despite the variety of definitions and approaches, what tragedy can do, as a literary tradition, is provide us with "some of the paradigms we use to understand suffering and the choices that suffering presents to us."[7]

Perhaps the most famous and oft-quoted view of tragedy comes from Aristotle's *Poetics.* The tragic for Aristotle is associated with a "serious action" that involves incidents that arouse both pity and fear in the audience (*Poetics,* XIII.2), and involves "a man who is not eminently good and just, yet whose misfortune is brought about not by vice or depravity but by some error or frailty." (XIII.3)[8] Such incidents generally lead to a change of fortune (a reversal) from good to bad which arouses pity, because of the unmerited nature of the misfortune, and fear, because of the occurrence of such misfortune to others we view as somehow similar to ourselves.[9]

Moreover, as Bouchard summarizes:

> a tragic drama represents a person's serious actions or choices that lead mistakenly or unwittingly to great misfortune and that the audience witnesses with compassion and horror. . . . Between the action onstage and the audience, the misfortune is witnessed by a chorus . . . [that] sometimes participates in the suffering, and . . . always provides a bridge to the audience. The chorus may articulate thoughts and emotions that the actions evoke, and may thereby help the audience confront painful limits of understanding.[10]

Bouchard contends that literary tragedy is best defined not so much in terms of what it *is* but what it *does.* For him, what tragedy does is inquire, explore, and probe the difference between how things are and how we believe life "should be." In so doing, it tests the limits of a culture's moral expectations and the limits of its

---

[6]Wendy Farley, *Tragic Vision and Divine Compassion: A Contemporary Theodicy* (Louisville, Ky.: Westminster/John Knox Press, 1990) 23.

[7]Bouchard, 2491.

[8]Aristotle, *Aristotle's Poetics,* trans. S. H. Butcher (New York: Hill and Wang, 1961). Cf. Weitz, 155.

[9]Weitz, ibid.

[10]Bouchard, ibid.

virtues and norms. This suggests that dramatic tragedy, as well as the tragic in life, "has as much to do with those who witness and reflect on suffering and moral choice, in the manner of a Greek chorus, as with the suffering and choices themselves."[11] One value of literary tragedy, then, is that it enlightens us about our own beliefs, invites us to reflect on our own values and limits, and enhances our reflection on suffering by raising critical questions about our abilities to avoid, control, and/or alleviate it.[12]

Four key themes, identified by Wendy Farley, are important to highlight from Aristotle's view, as well as from classical tragedy in general. First, in classical tragedy, *suffering is depicted at the very core of the human situation.*[13] Misfortune and suffering are central concerns of the plot, and usually (though not always) involve the downfall of a fairly good person, worthy of our respect and honor, and usually not deserving of the suffering s/he experiences.[14] It seems, then, the tragic hero/ine is usually someone we can identify with or, in some cases, wish to emulate, and one who the audience or reader views as an innocent (or at least, an undeserving) sufferer. These conditions make the events portrayed all the more fraught with pity and fear. As Farley notes:

> The suffering of the tragic hero evokes pity; it is painful to watch a good person suffer. This suffering uncovers a world order that is hostile to what is good or virtuous. The defeat of the tragic hero suggests that the cosmos is meaningless and violent. This is the horror of tragedy.[15]

---

[11]Ibid., 2491.

[12]Ibid., 2492. Cf. Tiina Allik, ". . . the suffering of the hero has a counterpart in the fear and pity of the audience. . . . For the audience, the intelligibility of the plot includes the suffering of the emotions of fear and pity, yet the audience also experiences pleasure in that the mimetic activity of the poet brings fearful and pitiable events to representation and makes possible the catharsis of those emotions, partly through their intelligibility," "Narrative Approaches to Human Personhood: Agency, Grace, and Innocent Suffering," *Philosophy and Theology* 1 (1987) 319.

[13]"This concern with suffering distinguishes tragedy from most Christian theology, which identifies guilt as the primary clue to the human condition." Farley, 23.

[14]Weitz, 156.

[15]Farley, 28.

Without much of a stretch of the imagination, this situation that classical tragedy depicts seems quite applicable to contemporary, postmodern times, as attested to by our daily news reports and as indicated by much of the literature reviewed previously in chapters 2 and 3 above.

Moreover, the suffering that classical tragedy depicts is characteristically triggered by some action of the hero or heroine that for any number of reasons goes awry—from misjudgment, to ignorance about the ramifications of one's actions, to a lack of other viable alternatives in a given situation.[16] A reasonably good person with limited knowledge or foresight, the tragic hero/ine loses control over a situation through a combination of what the ancient Greeks called *hubris* (zeal, excess, passion, acting like or equating oneself with the gods) and *hamartia* (error, ignorance, mistake, or "missing the mark").[17] Horrendous consequences ensue not only for the individual, but also for his/her family and extended community.

One focus of literary tragedy, then, is that tragic suffering can occur as a result of a moral zeal or passion, an over-extension of self, or an error in judgment that has unexpected and unintended destructive consequences. The misfortune and suffering are, thus, not the direct result of a conscious sin, disobedience, or depravity but are due to what is often referred to as a "tragic flaw" or fault—an *inevitable* human error or proclivity, conspiring with forces and conditions already present and beyond one's control. Thus, the tragic protagonists are both actors and acted upon, agents and victims, and their actions compound their and others' suffering, whether they are directly culpable or not.[18]

In this sense, then, the action that brings about tragic suffering is guiltless, and, accordingly, suffering of this sort cannot be adequately resolved by penalty or punishment. As Farley stresses, "since guilt is not the primary problem in this type of suffering, atonement and forgiveness cannot help transcend it."[19] Thus, tragedy speaks of a type of suffering that cannot be effectively ad-

[16]Bouchard, 2493.
[17]Farley, 24.
[18]Bouchard, ibid.
[19]Farley, 29.

dressed by the responses of many of the traditional theodicies outlined in chapter 2, especially those that emphasize punishment,
redemption from conscious sin or guilt, or even "soul making."
Such suffering requires a different kind of response than these
theodicies have thus far provided.[20] As Farley notes about the suffering that is involved:

> There is nothing to appeal to which would make this suffer-
> ing meaningful. . . . Tragic heroes and heroines are usually
> destroyed in the course of the story. . . . The suffering is raw,
> unmediated by justice or utility; it witnesses to the power of
> absurdity or malice or sheer force to bring down what is
> noble and good.[21]

Furthermore, the suffering that tragedy depicts is always interwoven with the lives of others. Individuals are rarely, if ever,
shown to suffer totally alone, but within a network of sociality that
is also subject to the effects of the tragic incidents. For instance,
tragedy speaks of broken relations when, due to the tragic events,
the sufferer is often cut off or forced into exile from normal social
relations (e.g., the story of Philoctetes)—incurring a social and
spiritual isolation that is quite typical of severe suffering, as seen in
previous chapters of this work. Moreover, the destabilizing nature
of the complex events that take place put at risk not only the individual and his/her frames of reference, but also those of his/her
family and whole communities of which the hero/ine is a part
(e.g., the stories of Medea, Agamemnon, and Oedipus).

Thus, tragedy extends our understanding of that form of suffering that has the power to degrade and dehumanize precisely
because it is simultaneously severe, life-defeating, and unmerited.
Not only does it affect the person directly involved, but can also
affect the community of which one is a part. Therefore, it seems
reasonable to say, also, that the suffering that tragedy considers is
very similar to that which Farley has defined as "radical" and Sölle

---

[20]In the next chapter we will look at some possible elements of an alternative
response to suffering. At present, it is important to identify both that suffering is
at the heart of tragedy's concern with the human condition and what kind of suffering tragedy attempts to depict and confront.

[21]Farley, 24.

has identified as "meaningless" suffering—both of which are the most resistant to eradication or to major change by human effort.[22] Perhaps, then, the central themes of tragic Greek literature can enlighten us about the conditions of such suffering, leading to the possibilities of alternatives for confronting and living with what seems a major challenge to theological reflections on suffering.

Besides this central concern with undeserved suffering, Farley also notes a second theme that emerges on a regular basis from classical tragic stories—that of *the limits of human freedom intertwined with the extent of human responsibility.* As noted above, tragedy speaks of suffering that ensues because of "chance, lack of full knowledge, negligence, misjudgment, as much as through conscious deeds of malice, oppression, and ill-will."[23] In so doing, it recognizes the role and inevitability of human error and limitation in our daily existence. No matter how intelligent, rational, and well-meaning one is, one's decisions and actions can set in motion disastrous consequences. As one author has noted:

> there is also a less easily formulated conception of heroism at work in the [tragic] genre . . . its scope is that of lives lived, whether in action or suffering, at or close to the limits of human possibility—a form of heroism, uniquely for the Greeks, discoverable in women as well as men, and one which, in its concern with human extremes, is inherently religious in its implications for tragedy.[24]

Tragic protagonists are usually portrayed as relatively free agents, able to choose a course of action among a number of alternatives. However, no matter how heroic or laudable, these protagonists are also portrayed as finite and fallible, insufficiently knowledgeable and insufficiently virtuous for the conditions at hand. Moreover, these very conditions that surround and affect the protagonist and the action are often shown as capricious, morally questionable, and even malevolent, and can significantly affect the suffering that occurs. Within this complex environment,

[22]See chapter 3, pp. 130–1, 134–6 above.
[23]Farley, 24.
[24]Stephen Halliwell, "Human Limits and the Religion of Greek Tragedy," *Literature and Theology* 4 (1990) 173.

the hero/ine still *must* act—i.e., the protagonist cannot abdicate the decision to act, or refuse to act in order to avoid responsibility. Thus,

> Freedom is confined within a preexisting situation and is hedged by ignorance and conflict. Tragedy requires of its hero action within a situation where all action leads to disaster. It is the genius of tragedy to recognize the complexity of responsibility.[25]

Not only, then, is the hero/ine in tragedy free and must act, but s/he is also limited and susceptible to dubious forces or conditions, and accordingly, the outcomes of his/her choices and actions are highly ambiguous, if not calamitous. Although the action that condemns the hero/ine to destruction is a guiltless one, the hero/ine remains, nonetheless, accountable on some level for what happens. As Kathleen Sands has identified so well, the genius of tragedies is that they "often center on the awful enigma of *nonculpable fault,* which deflates . . . morality and paralyzes movement until responsibility for evil is borne."[26]

In a tragic vision of reality, what one does matters, but the outcomes of one's actions are never fully predictable or guaranteed. Because of this dual aspect of tragic suffering, a sense of powerlessness, unfairness, and defeat in the face of tragic or radical suffering can arise, and yet the necessity to act and the responsibility for those actions remain intact. Here it is important to note, then, that contrary to some notions of tragedy, tragic heroes and heroines are not absolved from accountability for their actions, however innocently and unwittingly executed, and remain responsible for the consequences of those actions.[27]

Thus, whereas the tragic hero/ine is usually depicted as free and responsible, tragedy also speaks of the inability to determine culpable fault in every negative outcome—perhaps, what might be termed an inherent chanciness in life. Conversely, one cannot ignore culpability altogether—since that would be a denial of moral

[25]Farley, 24.

[26]Kathleen Sands, *Escape from Paradise: Evil and Tragedy in Feminist Theology* (Minneapolis: Fortress Press, 1994) 16 [my emphasis].

[27]Bouchard, 2493.

complexity and responsibility. In this way, tragedy "explores not only error but also choices structured by the moral life itself."[28]

A third predominant theme that emerges from classical tragic stories is that *the very constitution of the world order makes suffering inevitable.* Contrary to the view that human desires and actions (such as disobedience) are solely or primarily responsible for the suffering that occurs, tragedy identifies that something in the world order itself "makes an ethical passion for piety, justice, truth, or compassion self-destructive."[29] In addition to the hero/ine's own actions or agency, the very way things are structured in any social location or historical reality, is implicated as part of the origin of tragic suffering:

> . . . tragic vision locates the possibility of suffering in the conditions of existence and in the fragility of human freedom. The very structures that make human existence possible make us subject to the destructive power of suffering.[30]

Not only, then, is freedom constrained and responsibility intact, but also the environment of tragedy within which human action occurs is implicated as a source of suffering. This tragic environment within which the hero/ine must act is usually determined by "either an external, non-human power (such as the Fates or Zeus) or a set of intrinsic conflicting values," which constrains the person's freedom but also sets up a severe conflict of some sort.[31]

For example, in the first case, the moral passion of the hero/ine is in conflict with elemental powers and principles of the cosmos, usually depicted in terms of sheer power or omnipotence of a god or of the Fates. As in the story of Prometheus, his suffering comes about because of his kindness to the human race, and is exacted as punishment for defying Zeus' omnipotence. In the second case, tragedy is traced to "the irreconcilability of equally important obligations," as exemplified in such a character as Antigone who must honor her duties to the gods and to her family in burying her brother, which simultaneously challenges her loyalty to the

[28]Ibid.
[29]Farley, 26.
[30]Ibid., 29.
[31]Ibid., 26.

authority of government by disobeying the prohibition against burying traitors. "She exemplifies the passion for justice that is condemned by an environment that *requires* a betrayal of one fundamental value in order to pursue another."[32] In both cases,

> Tragedy recognizes something in the world order recalcitrant to human freedom and well-being, which qualifies and even corrupts obligation. But tragedy resists the temptation to elevate this enigmatic necessity to a strict determinism or predestination that would erode responsibility. The dialectic between freedom and fate remains ambiguous. Human beings are not absolved from responsibility, but actions are performed in an environment that is not morally neutral; it is already tainted, disguised, even malevolent.[33]

In a tragic vision of reality, then, human freedom is fragile and not absolute, and is exercised within a context that is already defined negatively in many essential ways, before any human will is exercised or any act occurs. In this way, tragedy recognizes and exhibits that the threat and reality of radical suffering is embedded in the very conditions of our embodied, social existence, and that human action occurs in an environment that is not entirely shaped by our control. Thus, it "places evil within a context that is more inclusive than human fault."[34]

As a result of such evil, the suffering that occurs in stories with a tragic sensibility is a way of exemplifying "a world order in which intolerable and unjustifiable suffering is inevitable. . . . The catastrophes that befall tragic heroes illuminate the *way things really are*."[35] Thus, tragedy speaks of suffering that originates, to some degree, in the conditions of his/her historical reality, over which the person inevitably has little or no control. To my thinking, in this way, a tragic vision speaks well to the experiences of natural evil and parallels well with Ruether's and Noddings' insistence on looking at evil as social and cultural, as well as natural and moral. As Walter Lowe has noted in *Evil and the Unconscious:*

[32]Ibid.
[33]Ibid., 25.
[34]Ibid., 31.
[35]Ibid., 28.

when one approaches classical tragedy from the side of the protagonist, one is struck that the individual is portrayed as caught up in events and yet responsible for them. There is a certain givenness to the situation, a certain *facticity;* and yet the tragic figure is somehow responsible, there is a certain *complicity.*[36]

What a tragic vision portrays, then, is that life is conflicted and reality, ambiguous. The conditions which hedge and circumscribe our actions for the good are always present, and as noted in chapter 3 with reference to systemic evil, are often bigger than the sum total of all human effort. Moreover, our very definitions of the "good," as Kathleen Sands also noted in the previous chapter, are variable due to their dependence on socially-determined constructs, so that we experience life as an arena of competing values or "goods," which can lead to various forms of radical suffering. As Sands suggests,

> *Tragedy,* as I understand it, is the inevitability of our involvement in evil, an inevitability that comes into focus only in a world unclouded by spiritual infinitism. In this world, where there is multiplicity but not infinity, . . . there can be delusion of sheer acceptance. In a radically plural and often conflicted world, we cannot be for everything and what we are against has a cost. Tragedy infects moral life with fault, and it troubles intellectual life with absurdity, since without negative moral judgments the plurality of truth would be benign and acceptable. . . . Those struggles are not of something against nothing, not of tolerance against intolerance or of bias against truth, but of power against power, truth against truth.[37]

It seems, according to such a tragic view, that because of who we are as humans we are inevitably in conflict with powers beyond our abilities to control, as well as subject to conflicts arising from competing "goods." We are part of, and vulnerable to, a world order that distorts our freedom and hedges our efforts to confront and eradicate the moral sources of evil and suffering.

Tragedy, though, also speaks of the necessity for acting, despite the limits and the potential hazards involved. In so doing, a

[36]Walter Lowe, *Evil and the Unconscious* (Chico, Calif.: Scholars Press, 1983) 11, 83, quoted in Allik, 324.
[37]Sands, 9.

tragic vision does not advocate a passive stance, as some might assume; it is built on acceptance of finitude and fragility, but also on such an acceptance that is characterized by defiance, resistance, and hope. This is the fourth key theme that Farley draws from her studies of Greek tragedies—that of *resistance to tragic suffering.*

As Farley stresses, "the tragedies of ancient Greece are unrelenting in their depiction of the downfall of the noble and virtuous, but they are not cynical. Tragic heroes are not resigned or stoic or glib; they are defiant."[38] They are not nihilistic, but often perseverant. For her, the very ethical integrity and vitality of the hero/ine signifies a moral order that is disclosed by his/her actions.

> Even in defeat, a vision of justice remains to vindicate the tragic hero. The defiance of the hero enacts and recovers human dignity even in the teeth of destruction. If suffering and destruction cannot be overcome, they can be resisted. It is in the resistance itself, in this refusal to give up the passion for justice, that tragedy is transcended.[39]

In these depictions, defiance and resistance are hallmarks of a viable response to tragic suffering that cannot be overcome solely through human agency or even in one's own historical framework. Partially because such a response returns dignity and power back to the sufferer, tragedy can be transcended in some cases, despite one's present defeat. Although the circumstances and the pain may continue, the way the person appropriates that pain is changed. In this way, suffering is placed within a different, more meaningful perspective, and may be modified or reduced through acts of resistance and defiance.

Moreover, in many tragic stories, Farley notes, "the brutality of power wins, but only by ensuring its own downfall."[40] This downfall may not occur within the confines of one story within a cycle of tragedies, but can become apparent in subsequent stories in the cycle. In a sense, then, a type of moral reckoning is assured, though not necessarily found in the protagonist's own lifetime. It may take longer than that tragic hero/ine's lifetime to work out the justice that is due. The parallels that this has with the stance of resistance

[38]Farley, 27.
[39]Ibid.
[40]Ibid.

depicted by womanist theologians and others in chapter 3 are quite obvious. In my view these women writers echo a sensibility and response toward suffering also found in many of the tragic dramas of ancient Greece.

Notwithstanding the power of external and internal forces to provoke evil and suffering, or the intrinsic conflict of values that exists in a world of diversity such as ours, the message of the tragic dramas, according to Farley, is that "some good persists that makes defiance of tragedy meaningful."[41] Classical tragedy for her, and I would concur, is therefore ethical rather than absurd or nihilistic:

> Tragedy presses upon us a dark vision of reality, but it is in turn transcended by the apprehension of ultimate goodness. Its appeal to justice and its evocation of compassion are traces of an ethical order that is frustrated but not destroyed by unjust suffering.[42]

And further:

> In tragedy, the power of evil to destroy what is good is present in the very structure of the cosmos. But then another layer of the world order is peeled back. One is permitted to glimpse something beyond the apparent finality of evil. The victory of the malignant power suddenly stands hollow. An ethical order reappears to stand in judgment on that which would defeat what is good.[43]

## THE TRAGIC STRUCTURE OF REALITY

In combination with these four themes (of tragedy's central concern with suffering, the limits of human freedom intertwined with the extent of human responsibility, a world order that distorts freedom and engenders suffering, and resistance as a key response to tragic suffering), Farley further elucidates what she defines as "the tragic structure of reality." This structure displays the dialectic between human freedom and finitude, and describes features of human existence that condition the possibility and occasion the destruction of human life.

[41]Ibid., 28.
[42]Ibid., 29.
[43]Ibid., 27.

This tragic structure of reality shares with Christianity the view that "creation is good, creatures are good, and their mutual relations are good"; but, those relations can be conflicted due to the structure of reality that encompasses those relations.[44] For example, cultural diversity can be both an occasion for celebration of the many gifts each of us brings to a situation, but it can also become an occasion for suspicion and violence due to social and ethnic prejudices that affect our relations. Important to note here is that in and of itself, this tragic structure that affects relations among humans is not evil, but it makes suffering "both possible and inevitable prior to any human action."[45] Let us see in more detail how this can happen by reviewing some of the insights regarding this tragic structure of reality found in the work of Farley and another theologian, Tiina Allik, as well as the contributions Paul Ricoeur has made in his early work on the symbolism of evil.

## Wendy Farley on This Tragic Structure

Farley identifies the following key elements as contributing to such a tragic structure of reality: finitude, conflict, and fragility. Because each can add to our understanding of radical or tragic suffering, I have discussed each briefly below.

*Finitude,* often thought of as the "limitedness" of human beings, is one key element in our lives that enables suffering to occur. Finitude is usually seen as "a function of human participation in the physical and biological, spatial and temporal world, . . . [and] has often been used to refer to the way in which human powers . . . never attain perfection but are always limited."[46] As Stephen Halliwell, discussing human limits and the religion of Greek tragedy, stresses:

> The limits against which the lives of the tragic hero or heroine press, or are pressed, lie across physical, ethical, psychological, and social regions of experience . . . [such as] meeting a particular kind of death, living with unbearable knowledge, . . . confronting an irreconcilable clash of values

---

[44]Ibid., 32.

[45]Ibid., 31–2.

[46]Tiina Allik, "Human Finitude and the Concept of Women's Experience," *Modern Theology* 9 (1993) 82, n. 1.

> . . . or sustaining a purity of dedication against all tempta-
> tion of self-preservation or compromise. . . . Tragic hero-
> ism is a discovery of the strengths and the limits of humanity,
> and their complex relations to the more than human.[47]

Finitude, then, is one quality of our lives that qualifies all our actions in the world, and forces us to recognize and acknowledge
our insufficiency and need.

For instance, finitude can involve the fact that our very embodiment constitutes both a boundless pleasure and a major limit
on our existence, and makes us subject to decay, disease, harm,
frustration, accident, and death. So, the threat of radical suffering
is actually embedded in us, in that we are bodies that have physical limits, that can suffer, and that are subject to mortality.

Furthermore, the anticipation of pain in such a body can lead
to a sense of anxiety and foreboding for the future, poisoning sat-
isfaction and enjoyment of the present. As Farley clarifies:

> when mortality is accompanied by nerve endings and self-
> consciousness, then physical pain, grief, fear, and anxiety will
> augment injury and sickness with deeper kinds of sufferings.
> Since human beings are always social and cultural, frailty will
> extend itself to include culturally determined meanings and
> threats. . . . Bodies equipped to experience pain and pleas-
> ure can also be tortured, raped, and imprisoned. . . .
> Embodiment and mortality are also the causes of the most in-
> tense pain and deepest sense of foreboding. . . . The inten-
> sity of enjoyment that comes from risk gives a greater
> perfection to creation than a flatter, if safer, world would
> allow. But this metaphysical conflict means that every good
> conceals a shadow side. . . . The conditions of finite exist-
> ence are tragically structured. Multiplicity, embodiment,
> mortality, historicity make human existence possible—but
> each of these structures makes certain kinds of suffering in-
> evitable.[48]

Tiina Allik also proposes another way to look at human finitude that conditions our experiences of evil and suffering. Finitude

[47]Halliwell, 174.
[48]Farley, 33–4.

for her can also be seen as "human openness to the world, the ability to be affected by things in the world which one has not willed, including one's own unwilled and unconscious aspects."[49] This openness, or vulnerability, can be seen either negatively or positively, depending on whether one values control over oneself and mastery of one's environment, or values spontaneity, as well as the "richness and the creativity that comes from a mix of contingencies." If one is interested in appropriating a variety of experiences, people, and unwilled aspects of the self, then

> one would never want to do away with the vulnerability which is also the sensitivity which makes possible these experiences and interactions. In other words, human finitude is not only human limitedness, but also an openness and receptivity to the world, a basis for creativity and spontaneity of human existence.[50]

Whichever view one takes, whether one sees it as a limitedness of one's freedom and powers, or an openness and receptivity, finitude makes one susceptible to both external and internal forces that can affect one's experience of evil and suffering.

Another element of the tragic structure of reality that Farley and others identify has to do with *conflict*. Even though tragedy depicts creation and creatures as good, as well as the mutual relations between those creatures as good, those relationships are, inevitably, conflicted. As Farley identifies:

> relationships can be conflicted and sometimes are necessarily so, as in the relationship between predator and prey. The multiplicity of religions, cultures, and nations gives depth to human life, but this plurality inevitably (if not necessarily) degenerates into competition, misunderstanding, and conflict. . . . Values, too, can be essentially incommensurate and conflicting. . . . Nicolas Berdyaev describes the moral life as fundamentally tragic because equally compelling values must come into conflict.[51]

---

[49]Allik, ibid.
[50]Ibid.
[51]Farley, 32. Cf. Nicolas Berdyaev, *The Destiny of Man* (New York: Harper & Row, 1960) 154.

Tragedy thus speaks of conflicts of purpose or between equally important and admirable values (e.g., benefiting the common good vs. respecting personal autonomy). As Hegel also pointed out in his assessment of the life and trial of Socrates in his *Lectures on the History of Philosophy,*

> in what is truly tragic there must be valid moral powers on both sides which come into collision; this was so with Socrates. . . . Two opposed rights come into collision, and the one destroys the other. Thus both suffer loss and yet both are mutually justified.[52]

Thus, tragedy deals with dilemmas wherein there are at least two *valid* ethical claims (two things one ought to do), but one cannot do both without sacrificing one for another.[53] Furthermore, no matter what choice one makes, either one involves some form of "wrongdoing" and/or guilt, and yet the protagonist must choose or act.[54] In this way, tragedy often deals with hard choices that arise from conflicting values or limited resources, and can even involve issues of just distribution of those resources. By so doing, tragedy can express for us the nuance and complexity of our existence and, perhaps, lead us to more satisfying resolutions and understandings of the suffering in our midst. As Sands states, in a slightly different way:

> Tragedies, as I define them, are stories or ways of telling stories that highlight elemental conflicts of truths, which I also call conflicts of powers. Elemental powers, in this definition, are the vital, integral dimensions of life in a particular context. They need not be permanent or eternal, and they are never beyond question. Tragedies illuminate the way in which such elemental conflicts afflict humanity with evil—that is, with negative moral judgments in which some elemental power must be opposed. In so doing, tragedies force their observers . . . to make their own judgments about the judgments of the

[52]G.W.F. Hegel, *Lectures on the History of Philosophy,* quoted in Weitz, 158. Cf. Philip Quinn, "Tragic Dilemmas, Suffering Love, and Christian Life," *Journal of Religious Ethics* 17 (1989) 151–83; Quinn, "Agamemnon and Abraham: The Tragic Dilemma of Kierkegaard's Knight of Faith," *Literature and Theology* 4 (1990) 182–5.
[53]Quinn, "Agamemnon and Abraham," 182.
[54]Ibid., 183.

tragic characters. Through confrontation with elemental conflict, the community can season its moral wisdom . . . and,
right within the narrow horizon of the possible, identify acts
and attitudes that warrant praise or blame.[55]

For Sands, then, tragic conflict is not necessarily a situation of social and moral disintegration, but more an essential element of our
lives as currently structured. It is not something that indicates evil
in itself, or something that we should flee from out of frustration
and exasperation, but is more an inevitable part of the fabric of
our lives that allows for suffering to occur. As she says:

Once society is apprehended as a network of diverse and often
conflicting powers, tragic conflict becomes a routine function
of social contradiction, not just an anomaly of social collapse.[56]

Thus, in taking both views of Farley and Sands here, conflict
within a tragic understanding of reality can involve both "a con-
stituent feature of existence and a corruption of variety and relationship."[57] Conflict makes human life possible in all its richness
and diversity, but, in some instances, it also makes suffering inevitable. Perhaps, no matter how good our theories about evil and
suffering are, or how much we strive to resolve conflict, we need to
accept on some level that tragic conflict is an inescapable part of
our lives.

Moreover, as depicted in many classical tragedies, reality is also
structured by a condition of human *fragility,* according to Farley.
Not only is our freedom subject to and limited by external forces,
but also by what Farley defines (and Allik echoes) as "an interior
unsteadiness" caused by anxiety and desire.[58] For instance, the apprehension of danger and a dread of possible deleterious futures
perennially haunt our lives, to the point that

Anxiety sickens freedom with an unpleasant suspicion that
possibility is a code word for nothingness. Anxiety is the

[55]Sands, 10.
[56]Ibid., 6.
[57]Farley, 32.
[58]Ibid., 34. Cf. Stephen Duffy, "Our Hearts of Darkness: Original Sin
Revisited," *Theological Studies* 49 (1988) 610.

apprehension of the future less as a tempting promise for happiness than as a concealed threat. It is that interior disquiet that accompanies contingency.[59]

In such a state of anxiety, one can be easily and unwittingly seduced by deception and wrongdoing, beguiled by an apathy or callousness to change situations that are destructive to the flourishing of the human person or succumb to despair and hopelessness.[60]

Walter Lowe seems to agree when he points out that conflict in tragedy can also arise not so much from

> a dualism which is a result of foreign impingement on the hero but rather as a dualism which consists of a genuinely internal conflict between different aspects of the hero. This has the effect of deepening the conflict and making it seem inevitable, because the hero is involved in and responsible for both sides of the conflict.[61]

Here, Lowe seems to support the view already discussed that the evil represented in a tragic vision is something for which one both is and is not responsible. But, Lowe also extends this into a discussion of the connection of the unconscious with some of the evils of human existence—extending the notion of our lack of control over conscious decisions and acts. The unconscious sets up internal conflicts that create an unsteadiness in the human agent *vis à vis* evil and suffering. Tragic suffering, then, can be a function not only of conflicts external to the human person, but also in part, can be a function of one's internal self-conflict.[62]

Desire, too, as an aspect of human fragility, can accentuate the unsteadiness of our freedom in the world to do what we consider "good." As Farley points out, desire is that sense of restlessness and yearning that constitutes much of human existence, and does not necessarily imply selfishness, but can also be the unfulfillable drive

[59]Farley, 35.
[60]"Freedom is always, because undetermined but hounded by its own finitude, permeated by an inescapable anxiety and hence a constitutive fallibility and vulnerability to sin. Human freedom is tragic as well as moral. Fallibility and anxiety are not the consequences of a primal fall; they are ontological constituents of freedom," Duffy, 611.
[61]Allik, "Narrative Approaches to Human Personhood," discussing Lowe, 324.
[62]Cf. chapter 2, pp. 29–30 above.

for various good endeavors. The problem with desire, as she notes, is that "no concrete desire ever perfectly coincides with its possible fulfillment."[63] Our desires are such that we are never fully satisfied.

Not only is desire unfulfillable by its very nature, but it is also ambiguous in its content. We have mixed desires (e.g., those who long for the end of physical and psychological violence toward women, but also desire to punish all rapists and abusers with the death penalty). Thus, this restlessness and ambiguity of desire "reinforce feelings of unease and dissatisfaction."[64] All our actions for the "good," according to tragic literature, are hedged by our fragility, by conflicting values, valid needs and desires, and by our very finitude. We are often caught in a situation between opposing forces and conflicted desires, between passions and responsibilities. Nonetheless, we must act in our world, in spite of our awareness of our limitations to carry forth our determined "goods." Thus, as depicted by tragic literature:

> It is often the case that freedom is more of a burden than a pleasure; we are enervated rather than exhilarated by the possibilities of life. It would be such a mercy, such a relief to hand freedom over to someone else. . . . The harshness of anxiety and the restlessness of desire condemn freedom to betrayal and defeat. Freedom is the tragic flaw of human existence, at once the stamp of its greatness and its destruction.[65]

## Tiina Allik on This Tragic Structure

Tiina Allik, writing on narrative approaches to human personhood, echoes many of Farley's and Lowe's insights into the tragic structure of reality and adds to our understanding of suffering by further showing compatibilities between tragedy and some aspects of Christian theology.[66] Intending to acknowledge the extent of human materiality and interdependence when looking at suffering and incorporating a view of the concept of concupiscence based on Karl Rahner's thought, Allik demonstrates some affinities between tragedy and Christian thought.

[63]Farley, 35.
[64]Ibid., 36.
[65]Ibid., 37.
[66]Allik, ibid., 305–53.

As she notes, concupiscence, in traditional Christian thought, usually refers to "the desires or appetites of the lower faculties of human nature that have not been brought under the control of the rational capacities." Concupiscence, in this traditional view, is thus often considered to be a "resistance of sinful desires and appetites to the rational decision of the person to live her life in a way that she believes is good."[67]

However, as Allik interprets Rahner, another view of concupiscence arises in which it is seen more as a permanent condition

> . . . rooted in our materiality and in the limitedness of our powers of self-control and self-determination that is due to our materiality. Concupiscence does not necessarily have to be sinful. Indeed, sometimes our concupiscent desires are good and our rational decision of self-determination is the element in the conflict that is bad. . . . [Rahner] also points out that the fact of having desires and appetites which are not under the control of the rational faculties is not in itself an indication of sinfulness.[68]

Because of the essential materiality of human existence, the integrity of the human to choose possible "goods" or even to love God above all other impulses cannot "consist of a deliberate and conscious control over every part of the human person or even that that state will have been achieved by those means."[69] For her, then:

> Given the essential materiality of human existence, there will always be involuntary and spontaneous actions and a person's integrity will not consist of, nor can it have been achieved by, a consistent and conscious ordering of all parts and aspects of the person.[70]

What is important for Allik about this permanent creaturely concupiscence is that it makes human beings "permanently vulnerable to destruction by external forces."

[67]Ibid., 313.

[68]Ibid. Cf. Karl Rahner, "The Theological Concept of Concupiscentia," *Theological Investigations,* vol. 1, trans. Cornelius Ernst (Baltimore: Helicon Press, 1961) 347–82; and Tiina Allik, "Karl Rahner on Materiality and Human Knowledge," *Thomist* 49 (1985) 367–86.

[69]Ibid., 313–4.

[70]Ibid., 314.

> If one envisions human persons as always having spontaneous
> desires, one also envisions them as always reacting to what is
> other or external to their volition, and often to their conscious-
> ness. In other words, the notion of a permanent concupiscence
> means that human persons are essentially a part of the world
> around them and genuinely open and vulnerable to that world.
> It then follows that the human capacity to be a self-determin-
> ing agent must correspondingly be envisioned as something
> that can be subject to such violence that it can be destroyed.[71]

Therefore, if one is truly "open" to that which is outside one's control or volition (either people or events), then one is also open to
"a kind of sin that would make him [or her] sin and violate his [or
her] conscience and character."[72]

If this view is correct, then, humans are constituted not only
by their consciously selected actions and potentially destructive
choices, but also by a permanent vulnerability, based in one's materiality and finitude.

> If this is in fact the case, human integrity and the capacity to
> be self-constituting would be partly dependent on God's
> providential care. This would be so, not only because of the
> prevalence in human beings of moral defect, but also because
> of the inherent fragility of the human person as a self-consti-
> tuting agent.[73]

It seems, then, that Allik is concerned that we not lose the
sense of real moral tragedy—"a situation in which a person is determined in a way that violates her moral integrity and in a sense
makes the person do what she does not want to do."[74] She is concerned that we not deny the permanence and radical nature of our
human vulnerability to non-voluntary forces, as expressed in
Rahner's concept of permanent concupiscence, and consequently,
also deny our inherent need for God's grace. What makes Allik's insights so important to a study of women and suffering is that they
caution us against giving too much credit to the power of humans
to overcome evil and suffering on our own.

[71]Ibid.
[72]Ibid.
[73]Ibid.
[74]Ibid., 315.

I concur with Allik in that some views of human personhood, whether they come from feminist circles or not, have the potential for claiming too much for human autonomy and agency, and the human capacity for self-constitution. The danger can lie in making inordinate claims for human agency in eradicating suffering, born out of the deep desire to make sense of and find justification for the radical suffering that assails us.

## Paul Ricoeur on This Tragic Structure

Corresponding to many of Farley's and Allik's insights are contributions to a tragic vision of reality in selected works of Paul Ricoeur. For example, in *Fallible Man,* Ricoeur identifies a "fatal flaw" in humans that allows evil to enter into the world. For him, as found in this work, to exist is to project oneself into the future; but, it is, at the same time, to recognize that there exists a rift between what we are at present and what we think we can be. This alienation from one's own deepest being, this discontinuity between existence and essence, constitutes a fragility, or vulnerability, in us which allows evil to enter into the world through us. This flaw or fallibility is not yet a moral flaw, but a condition of finite being which makes evil and morality possible.

> To say that man [sic] is fallible is to say that the limitation peculiar to a being who does not coincide with [her-]himself is the primordial weakness from which evil arises. And yet, evil *arises* from this weakness only because it is *posited.* This last paradox will be at the center of the symbolics of evil.[75]

For Ricoeur, as revealed by some of the symbols and myths of Western culture, evil appears inscribed in the innermost structure of human reality. We, by our nature, are fragile and liable to err. "For man [sic], as he [sic] is revealed by his symbolics, appears no less a victim than guilty."[76] Here, too, suffering is not only a product of human choice and action but a result of a basic condition of humanity.

---

[75]Paul Ricoeur, *Fallible Man: Philosophy of the Will,* trans. Charles Kelbley (Chicago: Henry Regnery Company, 1965) 224.

[76]Ibid., xxix.

In his influential study *The Symbolism of Evil,* Ricoeur elaborates on his views of the nature of evil and suffering through an extensive discussion of the symbols of defilement, sin, and guilt, as well as of four cycles of myths that he defines as theogonic, the myth of the exiled soul, tragic, and Adamic. Of interest here are his conceptions of the interactions amongst the three primary symbols of evil and the cycles of myths, most particularly the tragic and Adamic.

For Ricoeur, all three primary symbols of evil (guilt, sin, and defilement) come together dynamically in his notion of the "servile will." In a dynamic interplay, the three symbols tend toward a paradoxical concept of the human person as one who is both responsible and "captive."[77] The symbol of captivity is both communal (sin) and individual (guilt). Defilement enters into this concept in that, for Ricoeur, evil is not just a simple lack, an absence of order, a "nothing," but is the "power of darkness; it is posited; in this sense it is something to be taken away."[78] Thus, not only is evil a lack of being, but a "something" with substance that can infect and contaminate the person and his/her community.

Further, evil, as symbolized by defilement, is also external— "evil comes to man [sic] as the 'outside' of freedom, as the other than itself in which freedom is taken captive." Evil is characterized here by seduction, evil-already-there, enticing, as well as something brought about by human will and malicious action. "Evil is both something brought about now and something that is always already there; to begin is to continue."[79] Seduction and beguilement from the outside are ultimately an infection of the self, by the self (auto-infection), moving from the state of being bound to the binding of oneself.[80] Herein, then, is a depiction of our lives as a combination of being caught through our limitations and frailty, and yet still making choices that can lead to further suffering.

Without describing each of the four cycles of myth that he identifies, what is important for the purposes at hand is Ricoeur's understanding of the significance of the tragic and Adamic myths

[77]Paul Ricoeur, *Symbolism of Evil,* trans. Emerson Buchanan (Boston: Beacon Press, 1969) 100–1. See Simone Weil's notion of the afflicted soul as a parallel.

[78]Ibid., 155.

[79]Ibid.

[80]Cf. Farley, 44–9.

to our understanding of evil and suffering. For Ricoeur, in tragic myths, a tragic hero/ine is led astray or blinded by a jealous or wicked god and is subject to a fatal destiny. The tragic hero/ine does not commit the fault per se but is still responsible for allowing evil to enter the world by becoming the vehicle for fault.

In combination with his explication of the relation of the three other types of myths to the Adamic, Ricoeur seems to bring a sense of fatedness to our choosing evil—an anteriority of evil spoken of by the theogonic myths and a passivity and externality of evil, as spoken of by the myths of the exiled soul.[81] These aspects are further developed in the tragic elements taken up by the Adamic myth, a review of which summarizes some of Ricoeur's main points.

The tragic aspect can be seen in the figure of Adam [or Eve, in my view] himself. The mystery of evil is portrayed in Adam who initiates evil by a choice and action (in the instant of choosing evil over good), but also as an underlying "peccability" within his being. For Ricoeur, this is not quite the notion of a first (or original) sin which is transmitted to future generations, but what he calls a "horizon of actual evil . . . at the frontier of the avowal of present evil."[82] This is an evil which one confesses is already there in the very instant in which one confesses that one chooses it—an evil not posited by any particular person, but *assented* to by persons and communities:

> . . . the evil for which I assume responsibility makes manifest a source of evil for which I cannot assume responsibility, but which I participate in every time that through me evil enters into the world as if for the first time.[83]

This aspect of evil is, perhaps, best represented in the Adamic myth by the symbolic significance of the figure of the serpent.

> The serpent is more than the transcendence of sin over sins, more than the non-posited of the posited, more than the radical of radical evil; it is the Other, it is the Adversary, the pole of counterparticipation . . . about which one can say nothing

---

[81]Ricoeur, ibid., 311, 327, 333.
[82]Ibid., 311.
[83]Ibid., 312–3.

except that the evil act, in positing itself, *lets itself be seduced* by the counterpositing of a source of iniquity represented by the Evil One, the Diabolical.[84]

The tragic myths, correlated with the tragic elements within the Adamic myth, reaffirm the fateful side of any ethical vision and confession of sins in the midst of suffering.

> Here, then, is a fault no longer in an ethical sense, in the sense of a transgression of the moral law, but in an existential sense: to become oneself is to fail to realize wholeness, which nevertheless remains the end, the dream, the horizon, and that which the Idea of happiness points to. Because fate belongs to freedom as the non-chosen portion of all our choices, it must be experienced as fault. . . . This fateful aspect, joined to the aspects of antecedence and externality expressed by the other myths, points toward the quasi-nature of an evil already there, at the very heart of the evil that springs up now.[85]

A part of evil and suffering, then, is out of our control, and yet is at the very heart of that evil which we do choose. What these symbolic expressions of meaning point to, then, is a side of evil and suffering that is already present in the very structures of our existence and that we are all "caught by," and, arising out of this aspect, a side that we perpetuate through willful acts of discord and harm.

In this way the Adamic myth, for Ricoeur, reflects the polarization of two tendencies found within his typology of myths—those mythic representations that take evil beyond us and those that concentrate evil in an evil decision or choice—from which stem the pain of being human. This tension of the externalization and internalization of evil resists reducing evil and suffering to a transgression of some moral law, with suffering as mere chastisement for wrongdoing or as merely educative, and echoes Farley's and Allik's concerns over the value of incorporating a tragic vision of reality into discussions of suffering.

On the one hand, the ethical vision of evil and suffering resets evil solely within the context of our freedom to choose. Freedom, here, is the power to act and to be—a freedom capable of digression,

---

[84]Ibid., 313.
[85]Ibid., 312–3.

deviation, and subversion. Evil, then, is reduced to a moral vision of the world—or any deviation from a proscribed mean.

On the other hand, what this ethical vision does not take into account, according to Ricoeur, Farley, and Allik, is the "tragic" aspect of evil, which is expressed so eloquently in the symbols and myths that Ricoeur studied (e.g., preeminently for him in Job). The ethical vision of evil does not acknowledge "evil-as-already-there"—an evil into which we are born; an evil present before one's awakened conscience; and an evil which is unable to be analyzed or reduced solely into individual culpability and faults.[86]

Job, in particular, reminds us of the suffering of the innocent under the law, the shattering of the moral vision. With Job, as seen by Ricoeur (and similar to Sölle's contributions), suffering is not only undeserved but senseless—how can one comprehend the suffering of an individual who appears to be fully conversant and in agreement with the ethical vision of God? In Ricoeur's view, the suffering of Job is for the purpose of understanding—that is, to throw into question the God of the ethical vision of reality (as also paralleled in Sölle's admonishments to reappropriate God images in the midst of suffering). By so doing, one is then able to discover the tragic, inscrutable God of "unverifiable faith."[87] The God that the Job narrative portrays is one that must be approached through faith. As Ricoeur clarifies, God's answers to Job are not a reconstruction of or a resolution to the problems of evil and suffering, or even a higher degree of subtlety regarding the ethical vision of human-God interaction.

As exemplified by Job's case, in a tragic vision of reality suffering, then, cannot be eradicated by our merely becoming "better" or more "perfect" people—by doing the "right" thing. As Ricoeur notes, "suffering emerges as an enigma when the demands of justice can no longer explain it; this enigma is the product of the ethical theology itself."[88] Therefore, in radical suffering, as exemplified by Job's experience, nothing is ultimately explained or settled once-

---

[86]"Evil is choice, but more than choice, for evil is transubjective and other. There is a serpent within, but also without, always already there waiting. We institute evil, but we also discover it; we are responsible agents but also tragic victims," Duffy, 616.

[87]Ricoeur, ibid., 319.

[88]Ibid., 314.

for-all, but new insights (revelations) can be gained in the midst of suffering, which can change one's entire point of reference.

By taking a variety of myths together, in a dialectical process, one can see evil depicted not only as an act, as a transgression, but as habit, tradition, a condition which precedes one's awareness and one's individual acts (say, of sexism, racism, etc.), and leads to the pain of humanity. As Ricoeur notes, the tragic elements in mythic symbolization "speak of a 'mystery of iniquity' that man [sic] cannot entirely handle, that freedom cannot give reasons for, seeing that it already finds it within itself . . . a divine mystery of evil."[89] With the help of tragedy, we see that evil and suffering cannot ultimately be explained, ethically or otherwise. One must learn to live in their midst, at times, without explanation. As Stephen Duffy notes, "so we are encumbered with ambiguity."[90]

## AN EXCURSUS ON JOB AS AN EXAMPLE OF A TRAGIC SUFFERER

My own views of God's speeches from the whirlwind at the end of the Job narrative incorporate many of these insights from Farley, Sands, Allik, and Ricoeur, and further highlight the importance of utilizing a tragic vision when dealing with experiences of radical, unmerited suffering. As exemplified in these passages of Job's plight, one can see parallels with the suffering that many of the women in chapter 3 conveyed, as well as glimmers of possible responses to their suffering.

For example, in these passages, God does not bring forth a list of Job's failings in his dealings with the world (the "indictment" that Job has asked for) and identifies no "secret sin" that Job has done.[91] God seems totally unconcerned with this level of conversation. It seems, Job's sufferings were for "no reason" in the sense that Job was as blameless in God's eyes as he believed he was, and nothing he had done, per se, warranted the suffering he experienced. To the reader's profound disappointment, God does not *explain* in

[89]Paul Ricoeur, *The Philosophy of Paul Ricoeur: An Anthology of his Works,* ed. Charles E. Reagan and David Stewart (Boston: Beacon Press, 1978) 56.

[90]Duffy, 621.

[91]See concerns of abused women in section three of the schema of women's writings in chapter 3, pp. 101–3 above.

these final speeches what has happened (by giving reasons for Job's suffering), or reveal an underlying motive for Job's testing (perhaps, to see if his piety was based on a genuine service and love for God as God). Nowhere does God pronounce Job to be guilty of specific misdeeds, but neither does God acquit him of fault or guilt.

On the other hand, and in a more affirming sense, God also does not destroy or rebuke Job for his laments, questions, and protests. Nowhere does God tell him to stop complaining, to be silent in the midst of his anguish, or that he has no right to ask God directly for answers that cannot be found in the justifications offered by human counsel, as typified by his friends' discourses. God even confirms that Job has spoken the truth about himself, whereas his friends have not (Job 42:7).

Moreover, the very fact that God comes to Job is, in my mind, significant. Job has risked everything to come before God (including relinquishing some of his own long-held notions and images of God). God has heard him and responds—signifying God's desire to reestablish their relationship in a manner more evident to Job. And yet God responds in ways that are both unexpected and opaque to human understanding. On some level, though, it seems that God is saying that s/he has always been with Job, even though Job has felt abandoned (e.g., 30:11, 20) and persecuted (30:21), as well as scrutinized and attacked. But now, God comes forth more directly to Job, partly, perhaps, to keep him from letting his suffering overwhelm his faith in his own innocence, as well as in God's justness and goodness. I think, too, that part of the significance of God's enigmatic response is to help Job (in the very midst of his suffering) to know God as God is and not as a function of his own intellect, desire, or even his own anguish.[92]

Job has sought understanding of what has befallen him and, in this encounter with God, discovered there is no exact one-to-one correlation between what he has done and what comes his way. Thus, he can no longer live with the expectation that his ethical actions (no matter how laudatory) will necessarily produce and ensure positive, pain-free results. As Francis Andersen notes, "Job

---

[92]Cf. Sölle's discussion in chapter 3 on mystical acceptance of suffering, pp. 125–30 above.

now must realize that he is no more able to exercise jurisdiction in the moral realm than he is able to control the natural. . . ."[93]

Moreover, God calls into question Job's own knowledge (38:2) and understanding (38:4) of the activities and concerns of God—depicting the vastness of God's concerns in the universe and the limitations of human knowledge and power to do the same (38–39). God shows Job the expanse of God's concerns, from the creation and maintenance of the earth, the seas, time, of darkness and light, the weather, to God's care of animals, both domestic and wild, and of monstrous beasts that can symbolize the forces of chaos and evil (40:15–41:34). While not speaking at all of the moral order that has so consumed both Job and his friends (and consumes sufferers to this day), God speaks of a natural order and a purposefulness in creation (one that may only be to allow the cosmos in all its wide diversity, with all its competing "goods," to be held in balance). It seems that one of the messages here from the writer(s) of Job is that although evil and suffering are present in this order, God encompasses and orders it all (39:14-18; 40:11-13). Job is thus taken up into a vision of reality from God's perspective —one of primal energy, "among the most elemental realities, at the center of which there is an indestructible power, and indestructible joy."[94] But, why would God show this to Job? How does it speak to his own tragic suffering and anguish, if at all?

To begin, God's showing Job the immensity and majesty of creation and God's role in keeping it functioning is partly a way to highlight the close link God has not only with the human sphere, but also with everything in creation. Humans, though an important part of the universe, are not the only significant beings with whom this God is concerned, and therefore, are not always at the center of God's concerns. Rather, humans are a vital part, if not a pivotal point, of a larger confluence of life and energy.

To speak of the subtlety and richness of creation *vis à vis* Job's suffering is not necessarily to discount that suffering or make Job small and insignificant, in my view, but to show Job where he fits—

---

[93]Francis I. Andersen, *Job: An Introduction and Commentary* (Leicester, England: InterVarsity Press, 1976) 287.

[94]*The Book of Job,* trans. Stephen Mitchell (San Francisco: North Point Press, 1987) xx.

to allow him to have genuine humility and true understanding of who he is, in relation to the rest of creation. God's creation, as depicted in these passages at the end of the book of Job, includes not only the highly developed human, but also animals that were created not for the service of humans but for their own being (38:26-27); and includes activities that order that very creation and to which humans are subject (38:12-15). It seems that God tries to show Job creation from a more comprehensive perspective than he has had before such a theophany—not merely to overwhelm him, but to reassure him, in that God orders all of this with care and justice.

This does not mean that there is not evil or pain or death, but that it is all part of a larger, meaningful whole, a larger context of significance. Perhaps, this is part of the problem for all of us to accept: that humans are not the center of the universe, even though we are a significant part of it. Our *"hubris"* and *"hamartia"* as the ancient Greeks might say, in believing that we are the center can lead us, at times, to monumental suffering.

Falling out from this understanding of our location within this broader creation is also the point that the universe as a whole does not necessarily operate on the moral and ethical codes humans have developed to order our relations with one another. Again, this is not a sign to dispense with all ethics or codes of behavior; it is not a sign to stop pursuing social justice in our day-to-day activities. It is more to see these ethics and codes within a broader context, and to allow, at times, that they cannot explain all of life and suffering to us, nor function at certain levels of our experience. It seems, by the example of Job's story, God transcends those human constructs and may even present to us situations that require us to do things contrary to those accepted human norms.

Further, the story of Job portrays the situation where we may also feel tested to our limits by God, in ways that do not make sense given those human norms. But as our maker and sustainer, this enigmatic God requires, if Job serves as one model, not only our candid laments and protests, but also our trust and faith in those times. Ultimately, if Job's experience can be used as a guide, we are brought, in and through suffering, to an encounter with God that results in a greater state of blessedness. To me, at the level of such radical, unmerited suffering, the sufferer's response then becomes a series of questions and protests, as well as a response of faith. Perhaps, then, this narrative is pushing us to recognize evil and consequent suffering as part of a meaningful totality. As Ricoeur states, "one must, then, come to this point where he [sic] sees evil as the adventure of being, as part of the history of being."[95]

Moreover, in terms of Job's suffering, I do not believe that what he saw with God removed all his pain, or even made it "alright" in terms of a moral or ethical understanding of reality. Perhaps what the encounter with God did, though, was help him to see God and his relationship with God in such a new way that his pain took on new meaning—in a way that it never did before—and reduced or changed his suffering. Since the reader (or as the one who stands outside the sufferer) cannot perceive the full content or extent of Job's experience, it can only be said that for some reason(s), through a direct revelatory encounter with God, Job was satisfied. Despite all expected outcomes, Job experienced a grace that moved him from meaningless, radical suffering to life renewed. Thus, God met Job in his tragic suffering, even in his anger and protests toward God, and provided him with such a view of God's self ("but now my eye sees thee") that he is at peace, vindicated on some level. The turmoil of his former state is somehow abated. As Ricoeur noted above, so too does Ernest Becker state:

> One goes through it all to arrive at faith, the faith that one's very creatureliness has some meaning to a Creator; that despite one's true insignificance, weakness, death, one's existence has meaning in some ultimate sense because it exists within an eternal and infinite scheme of things brought about and maintained to some kind of design by some creative force . . . one is a creature who can do nothing [at times], but one exists over against a living God for whom "everything is possible."[96]

A tragic vision of reality, then, is an understanding of life that involves a sense of individual and communal powerlessness and/or loss of control over the outcome of one's actions and over one's environment. With such a vision, one learns to relinquish the sense

---

[95]Ricoeur, ibid.
[96]Ernest Becker, *The Denial of Death* (New York: The Free Press, 1973) 90.

that s/he or we have or will have evil and suffering "figured out," or that we can somehow "fix" suffering through rational explanations and justifications. This does not mean that one ceases pursuing understanding or changing unjust conditions; it means, partially, that our expectation with regard to the resolution of suffering must always remain open-ended, accepting of limitation, and akin to the distinction made earlier by David Morris between a puzzle and a mystery.[97]

Thus, in this view, no matter how hard one tries, one cannot know enough or always do "the right thing" because of the very way things are ordered in our world and the very limits of our existence. Our actions are always constrained by a context that is already disordered by an "evil-already-there," by forces that must be recognized for their powerful destructiveness over the vulnerable and the innocent, over the virtuous and noble, and over which we inevitably have little or no control. A tragic vision of reality depicts our actions (no matter how moral, ethical, well-intentioned) as always contingent, circumscribed, and fallible.

Tragedy also speaks of a complexity of responsibility and yet reminds us of the ambiguities of our intentions and ethics. To use Martha Nussbaum's phrase, tragedy speaks of the "fragility of goodness," a fragility that afflicts even the best among us, and if the Greek tragedians are correct, particularly puts the virtuous at risk.[98] Perhaps, the lack of acknowledgment of this fragility underlies the why me?/why us? questions of faith in suffering. For no matter how good or ethical one is, no matter how hard one tries to do the "right thing," such goodness does not guarantee immunity from suffering and disaster. Radical suffering is just that sort of suffering that can permeate even the best of lives.

Thus, a tragic sensibility also reminds us that we are not in ultimate control of our lives, contrary to so much of what our North American culture strives to convince us, as noted by Eric Cassell and David Morris earlier in this work. Such a vision runs counter to our North American rugged individualism, our pursuit of self-reliance to the exclusion of building community, and to our "can

[97]See chapter 2, pp. 17, 19–20 above.
[98]Martha C. Nussbaum, *The Fragility of Goodness: Luck and Ethics in Greek Tragedy and Philosophy* (New York: Cambridge University Press, 1986).

do" popular culture wherein if we only locate the "right" program of personal development, our problems will disappear. But, as Kathleen Sands states:

> The heuristic purpose of tragedy is to discern in the moment and for particular historical agents what is within our control and what is not, forming responsible judgments on the one side while holding compassion and desire open to what remains beyond.[99]

What a tragic vision of reality emphasizes, then, is that the central human condition is not so much guilt as suffering and the fear of suffering. Further, it does not emphasize nihilism or even punishment of sins. It is concerned with illuminating our inherent suffering and with seeking justice in spite of the limits of our existence. Tragedy values creation and is driven by a keen desire for justice, but it faces the reality that this desire for justice is not often satisfied in history, in our lifetimes, or even in our descendants' lifetimes. Wendy Farley sums it up well when she says:

> The more characteristic ethical problem both [biblical stories such as Job and Greek tragedies] address is the *injustice* of certain events and sufferings rather than the *justice* of punishing sinners. Justice is restored not so much when [the protagonist] is punished, but when [a people or individual] is vindicated and relieved of persecution.[100]

So, why, then, is such a tragic vision important to the development of theological responses to women's suffering?

## IMPORTANCE OF TRAGIC VISION TO THEOLOGICAL DISCUSSIONS OF SUFFERING

As proposed by Wendy Farley, Tiina Allik, and Paul Ricoeur, a tragic vision of reality provides an alternative conceptual framework for reflecting on and addressing the complexity of evil—one that does not merely justify and explain, and thereby, minimalize or discount radical suffering. A tragic vision, unlike many traditional

[99]Sands, 14.
[100]Farley, 29.

explanations of suffering, squarely looks into the face of a cosmos that, at times, appears empty and desolate, and into our lives that consequently appear futile and meaningless. It faces radical, unmerited suffering directly and seeks a response that keeps the inconsolable qualities of that suffering alive and active—i.e., it does not attempt to come away with easy explanations for hard questions, to blame victims for their suffering, or to see the world itself simplistically as one homogeneous unity and whole.

A tragic vision is important for Christian responses to the suffering of women because it centers its concern not so much on guilt and depravity of the human person, but on suffering as the human condition from which we desire and need salvation. It profoundly acknowledges the destructiveness and injustice of radical suffering, while also acknowledging and exploring the notion that this type of suffering does not always arise from conscious wrongdoing or wicked intent. Such suffering may occur because something is wrong or distorted with the very way one's life is conditioned, structured, or constrained. Such suffering may occur because of one's limitations and fragility, or because of conflicts arising from choices that involve more than one valid "good."

Such a view echoes many of the writers reviewed in the previous chapter, and reminds women that in seeking viable responses to suffering, we cannot assume that all suffering is the same and thus, that all suffering requires one, universal response. For instance, some suffering can be eradicated by human efforts to change unjust circumstances, distorted social and political values and policies, and oppressive mindsets. Other types of suffering, however, may resist all efforts to change the situation, and may require a very different approach that incorporates notions of human finitude, conflict, and fragility. A tragic vision of reality recognizes the conflicted context within which suffering occurs, wherein ". . . we must create what right and reason we can."[101]

What a tragic view of reality and suffering might do, for example, is move one from self-blame or from the projection of responsibility to change things outside oneself to a more mature realization of one's own *appropriate* responsibility within a context of limitation and finitude. It acknowledges that we are limited

---

[101]Sands, xi.

creatures, vulnerable to the conditions that order our lives as finite, to a systemic evil already embedded in the social and cultural structures that both give us life and destroy us, and to the radical destructiveness of natural evils that we cannot contain or do not yet comprehend. Thus, tragedy speaks to us of a life of radical contingency and vulnerability to evil, suffering, and a destructiveness that may not only take one's life but may destroy her humanity, dignity, and social connections along the way.

Tragedy also speaks of this life of contingency and vulnerability as inevitable—i.e., not dependent on virtue or good will or political ideology. What a tragic vision of reality can therefore bring us to is the realization that all humans (including oneself and one's own virtues), all human institutions (including one's family and the Church), all political and social ideologies (even feminist) are fallible and susceptible to evil. A tragic sensibility unmasks the truth that at certain critical points, they all can and do fail the radical sufferer.[102]

In the previous chapter it was noted that many women's writings on suffering call for not only a rethinking of traditional views on suffering, but also of theological categories such as original sin, anthropology, and grace. As illustrated by Pamela Dickey Young, for the Christian, the saving work of Jesus must be reenvisioned within a context wherein the human predicament (that from which we need saving) involves not only a lack of integrity but also what Farley, Allik, and Ricoeur have identified as the tragic structure of reality. As humans, we are conditioned and circumscribed by our embodiment, our fragility, and vulnerability to evil that seduces our consent and by radical suffering itself which cripples our very existence by the action of paralysis and despair, disease, accident, and death itself. I propose that this way of looking at reality is important for women who reflect on suffering and attempt to find adequate or viable responses for radical suffering because it helps us see the limits of all our efforts to eradicate all forms of suffering. It does so, also, with the reminder that despite those limits,

---

[102]"In this sense original sin is an ineradicable bias or complicity, a dark involuntary at the heart of the will, eluding conceptual clarity and fast becoming voluntary in the conspiracy of impotence and cowardice against growth. Each one feels the undertow of an evil that is his [hers] and not his [hers]," Duffy, 620.

we must still act, we must still *do* something to change suffering for ourselves and for others.

It is one of my concerns that interwoven within many feminist theologies and ideologies up to this point is an implicit or invisible thread—that of a romanticized, somewhat naive notion that women are somehow exempt from fallibility, limitation, and in some cases, the seduction of radical evil. In my observations, it seems that some feminists imply, if not directly state, that only if we can arrive at a point where women are again in power, are able to control a greater proportion of the socio-economic and political environment, then a "golden age" of humanity will occur.[103]

And yet it is also my observation, even when we gain some of these inroads women still oppress each other, their children, and, sometimes, even the men with whom they relate. No more obvious a point can be made to support this than the long history of Caucasian women's oppression of women of color, or the lateral sexism that occurs among women of every color.

Even when inroads are made against patriarchy and the sin of sexism, we still inflict on one another and experience ourselves the suffering that seems inescapably a part of our existence. To a certain degree, we are caught in the limitations common to all humans—caught by the reality that tragedy speaks of so eloquently. What a tragic vision of reality can do is help us understand our own realistic limits, which may reduce the possibility of despair when our efforts fail to elicit a desired end and of an attendant paralysis of action. It may provide a way of looking at one's experience that helps her to continue on and build resilience in the face of radical suffering.

For a tragic vision of reality does not necessarily encourage a passive stance toward suffering, but can illumine alternatives to the situation and provide replenishment through imagination, creativity, protest, and resistance. It should be noted that even some Greek tragedies do not end unhappily, and can point toward an experience of transformation (e.g., the story of Philoctetes), or a vindication that comes later in time.

---

[103]E.g., see Sands' discussion in chapter 3 on the second pattern of responses to evil by religious feminists who defend an immanent good, pp. 81–3 above.

Furthermore, as Sands points out, although we are not all facing catastrophic suffering in our day-to-day lives, we are all to some extent "unmoored," and endangered as human beings. Humans are endangered not only by our very embodied existence but also by forces beyond our control. "Not only are [our] distinct powers and goods separately vulnerable; so is our ability to weave them into some integral whole that does more good than harm."[104]

Thus, one of the values of seeing life through a tragic lens is that it does not lead to false hope in human actions, constructs, and institutions. Such a view acknowledges the fragility of even our best intentions and well-laid plans. What a tragic vision of reality can do is correct an over-emphasis on our abilities to be self-constituting agents for moral good that I see as problematic in some feminist literature. This over-emphasis extends to a false sense that we can somehow eradicate suffering. What a tragic view can do is help one recognize and acknowledge the complexity of evil to which suffering is connected. It, thus, acknowledges the complexity of our postmodern existence.

It acknowledges an existence that involves the difficulties of making life-threatening decisions amidst a conflicted environment of sometimes competing, antagonistic, and antithetical "goods." It also recognizes the complexity of choices, judgments, and decisions wherein we, no matter how well-intentioned, self-reflective, socially conscious, are still subject to our own latent racism, sexism, classism, etc. We are still subject to our own "fragility of goodness."

What a tragic vision of reality also helps us recognize is that we cannot approach some of our deepest experiences with rationality and reliance on our virtue alone. It encourages in us, at times, a willingness to relinquish explanation and a desire to find cause or fault when they no longer enlighten our suffering or move us to make concrete changes to alleviate our own or others' suffering. In so doing, a tragic vision can move us into an approach toward suffering that incorporates ambiguity, paradox, and mystery. Such a view of reality can lead, paradoxically, away from despair when all one's best efforts fall short and can lead to placing one's trust and hope in something beyond this radical contingency.

Of course, the danger always arises that one can choose or be swept into despair and meaninglessness at this juncture. However,

---

[104]Sands, 12.

within a Christian faith context, embedded in an understanding of God as triune and interactive with this historical plane (as a creator concerned with creation, as companion-sufferer and redeemer, as sustainer particularly in the midst of the most horrific suffering) one is given the divine promise of comfort and hope, despite all rational probabilities to the contrary. To me, at this juncture between despair and hope is exactly where one's faith and one's community of faith can provide a needed alternative. It is here that God may come in a new way to us, to enliven our suffering with comfort, resilience, strength, and hope. Therein lies the possibility that one will not be crushed by the inherent and inevitable limitations of self and others.

Moreover, in utilizing a tragic vision within a Christian feminist theology of suffering, one also does not negate the validity of human responsibility for some forms of evil. What I propose here is that one needs to incorporate *both* a view of evil as moral (and therefore, something that can be changed by human efforts to eradicate the suffering that occurs), *and* a view of evil as natural and tragic. As Tiina Allik has emphasized:

> . . . attempts to analyze human evil solely as moral evil, or in terms of deliberate, autonomous agency, and also attempts to analyze human evil solely as natural evil, in terms of a second nature over which human beings have no control and for which they have no responsibility, miss the mark. . . .
>
> If one focuses on natural evil, the tendency is to see all evil in terms of the natural conditions of human existence; as a result, all is forgiven and no one is held responsible. . . . In this approach, evil is usually justified by saying that it is a necessary result of conditions which are necessary for arriving at certain goods in human life. If, on the other hand, one focuses on moral evil, there is the tendency to feel that there are no limits to the improvements that human beings can make on themselves and on the world. The tone of this kind of theodicy is often rather moralistic—human beings are simply what they choose to make of themselves. In this approach, evil is usually justified as usefully instructive and as a just punishment for human failures.[105]

[105]Allik, 326.

Using her understanding of Lowe's work, Allik points out that both approaches are attempts to resolve the problem of evil completely, or to explain the presence of evil "without remainder." One is fatalistic, explaining evil as a natural condition and because of that, absolving human beings of responsibility. It disavows that we have direct control over evil, but it seems to affirm a kind of human mastery over evil as a mastery of explanation. The other approach, optimistic in its orientation, claims that we have direct control over evil and provides a means for control by explanation and rational justification. However, the excess of suffering that we experience in our postmodern times is not adequately accounted for by either alone.[106]

Tragedy, though, acknowledges that sin, guilt, cruelty, and indifference play a major role in evil and suffering, but it also places evil in a context that is more inclusive than human fault. As Stephen Duffy says:

> Sin is one's true situation before God . . . sin is more than sins, more than individual conscious acts or deviations of the will. It is a radical mode of being; it is Ezekiel's "heart of stone." Sin arises at a deeper level than that of conscious intention and explicit choice. . . . Sin is located along a graced horizon that humans are struggling toward. It is less lost innocence than incompleteness.[107]

Human fault and responsibility are still retained in a tragic vision, but tragedy acknowledges the reality of an existence conditioned by finitude, conflict, ignorance, deception, fragility, and limitation. As Duffy has also pointed out:

> two types of language have to be dialectically related in speaking of evil as both moral and tragic: that of freedom and that of inevitability, contingency, and universality, responsibility, and inescapability.[108]

But, perhaps more significantly, what tragedy can do is bring one to a shift in how she views her own or others' suffering. If one

---

[106]Ibid., 326–7.

[107]Duffy, 617–8.

[108]Ibid., 600. Note, too, that when he speaks of universality, he means universal in its range, and not necessarily synonymous with an essential humanity.

thinks in terms similar to Eric Cassell's distinction between pain and suffering as defined in chapter 2, perhaps what a tragic vision of reality can also do is help lighten or ease the suffering even though the circumstances that lead to suffering are still active. Perhaps, rather than attempt to remove or resolve the pain, what a tragic vision can do is help the sufferer find new meaning (her own meaning) in the very midst of her affliction, and bring her to a place of "unverifiable faith," as Ricoeur would say. As Allik notes:

> The task of theodicy seems more feasible if one can say that human beings, despite the violence that is done to them and the depth of their suffering, at least never lose their capacity to freely interpret their suffering and to appropriate salvific and/or adaptive narratives that, on some level, make sense of human suffering and tragedy.[109]

Tragedy can move us, perhaps, to reflect ever more concretely and deeply about our images, metaphors, and experiences of God in our particular historical realities and social locations, and to weave these into a tapestry that includes all aspects of life as we know it. Tragedy gives no easy answers and can lead us into a depth of religious understanding of suffering wherein not all tensions or questions generated by suffering can be "resolved into unambiguous acts of causation and responsibility."[110] I believe such a stance is more relevant in our times to those hungering for a religious/ spiritual center in the midst of radical suffering.

Moreover, as Sands points out:

> In commending theological attention to the tragic, I am proposing a style of theology that is founded more on questions than on speculative or doctrinal claims. Tragedies foreclose the faith that forecloses questioning. Instead, they find every form of conflict and suffering *question-worthy* and *wonder-worthy,* especially those that present themselves as elemental and immovable.[111]

[109]Allik, 315.
[110]Halliwell, 177–8.
[111]Sands, 11. "Tragic knowledge always contains the final release from tragedy, not through doctrine and revelation, but through the vision of order, justice, love of one's fellow man; through trust; through an open mind and the acceptance of the questions as such, unanswered," Jaspers, 102, quoted in Farley, 27.

Thus, a tragic sensibility keeps the question of "why suffering?" open, and reduces the possibilities of doctrinal triumphalism and claims to absolute truth that do less to help a radical sufferer than to shore up rational justifications for violence, self-sacrifice, passive acceptance, and silence.

Finally, and perhaps most significantly, what radical suffering and a tragic vision of reality can also bring us to is the realization of our need for something transcendent, for a larger context of meaning and significance, that encompasses these tragic events and radical suffering and is yet beyond the contingencies that we experience. To my mind, radical suffering and a tragic vision speak of our inherent need for something "outside" (or not contained by) the tragic structure of reality, that interacts with us, that comforts and sustains us in the midst of what we do to one another and what the world does to us. Tragic stories often speak of this reality as a larger context of meaning or significance, of a moral/ethical order outside the action of the story—of a reality that I will here call God, that interacts positively with our world of finitude, contingency, and suffering. Tragedy, as Allik states, can help us recognize our radical "need for dependence on God's help for making sense out of evil."[112]

She further identifies this need as our need for grace:

> The affirmation that human beings need grace, not only because of the incapacitating qualities of sin, but also because, as material creatures, they are dependent on God and interconnected with the rest of creation, just by virtue of their creatureliness, is another important theme, one which is based on the biblical stories of creation. It is not that human beings need to be redeemed from their creatureliness but that the creaturely dependence of human creatures on the world and on God affects the nature of God's graciousness in redemption. The need for God's grace, even in the appropriation of his gift of grace, is the result, not just of our sinful self-deception, but of our human limitations as agents and thinking beings as well. We can never fully know our own motivations or know them with complete certainty, even if they are good. Nor can we ever hope to achieve or maintain our unity and

---

[112]Allik, 327.

integrity as agents through a self-conscious and deliberate ordering of our multitudinous actions.[113]

Thus, an encounter with grace, an experience of God's presence in the midst of radical suffering, may be the only viable means of healing for radical sufferers because only grace can meet tragedy on its own terms—in the realm of the unexpected, the paradoxical, and what I like to think of as the "supra-rational." "Thus the depth of sin and its rootedness in a preconscious matrix needs to be matched by a corresponding depth in the scope of God's grace."[114]

Perhaps, then, the most important aspect of a tragic vision for radical sufferers is that it leads one to recognize, acknowledge, and accept one's insufficiency and therefore, one's need for the transcendent, for God. In so doing it opens us to the activity of God's grace in our lives in new ways, and may, in some cases, enhance a movement from meaningless suffering (in Sölle's sense) to meaningful suffering. Through a recognition of one's need for and an actual encounter with God's healing presence, one may move from a place of despair, powerlessness, and confusion to a place of strength, protest, solidarity with others, and transformation.[115]

As can be seen, then, a tragic vision can provide Christian faith with valuable insights into the nature of evil and suffering, and these insights can be used as a foundation to construct a variety of theological and spiritual responses to radical suffering. In the following chapter I shall utilize the notion of a tragic vision of reality to identify components of a spirituality that might assist some sufferers in confronting and coming to terms with their difficulties and to move from despair to hope, resistance, and compassion.

---

[113]Ibid., 312.

[114]Ibid., 331.

[115]Similar to the movement from Phase One to Phase Two of Sölle's process out of suffering.

# 5

# Elements of a Proposed Spiritual Response to Suffering

I N AN ATTEMPT TO INTEGRATE THE CONTRIBUTIONS PROVIDED BY the writers previously discussed, this final chapter will now look at the implications of the above exploration and focus on the role of spirituality in responding to women's experiences of suffering. It is hoped, in particular, that the insights of the women writers in chapter 3 and the tragic vision discussed in the previous chapter will assist in identifying aspects of a spirituality that lead one not to passivity and despair in the face of radical suffering but, in some cases, to a deeper connection with God, with one's own self, and with others in creation. It is not assumed such a spiritual response will necessarily totally eradicate the pain that many women experience in this life, but perhaps, it will provide a foundation to aid some in viewing their suffering differently.

In this chapter I hope to identify what I call a "mystical-political" spirituality, which might empower one to consciously confront, bear, and work through suffering when possible; to see life as containing choices even when one has little control over changing a situation; and to be responsive to the needs and contributions of others who might also be suffering. It is believed that a form of this mystical-political spirituality might move one from a personal, private, and individual realm to a more communal, interdependent, and interconnected realm. By so doing perhaps this movement might break the experience of loneliness, secrecy, and isolation that is often such a key destructive element in experiences of radical suffering. By using the work of the writers already discussed at length above, as well as works by Anne Carr, Constance FitzGerald, and others, I hope to begin formulating a spirituality that is characterized by two poles: protest, solidarity, and resistance (the active or "political" pole), but also by another, which acknowledges our inherent lack of control over our lives and thus, of our need for and openness to God's activating presence in alleviating or transforming suffering (the contemplative or "mystical" pole).

However, before embarking on the identification of specific elements that might be incorporated into such a spiritual response, it might be wise again to define my terms here—in this case, to clarify what I mean by "spirituality."

## SPIRITUALITY DEFINED

Spirituality, in the words of Sandra Schneiders, can be thought of as "a fundamental dimension of the human being," as well as "the lived experience which actualizes that dimension."[1] According to this view, not only is spirituality constitutive of humans, it can be developed and expressed in a person's life through such activities ordinarily associated with spirituality (such as prayer, spiritual exercises, liturgy), as well as through the whole of the life of faith, including its bodily, psychological, social, and political dimensions. Spirituality, then, is not limited simply to a person's life *vis à vis* the divine or God, but is more one's life lived *in* God.

In addition, as noted by Schneiders, there is no "generic" spirituality. It is always determined by a movement toward a particular ultimate value or focus of one's life. Spirituality, for her, is

> . . . the experience of consciously striving to integrate one's life in terms not of isolation and self-absorption but of self-transcendence toward the ultimate value one perceives. [It is] progressive, consciously pursued, personal integration through self-transcendence within and toward the horizon of ultimate concern.[2]

[1]Sandra M. Schneiders, "Spirituality in the Academy," in *Modern Christian Spirituality: Methodological and Historical Essays,* ed. Bradley Hanson (Atlanta: Scholars Press, 1990) 17.
[2]Ibid., 23.

Thus, as Anne Carr also describes it, spirituality is "the whole of our deepest religious beliefs, convictions, and patterns of thought, emotion, and behavior in respect to what is ultimate, to God."[3] In Carr's view, because spirituality is more encompassing than a set of values, or even theology as an explicit intellectual position, it

> . . . reaches into our unconscious or half-conscious depths. And while it shapes behavior and attitudes, spirituality is more than a conscious moral code. In relation to God, it is who we really are, the deepest self, not entirely accessible to our comprehensive self-reflection. . . .
>
> Moreover, spirituality can be a predominantly unconscious pattern of relating seldom reflected on, activated only in certain situations . . . a dimension of life for the most part unexamined. . . . But spirituality can also be made conscious, explicitly reflected on, developed, changed, and understood in a context of growth and cultivation of the fundamental self in a situation of response and relationship.[4]

Furthermore, although it is deeply personal, spirituality is not necessarily individualistic or privatized. As Carr also stresses, "it touches on everything: our relations to others, to community, to politics, society, the world. . . . [It] is expressed in everything we do." Since spirituality involves a real transformation of one's character, it can have as much to do with ethics as it does with individual spiritual formation. Conversely, informed by family, friends, community, class, race, culture, gender, and shaped by the historical period in which one lives, spirituality is also "individually patterned yet culturally shaped."[5] Spirituality, then, can affect all our relations in the world and is so affected by those relations.

Thus, it can be said that spirituality entails a capacity or dimension within the human person to come to a fullness of being, that is, to know and experience the divine. This involves a conscious

[3]Anne Carr, "On Feminist Spirituality," in *Women's Spirituality: Resources for Christian Development,* ed. Joann Wolski Conn (New York/Mahwah, N.J.: Paulist Press, 1986) 49.

[4]Ibid., 50.

[5]Ibid.

experience of self, but also of something/someone beyond the self which, together, provide one with a growth toward wholeness, a consciousness of connection with that which is "other," and with the rest of creation. It involves experiences of self-understanding and self-determination, as well as of self-transcendence and self-in-relation.

For me, spirituality is also frequently, if not always, grounded in an experience or encounter with the divine—however one may define that, or better, however that is revealed to us. This encounter is one of "the Other," that which is not totally of the self but comes through and integrates the self. This encounter may occur once or several times in a person's life, but it can have life-altering ramifications. Such an experience can be transformative and lead one to a radical re-orientation of one's life according to the values and truths experienced in the encounter with the divine.

Furthermore, spirituality is also a "lived" experience in the sense of an ongoing development of the "new" life that is instigated by the encounter with the divine. One seeks to be in greater contact or relationship with the divine and with one's deepest self, and may develop practices to enhance such a relationship—such as spiritual disciplines, devotions, prayers, rituals, etc.

Spirituality, in my view, is also "lived" in the sense that the growth toward wholeness moves one to share those experiences with others, to fit them into a larger context, and to determine, at times, the authenticity or genuineness of those experiences through various techniques of individual and collective discernment. Thus, one is often motivated to seek a larger framework or tradition which resonates with one's experience, and looks to others who have and are reflecting on their own experience in a similar vein. In this way, one becomes a part of a larger communal base, which can include oral stories and written documents that embody and discern faith experiences both historically and contemporaneously. The individual both learns from and contributes to this body of teachings and record of faith.

Moreover, spirituality for me is also "lived" in the sense of worship—both in terms of adoration, praise, and thanksgiving for the divine-human encounter and as "worship" in the secular world. This latter point has a sacramental aspect of assisting the divine to be made manifest in history and creation, and of expressing the truths one has experienced in works of compassion, charity, and loving-kindness. Not only does one worship, then, in the sense of gratitude and praise for the experience of the divine, but one also is moved to worship through concrete works of social justice, care, and nurture of God's creation. Spirituality, therefore, connects us both on a vertical plane to the divine and a horizontal one to the rest of creation.

More specifically for me, a *Christian* spirituality articulates this "ultimate concern" that grounds one's life as God, revealed in Jesus Christ and experienced through the gift of the Holy Spirit within the life of the Church, broadly conceived. What makes a certain spirituality Christian for me is that it is both personal and inter-personal and is oriented toward a God that is explicitly trinitarian in expression.[6] As Carr notes, "Christian spirituality entails the conviction that God is indeed personal and that we are in imme-diate personal relationship to another, an Other who 'speaks' and can be spoken to, who really affects our lives."[7] Accordingly, in my view, Christian spirituality particularly emphasizes the primacy of love-in-relation, as demonstrated more directly by Ewert Cousins:

> whatever path one takes, or wherever one arrives, love cannot be absent. . . . The Christian path consists of the awakening of the personal center of the human being, by God's personal grace and Christ's compassionate, redemptive personal love, within the Christian community, in a journey that leads to personal union with the tri-personal God.[8]

Thus, Christian spirituality, for me, emphasizes that the source, the very secret and heart of the universe is a mystery of in-terrelational love. And, because this is so, we who have come from

[6]E.g., see Catherine Mowry LaCugna, *God for Us: The Trinity and Christian Life* (San Francisco: HarperSanFrancisco, 1993); "The Practical Trinity," *Christian Century* 109 (July 15–22, 1992) 678–82; LaCugna and Michael Downey, "Trinitarian Spirituality," in *The New Dictionary of Catholic Spirituality,* ed. Michael Downey (Collegeville: The Liturgical Press, 1993) 968–82; Mary Ann Fatula, *The Triune God of Christian Faith* (Collegeville: The Liturgical Press, 1990); and Mary Timothy Prokes, *Mutuality: The Human Image of Trinitarian Love* (New York/Mahwah, N.J.: Paulist Press, 1993).

[7]Carr, ibid.

[8]Ewert H. Cousins, "What Is Christian Spirituality," in *Modern Christian Spirituality,* 44.

love cannot find joy or fulfillment except in knowing and living this love in fact and action—in relation with God, self, and others.

As modeled by the Trinity itself, a Christian spirituality is, thus, ultimately characterized by a dimension beyond the solitary and individual. Because the triune God is in his/her essence a being-toward-another in love, freedom, and mutuality, this spirituality entails a life which flows out toward others as gift, as self-bestowal, as an intentional giving of oneself in freedom to another with respect and care for both oneself and for the other.

Now, with these foundational points in mind, what might a spirituality look like that attempts to respond to the radical suffering of women? What elements or characteristics of a spirituality might be critical in addressing concrete situations of women in pain?

### A PROPOSED SPIRITUAL RESPONSE
### TO SOME FORMS OF WOMEN'S SUFFERING

To begin, a spirituality specifically related to the concerns of women in pain would incorporate Anne Carr's contention that we need to take ever more seriously the situation of sexism in our various cultural contexts. Such a spirituality would incorporate a way of

> relating to God, and everyone and everything in relation to God . . . [that is] aware of the historical and cultural restriction of women to a narrowly defined "place" within the wider human (male) "world." Such awareness would mean that we are self-consciously critical for the cultural and religious ideologies which deny women full opportunities for self-actualization and self-transcendence.[9]

This critical stance, in her view, needs to include not only a healthy suspicion and vigilance toward "taken-for-granted cultural and religious views that, in a variety of subtle ways, continue to limit the expectations of women to passive, subordinate, auxiliary roles and rewards," but also, more positively, a "vision of the world in which genuine mutuality, reciprocity, and equality might pre-

[9]Carr, 54.

vail."[10] Although many may think that sexism is no longer "an issue," it seems, based on the statistics and some of the situations of suffering depicted earlier, women still experience their suffering and the world itself quite differently than many men.

Moreover, a spirituality that takes seriously the concerns of women in pain would recognize and affirm the importance of the supportive network among women of various ages, races, and classes, and yet acknowledge and critically confront the prejudice and lateral sexism that continues to occur *among* women. As Carr stresses, such a spirituality would

> espouse non-competitive, non-hierarchical, non-dominating modes of relationship among human beings. . . . [It] would recognize the competitive and non-supportive ways in which women have sometimes related to one another in the past and would consciously struggle to achieve authentic, interdependent modes of relationship.[11]

Such a spirituality would be genuinely and continuously self-critical, seek to understand the wider aspects of human oppression, and determine how racism, classism, and elitism of any kind relate to specific experiences of women's suffering in North American society. A genuine effort to move from elitism to inclusivity might be a hallmark of a spirituality seeking to address women's experiences of suffering from a Christian perspective.

Beyond that critique, however, is also the need to build community across differences, on the basis of mutuality, reciprocity, and interdependence. Thus, a spirituality that seeks to help women in pain needs to address not only the problems that we are imbedded in but also needs to envision effective ways of relating with others that do not dismiss or trivialize another's pain. We need to learn from each other's stories of pain in order to build solidarity but also to identify areas of needed change and conversion in how we respond to suffering that might be quite different than our own or for which we might be partially responsible.

---

[10]Ibid. For some ideas on how this might be done, see Prokes reference in n. 6 above.
[11]Ibid.

Moreover, such a spirituality would also encourage the autonomy, self-actualization, and self-transcendence of women, as well as men, before a God who desires our wholeness. It would recognize the uniqueness of each individual, assist each one to see the variety of choices one might have in a given situation, and affirm the individual as she struggles to make her own choices in terms of her suffering. As Marie Fortune and Joy Bussert have already stressed, it would provide women who suffer with resources for strength and transformation and not solely for endurance.

In addition, a spirituality that takes into consideration the variety of women's experiences of suffering would not only consciously struggle to free itself from the cultural and religious limitations placed on women in the past, but would also do so with respect to *any* ideology that becomes oppressive to one's growth toward wholeness in God. As Carr notes, it would also

> consciously struggle to free itself from ideologies in favor of the authentic freedom of the individual and the group as it attempts to be faithful to its own experience. As religious and as Christian, [it] would strive for an ever freer, but always human, self-transcendence before a God who does not call us servants but friends.[12]

Mary Giles also raises this issue further in an article on suffering in a "mystical-feminist key." She cautions us against allowing any ideology, including one such as feminism, to convince us that we have ultimate control over our lives. As discussed in chapter 4, even a well-constructed feminist ideology can fail us at times in dealing effectively with situations of radical suffering that women encounter. As Giles cautions:

> A peril of contemporary feminism is that its heart tends to be obscured by the political agendas that typify its exterior. The heart of feminism is each woman's awareness of herself as a uniquely gifted human being whose destiny is to realize that awareness in actions that enhance and nourish uniqueness. Although agendas may help us live out this destiny, their specific and particular nature inclines to dogmatism. Excessive attachment to agendas . . . deludes us into believing that we

[12]Carr, 55.

> are ultimately in control of our lives insofar as we follow the
> dictates of an agenda. This attitude of excessive attachment
> . . . must be broken down if we are to see the spirit of femi-
> nism, which . . . is the presence of God within each one of us.
> Of course, we must reject with all our might any suggestion
> of the victim or the masochist within, for the pain produced
> by living out those roles is anything but [a] potentially trans-
> formative suffering. . . .[13]

What this implies to me is that in any spiritual response to the suffering of women a key component must be the development of
techniques and practices of discernment.[14]

Connected with the development of discernment practices is
another aspect of this mystical-political spirituality that critically
reevaluates one's images, metaphors, and understanding of God.
In such a spirituality, work might be done, both collectively and
individually, on reassessing and relinquishing images of God that
compound suffering, as exemplified by Dorothee Sölle's discussion
of Job and Carter Heyward's and Marie Fortune's admonishments
described in chapter 3.[15] Perhaps, in so doing, one might move
away from the view that God wills such radical suffering to occur
for whatever "good" purposes, and move toward a God who desires our authenticity, healing, and vindication. One concrete way
that might be used to see God's presence in a person's life is to encourage the sufferer to be attentive to the "phenomena" of divine
compassion in the midst of her suffering—to ask the question
where *is* God in all this? Who suffers *with* her and yet calls her into
new life beyond that suffering?

---

[13]Mary E. Giles, "Reflections on Suffering in a Mystical-Feminist Key," *Journal
of Spiritual Formation* 15 (1994) 146.

[14]Some time-honored guides in the discernment of spirits might be helpful as
starting points, such as Jonathan Edwards' "Treatise Concerning Religious
Affections," in *The Works of Jonathan Edwards*, vol. 2, ed. John E. Smith (New Haven:
Yale University Press, 1959) and Ignatius Loyola's "Rules for the Discernment of
Spirits," from *The Spiritual Exercises*, trans. Jules J. Toner, in *Women's Spirituality*,
209–18. For some ways that women have modified Ignatius' contributions, cf.
Joann Wolski Conn, "Revisioning the Ignatian Rules for Discernment," in *Women's
Spirituality*, 312–6, and Elisabeth Tetlow, "An Inclusive-Language Translation of
the Ignatian Rules for Discernment," in *Women's Spirituality*, 219–25.

[15]Cf. Marian F. and Santiago Sia, *From Suffering to God: Exploring Our Images
of God in the Light of Suffering* (New York: St. Martin's Press, 1994).

Such a spirituality that attempts to address the concerns of women in pain might also focus on helping the person regain a sense of self-esteem, dignity, and purpose, particularly in situations of physical and sexual abuse and social and racial prejudice. By refashioning an inner world of revised values and standards from which to judge herself and others, the sufferer may relinquish her self-definition as one of "victim," regain her sense of self, and move toward defending herself and others in situations of unmerited suffering. One key aspect of this recovery of self-esteem and dignity (as highlighted by such writers as the womanist theologians in chapter 3) is, perhaps, to see oneself as a partner with God in effecting divine justice in history, in removing the ability or power of radical suffering to debilitate the sufferer, and in actively resisting manifestations of evil in one's life. In so doing, such a spirituality might help restore self-respect and power back to the sufferer and reduce one's complicity with the affliction.

In order to do this, such a spirituality, as noted by some of the womanist theologians surveyed, might emphasize the role of memory in effecting a changed perspective toward one's suffering—i.e., remembering and retelling stories of others who experienced similar deprivation and suffering and yet "made it through." In so doing the sufferer may learn from their strategies of strength and resistance in confronting and dealing with that which can be changed and living with that which cannot be immediately changed.

Such a mystical-political spirituality would also accentuate the need for expression, verbal and nonverbal, of one's condition. Lament, petitioning, prayers, protest, and the like would be encouraged, particularly for women who have been silenced in the past. Moreover, when the sufferer herself is unable to communicate or protest, then, the community around her might take over and, in the manner of the Greek chorus, both express her pain and seek meaning with/for her. One example of ways that the faith community might assist the radical sufferer might be through the development of wailing/grieving/mourning spaces, rooms, or places in nature (e.g., mourning pits) wherein the sufferer could freely give vent to the inconsolable qualities of her suffering.[16]

---

[16]One of the most intriguing and powerful segments of a contemporary film *Breaking the Waves* is when the female protagonist, experiencing deep anguish,

Through a valuing of one's embodiment, incorporating the goodness and worth of our bodies and emotions, such a spirituality would thus move away from the repression and denial of one's feelings and seek ways to express, release, or transform the pain through verbal expression, creative pursuits, movement (such as dance), physical exercise (e.g., tai chi), and attention to the bodily memories of suffering (through massage, body work, boxing, etc.). A spirituality particularly aware of and responsive to women who suffer in their bodies, through disease, rape, torture, and the like, might address the needs of the body to heal, as well as the needs of the mind and spirit.

Moreover, such a spirituality that seeks to resist evil and the suffering incurred might entail using verbal self-defense or defiance to establish psychological distance from the suffering and from the perpetrator of the suffering. As noted by the studies done by womanist theologians, verbal defiance and acts of resistance such as bold, audacious behavior ("sass") and physical removal from the suffering situation might be highly effective forms of confronting situations in which the sufferer feels otherwise powerless. The recovery of anger, wit, cunning, cleverness, and moral courage as valuable womanly virtues and the reevaluation of such traditional Christian virtues as obedience and self-sacrifice may also serve women in pain as viable mechanisms for resistance in the midst of radical suffering.

Such a spirituality would also utilize Dorothee Sölle's (and others') insights about joining with others in solidarity to share, protest, and formulate solutions to the suffering that can be alleviated, and to deal with forms of suffering that often times seem insurmountable alone. By developing productive, meaningful ties with others, as well as various forms of consciousness-raising and expression, the sufferer might work her way out of isolation and despair. Thus, such a mystical-political spirituality would find a variety of ways within Christian communities to assist the sufferer to express and protest her experiences, to deal with her suffering pragmatically, to build coalitions with others who suffer, and to call the community itself and the wider society to conversion and change.

---

howls into the surf along a rugged coast. When she has reached her limits of verbal self-expression, she returns to a primal howl to give voice to her anguish.

Most of the foregoing seems, to my mind, supportive of the "active" or "political" pole of the spirituality that I propose here. More on the side of the "mystical" pole and, perhaps, most frequently in the place of Phase One of Dorothee Sölle's process through suffering, one aspect of this proposed mystical-political spirituality might also be the activity of "vigil" with the suffering. What I mean by this is an "activity" that occurs in silence, a listening for and a waiting on God. One element of this spirituality, then, in the midst of radical suffering, might be the development of a "receptivity," or a way of staying with the anguish long enough in order to know it differently and to experience God's healing presence. As Melanie May expressed earlier, "presence heals hopelessness."[17]

For example, in a recent survey done by *U.S. Catholic* magazine, many respondents, like May, noted that the most helpful thing another did for them during a time of great personal suffering was to be present, listen, and pray with that person. What was helpful for many survey respondents was that another person showed concern and support, did not pass judgment, and, at times, suffered along with the individual. By so doing, the sufferer was better able to enter into her own anguish and was aided in her struggle to find some meaning in the midst of the situation.[18] What Karen Smith also found in these survey results was that what helped some women respondents, in particular, were opportunities to cry and lament in a "safe" environment, their ability to get angry at God and/or with the relationship between God and that person, and a reassurance that God "was to be known more completely through this experience."[19] Notably, what also "made all the difference" to many who responded to this survey was the realization that God was still with them in the midst of the suffering, through an experience of what they termed "presence."[20]

It seems, then, cultivation of such a receptivity to presence is not an attempt to trivialize the suffering, or whisk it away by a ra-

---

[17]For a clinical study of presence, see Jan McCrary Pettigrew's dissertation, *A Phenomenological Study of the Nurse's Presence with Persons Experiencing Suffering* (Denton, Tex.: Texas Women's University, 1989).

[18]Karen Sue Smith, "Can You See the Good in Suffering?" *U.S. Catholic* 59 (1994) 8.

[19]Ibid., 12.

[20]Ibid., 11.

tional explanation of the situation, but to "sit" with it, to contemplate it, inviting it to "speak" to the sufferer. In such a way the sufferer may learn to cultivate a willingness to experience her suffering, not as a debilitating force or as definitive of the self, but more as something she can "take on" in a new and different way and within which new possibilities might arise.[21]

Furthermore, this form of vigil is not necessarily for the purpose of waiting for God to resolve it all, but more, one waits to be healed by God, in order to act on her own and others' behalf. One waits for God to assist, enliven, and to provide hope. Such a spirituality might assist one in surrendering her suffering to God—which is not the same as yielding to the suffering itself or to an abuser who inflicts the suffering, but more, offering the suffering itself up to God (as noted already by Jean Blomquist). In so doing, one might break the hold that radical suffering has on the sufferer through a process of acceptance and release.

Thus, in such a spirituality one does not resign, extinguish, or abandon oneself in the face of severe suffering, but more, yields (or sacrifices) to God her suffering, as well as her protest. This is

---

[21]Another recent example that attests to the possibilities of positive transformation in the wake of extreme adult trauma is a doctoral study in clinical psychology conducted by Mary Margaret Baures. The major finding of this study of 20 individuals was that "all the survivors, in contrast to repressing the trauma, transformed themselves around its horror." They used a variety of attitudes, behaviors, coping skills, and cognitive abilities to approach their suffering. These included "creativity to create a new reality, to convert pain and waste into truth and beauty, to give the dead a posthumous life, and to create a symbolic immortality. They aligned themselves with forces larger than themselves (some called these forces spirituality, others God, others mysticism, others fate), and brought their strength to others who were suffering what they suffered. Some form of denial allowed them to pace themselves through the process of adjusting to catastrophic loss. They focused on hopeful visions of the future . . . they accepted what they could not change and changed what they could. They became skillful at both agency and communion or independence and intimacy . . . cognitive abilities included the ability to choose an attitude toward their suffering, to make a conscious decision to give up bitterness and hate, and to give up previous expectations for their lives. They accepted the dark parts of life . . . without being defeated by them. Direct contact with the dark parts of life seemed to motivate them to create a world where tragedy is not the final experience." Mary Margaret Baures, *Positive Transformations after Extreme Trauma* (Keene, N.H.: Antioch University/New England Graduate School, 1994), abstract, quoted in *Dissertation Abstracts International* 56B (September 1995) 1691.

more a passing over to God the suffering that seeks to take away one's dignity, freedom, hope, and compassion for self and others. This is more a surrender in faith into the promise and power of God to heal, into the realm of possibility, as May and Ernest Becker might say.

Because the activity of acceptance, surrender, and receptivity are so critical to a movement out of despair and passivity in circumstances of radical suffering, this proposed mystical-political spirituality needs to address a reformulation of these components. Help in doing so comes from not only the writers already discussed but by a pivotal essay by Constance FitzGerald, wherein she constructively links what she terms experiences of "impasse" with the symbolism of the "dark night of the soul," developed by the sixteenth-century mystic St. John of the Cross.[22] A review of her key points here may help clarify the mystical pole of my proposed spirituality.

FitzGerald observes that many of our present personal and societal experiences open into a profound experience of, in her terms, "impasse." What she means by this is similar to what we have already heard from other writers surveyed in this study, that is that in some experiences of suffering, one sees

> no way out, no way around, no rational escape from what imprisons one, no possibilities in the situation. In a true impasse, every normal manner of acting is brought to a standstill, and ironically, impasse is experienced not only in the problem itself but also in any solution rationally attempted. Every logical solution remains unsatisfying, at the very least. The whole life situation suffers depletion, has the word *limits* written upon it . . . [it is an] experience of being squeezed into a confined space. Any movement out, any next step, is canceled, and the most dangerous temptation is to give up, to quit, to surrender to cynicism and despair, in the face of the disappointment, disenchantment, hopelessness, and loss of meaning that encompass one.[23]

[22]Constance FitzGerald, "Impasse and Dark Night," in *Women's Spirituality*, 287–311. Originally published in *Living with Apocalypse: Spiritual Resources for Social Compassion*, ed. Tilden Edwards (New York: Harper & Row, 1984). I am most grateful to Steve Krupa, S.J., for reference to this essay.

[23]Ibid., 288.

Since impasse can generate a sense of failure and the recognition that even one's "own mistakes have contributed to the ambiguity," such an experience leads one to question everything—including the trustworthiness of other people, concepts, and one's own motivations and actions. In this experience of disintegration and deprivation of worth, reason, logic, analysis, and planning no longer function effectively to resolve the issues surrounding suffering, and such a situation leads one to a deep sense of powerlessness and immobilization. But, the impasse may

> . . . [also] force us to start all over again, driving us to contemplation. On the other hand, the impasse provides a challenge and a concrete focus for contemplation. . . . It forces the right side of the brain into gear, seeking intuitive, symbolic, unconventional answers, so that action can be renewed eventually with greater purpose.[24]

Because such a "negative situation constitutes a reverse pressure on imagination," it forces one to break out of conceptual blocks that limit one's thinking and actions "so that imagination is the only way to move more deeply into the experience"—such that the intuitive, unconscious self becomes more operative. In this way, according to FitzGerald, an impasse situation can then become an opportunity for the "reconstitution of the intuitive self," and thus, "the situation of being helpless can be efficacious, not merely self-denying and demanding of passivity."[25]

At this critical juncture in order for the intuitive, unconscious self to become operative, one needs, according to FitzGerald, to "yield in the right way, responding with *full* consciousness of one's suffering in the impasse yet daring to believe that new possibilities, beyond immediate vision, can be given."[26] This yielding allows one to move from sole dependence on rational approaches to suffering and allows for unexpected, even paradoxical, alterna-

---

[24]Ibid., 289, quoting Belden C. Lane, "Spirituality and Political Commitment: Notes on a Liberation Theology of Nonviolence," *America* (March 14, 1981) and citing Urban T. Holmes, *Ministry and Imagination* (New York: Seabury, 1981) 88–93, for a good treatment of right- and left-brain thinking.

[25]Ibid.

[26]Ibid., 289–90.

tives to surface via the unconscious and the creative imagination—through a form of contemplative reflection.

> The psychologists and the theologians, the poets and the
> mystics, assure us that impasse can be the condition for crea-
> tive growth and transformation *if* the experience of impasse
> is fully appropriated within one's heart and flesh with con-
> sciousness and consent; *if* the limitations of one's humanity
> and human condition are squarely faced and the sorrow of
> finitude allowed to invade the human spirit with real, existen-
> tial powerlessness; *if* the ego does not demand understanding
> in the name of control and predictability but is willing to
> admit the mystery of its own being and surrender itself to
> this mystery; *if* the path into the unknown, into the uncon-
> trolled and unpredictable margins of life, is freely taken when
> the path of deadly clarity fades.[27]

If one does not or cannot yield in this way and represses the suffering, then one runs the risk of being swallowed up by complicity and/or apathy, as Weil and Sölle have earlier noted. Thus, for
FitzGerald, "every attempt to humanize impasse must begin with
this phenomenon of experienced, acknowledged powerlessness,
which can then activate creative forces that enable one to overcome the feeling that one is without power."[28]

Based on her extensive work in spiritual direction, FitzGerald
further notes that when one sets the impasse experience within an
interpretive framework, such as St. John of the Cross' "dark night
of the soul," "the impasse is opened to meaning precisely because
it can be redescribed," and thus, reappropriated—providing the
sufferer with reassurance and new energy to live.

This "dark night," as FitzGerald interprets it, is a "kind of affective education . . . carried on by the Holy Spirit over a lifetime,"
and is characterized by a movement from desire and anxiety that
is "possessive, entangled, complex, selfish, and unfree," to a "desire
that is fulfilled with union with Jesus Christ and others."[29] In this

---

[27]Ibid., 290–1.

[28]Ibid., 290, selectively quoting Dorothee Sölle, *Suffering,* trans. Everett R.
Kalin (Philadelphia: Fortress Press, 1975) 11.

[29]Ibid., 291. Compare with Farley's views of desire and anxiety outlined in
chapter 4, pp. 179–81 above.

process of "affective redemption," as she calls it, desire and anxiety are not denied, suppressed, or destroyed, but are "gradually transferred, purified, transformed, [and] set on fire."

> Night in John of the Cross, which symbolically moves from twilight to midnight to dawn, is the progressive purification and transformation of the human person *through* what we cherish or desire and through what give us security and support. We are affected by darkness, therefore, where we are most deeply involved and committed, and in what we love and care for most. Love makes us vulnerable, and it is love itself and its development that precipitate darkness in oneself and in the "other."[30]

It seems, then, through an experience of limitation and exhaustion of previous methods of dealing with suffering, one is called and carried to a deeper perception, to what FitzGerald describes as a "deeper, stronger faithfulness and to the experience of a love and a commitment, a hope and a vision, unimagined and unexpected on this side of darkness."[31] Through such experiences of impasse, one's desire and anxiety are thus purified and freed; one goes *through* the struggles and ambiguities to reach integration and wholeness.[32]

What this process also entails, then, is an encounter with ambiguity. Ambiguity, as FitzGerald notes, arises from human finitude and inadequacy. But, it also arises, if St. John is an appropriate guide, from the

> Spirit of God calling us beyond ourselves, beyond where we are, into transcendence. We are being challenged to make the passage from loving, serving, "being with," because of the pleasure and joy it gives us, to loving and serving regardless of the cost. We are being challenged to a reacceptance of the "other" . . . to a new experience of God, a quieter, deeper, freer, more committed love.[33]

In this experience of impasse, then, comes the realization that "there is *no* option but faith," which for FitzGerald "triggers a deep,

---

[30]Ibid., 291–2. Cf. John of the Cross, *The Spiritual Canticle*, stanzas 3–7.
[31]Ibid., 292.
[32]Ibid., 291.
[33]Ibid., 292.

silent, overpowering panic that, like a mighty underground river, threatens chaos and collapse."[34] At this extreme limit of one's life, in this experience that can be likened to the cross of Jesus, John of the Cross defines this as the place where the soul feels most rejected and abandoned by God. As Sölle has also highlighted:

> All extreme suffering evokes the experience of being forsaken by God. In the depth of suffering people see themselves as abandoned and forsaken by everyone. That which gave life its meaning has become empty and void: it turned out to be an error, an illusion that is shattered, a guilt that cannot be rectified, a void. The paths that lead to this experience of nothingness are diverse, but the experience of annihilation that occurs is the same.[35]

What FitzGerald and others seem to be saying is that somehow, ironically, it is this very experience of abandonment and rejection that is "transforming the human person in love." Through such experiences we come to a healing of our selves, as well as a solidarity with others who suffer. As she notes of John of the Cross' insights:

> John seems to say that one leaves the world of rejection and worthlessness by giving away one's powerlessness and poverty to the inspiration of the Spirit and one moves into a world of self-esteem, affirmation, compassion, and solidarity. Only an experience like this, coming out of the soul's night, brings about the kind of solidarity and compassion that changes the "I" into a "we," enabling one to say, "we poor," "we oppressed," "we exploited." The poor are objects until we are poor, too. This kind of identification with God's people, with the "other," is the fruit of dark night.[36]

It seems, then, that some suffering experiences can be a sort of crucible wherein faith is refined in us and the faithfulness of God is made known or disclosed to us. It seems, in times when reason and rationality seem paralyzed, when intimacy is eroded, and when desire feels most confused or dead, we can learn both of our

[34]Ibid., 297–8.
[35]Ibid., 298.
[36]Ibid.

own faithfulness in response to God, but also of God's compassionate responsiveness to us. Such a "mystical" encounter can lead to a strengthening and a spiritual deepening in the very midst of suffering and exile, which then allows the sufferer to take a more active, political stance toward her suffering situation.

### CONCLUDING REMARKS

If one takes into consideration the wide range of theological writings on suffering by women, and incorporates a tragic vision of reality into those considerations, one potentially valid spiritual response to the radical suffering of women can be broadly characterized by the triple aspects of surrender, faith, and protest, working in combination with one another—a paradoxical and somewhat dangerous response, similar to the contradictions conveyed in the cross and the resurrection.

For instance, through surrender (in those terms defined by such writers as Melanie May, Elizabeth O'Connor, Jean Blomquist, Dorothee Sölle, and Constance FitzGerald), we come to the point where the cry "My God, my God, why have you forsaken me?" becomes both *my* and *our* cry.[37] In it comes all our fragile humanity—our being "caught," our inability to live the way we want and know we should, our inability to effect change or to fully love. In it comes all our disappointments, discouragement, and outrage with the limitations of our society and ideologies, with our religious and cultural values, with our trusted friends and family, and even with ourselves. We call out in anger and demand explanations like Job; we cry for mercy, resolution, and peace.

And further, through a vigil with one's suffering, we may come to suspend our need for rational explanations of the "why" of suffering and move into the realm of radical faith—or a trust in the promise of the efficacy of God's justice and compassion, and that somehow our and others' suffering really matter and will one day be vindicated (although, perhaps, never fully "justified"). Thus, the promise that faith adheres to is that this anthropotropic God of

---

[37]A surrender to our limitations to the inescapability of suffering in our lives, and even a surrender to the willingness to share in the suffering of others for their sake.

Christian faith hears us, suffers with us, takes our part, and heals and liberates us in the very midst of our suffering. And, in that healing we come to the other side of suffering.

What I am advocating in this mystical-political spirituality is the retrieval of such a spirituality that incorporates the ambiguous and paradoxical qualities of our living, which includes a type of surrender to the mystery of God's presence and action within the suffering. It is my belief that we are not called necessarily to endure or remain in suffering but, more often, are called, in our faith, to allow God to bear us through the suffering by being present with us.[38]

Thus, through faith, we come to an unexpected experience of God. This encounter allows us to see God and ourselves in a new way, which may move us into a different state from the one we experienced before such a theophany (as exemplified by the story of Job). In such a way, we may then stop running from the fear of suffering and be enabled to face the evil in our world in a new, more constructive way.

So, not only does grace meet tragedy on its own terms, as highlighted in the previous chapter, we, too, must meet tragic suffering on its own terms, with our "unverifiable" faith—a faith that is honed by a love both for ourselves and for others, a faith that does not settle for a learned helplessness or a self-sacrificing masochism, a faith that yearns for justice in spite of what the world offers. In so many ways, the "mystery of iniquity" always exists, but this faith brings us closer to an acceptance of the inescapable suffering in our lives that is not passive or masochistic but is more of an understanding, an integration, and a wholeness.

Moreover, this faith is based in an actual experience of God as companion-sufferer who "knows" our experiences of suffering and yet somehow overcomes our captivity in them. Through faith, we are brought to the promise, as delineated in the writings and records of the Christian community, that God (along with our efforts) will liberate us from our suffering, although, perhaps, not in ways we have originally desired or anticipated. In the end, as May

---

[38]E.g., see statements by a group of mothers whose husbands had sexually abused their children, in Marie Fortune, "My God, My God, Why Have You Forsaken Me?" in Ann Greenwalt Abernethy, et al., *Spinning a Sacred Yarn: Women Speak from the Pulpit* (New York: Pilgrim Press, 1982) 70–1.

and Becker say, we arrive at faith and hope, at the mystery of iniquity and suffering, and at the inscrutable, living God, for whom "everything is possible."

And yet, despite this type of surrender and faith, our response need also be one of protest and resistance to evil, however it manifests itself to us, and a "wrestling with God" toward understanding. As writers such as Joanne Carlson Brown and Rebecca Parker, Carter Heyward, and Marie Fortune stress, we must never minimize or accept the actual suffering itself, or settle for a suffering that we can eliminate. Through the "political" pole of our varied spiritualities, which is enlivened and sustained by the "mystical" pole, we must therefore actively plan and organize for liberation from the suffering situations that attempt to take away our dignity, hope, and life.

Thus, my proposed spiritual response to suffering has two poles: the mystical and the political—a contemplative and an active response. Neither one alone is sufficient in dealing with the suffering that women experience; both must work in tandem to bring hope out of despair, strength out of powerlessness, and responsible action out of helplessness. Obviously, more critical discussion needs to be raised around such a spiritual response, but at the end of this study, I offer this response as a modest beginning to such ongoing, thoughtful debate. Perhaps, through such continued discussion that incorporates the insights of feminist theory, cultural studies, theology, and spirituality, women in pain may be helped by a response to their suffering that holds their humanity and dignity in place, while also acknowledging their real need for God's activating presence in their lives.

# 6

# Conclusion

LMOST A YEAR HAS PASSED SINCE I BEGAN THIS STUDY IN EARNEST, but, it seems, this has been a work in progress for over thirty years. In its present version this study began with a review of contemporary definitions and understandings of suffering from various disciplines, including bioethics, historical/cultural studies, psychology and pastoral care, and traditional theodicies. Based on the works studied, it was found that suffering is a fundamental human experience and attempts to avoid it lead to apathy, trivialization, and an emphasis on the banal, which ultimately destroys our humanity.

Not only is it inescapable, suffering is also characterized by its inexpressibility, unsharability, and its ability to isolate and alienate people one from another. It can destroy self-purpose, lead to individual and collective brokenness and loss of agency and hope, and can culminate in despair and death. Suffering can dehumanize to such an extent that one complies with one's own affliction, which leads to a lack of desire to alleviate one's own or others' suffering— exhibiting a lack of compassion for oneself and others. Sufferers also frequently describe their situation as one of powerlessness, weakness, and abandonment by others and, ultimately, by God. Thus, regardless of the perspective, suffering is, most notably, an experience of isolation and a threat to the very existence of the individual or group.

Moreover, suffering is a complex, multidimensional experience that is a function both of painful physical and psychological experiences and, primarily, of the meaning we give those experiences.

This meaning is affected by such things as physical sensation, emotions, social location, cultural factors, awareness of the future, anxiety, loss of choice and control, self-hatred and guilt, hope, and the beliefs within which one places the experience of suffering. The society and culture in which one lives, at a given time in history, as well as one's political and social conditions can affect the existence, degree, and meaning of suffering in one's life. Thus, only persons (and not just bodies) suffer for many of these writers, and "person" includes one's body, personal history, interior life, associations with others, and beliefs. Suffering, then, is always individual and unique because the person experiencing pain and ascribing meaning to pain is unique and particular. Any and all of these dimensions that make up the "whole" person are at risk and susceptible to change that can threaten one's cohesiveness and integrity—thus initiating suffering.

In an attempt to understand how a good, just, and omnipotent God can allow or permit evil and suffering to occur in a basically good creation, Christian theologians have long attempted to understand and explain suffering by developing a variety of theodicies, also outlined in chapter 2. These theodicies have explained suffering as a consequence of dualistic forces, disobedience, ignorance, or disregard for God's intended good purposes that leads to punishment and retribution, and for purposes of atonement, redemption, human development, and instruction. However, for many in this century of prolonged and horrific innocent suffering, most of the traditional theodicies fall short in their efforts to justify God with regard to the existence of continued evil and suffering. Perhaps, the most lasting or viable traditional theodicy is still the faith solution, wherein no ironclad explanations or adequate rational explanations are given for the continued existence of suffering in a world created and governed by a good, just, and powerful God. In the midst of innocent suffering and *vis à vis* such a God, this theodicy admonishes one to resort to petition, lament, and responses based on trust and faith in God's justice and loving-kindness.

Some of the critiques raised by process, suffering-God, and liberation theologians regarding the limitations of these traditional theodicies were also noted in this chapter. Generally, the emphasis in these critiques is more on concrete experiences of suffering and the social and historical structures which enable such suffering to occur, and less on abstract, theoretical justifications for God's actions or lack thereof. These alternatives center around more pragmatic, praxis-centered approaches, and focus on human responsibility for eradicating or overcoming evil and suffering, as well as how God assists in that process.

From there, chapter 3 consisted of reviewing a number of women's "theological" writings on suffering, to determine what was similar to and different from the responses to suffering given by the writers discussed in chapter 2, and of developing a schema for organizing those writings. This schema consists of six categories of writings from different Christian feminist/womanist perspectives, including reconsiderations of evil, critiques of traditional theodicies, those reflections which uncover areas not formerly considered in theology, the "wrestling with God" writings, extensive theological inquiries into suffering which incorporate women's stories and experiences, and finally, those writings which point toward the development of future feminist theologies of suffering.

From these writings, I noted five general trends that differ from the traditional approaches to the questions of faith raised by suffering, and paralleled those approaches of process, suffering-God, and liberation theologies in general. These trends included (1) a shift from the abstract theodicy question to more practical, concrete discussions of evil and suffering; (2) a shift from looking at sin, evil, and suffering as one, monolithic experience to differentiating among various types of suffering; (3) a shift in focus of the meaning and significance of relationality in one's faith journey; (4) an identification of which part of the traditional theodicy question—God's justice, goodness, or power—is most often relinquished or rejected in women's depictions of evil and suffering; and (5) the development of different ways of viewing the human person that are intended to be more helpful to women who suffer. I also identified a few areas that are not covered in this literature, as well as noted the lack of general consensus regarding the value of suffering from these women's perspectives.

Out of this review of writings, I also observed that the suffering that resists eradication by changes in social, political, and religious systems has been given less attention, at present, in women's theological reflections on suffering. Little was found related to how one might actually come to terms theologically and spiritually with "radical" suffering, as defined by Wendy Farley.

This situation led to a discussion in chapter 4 on the usefulness of incorporating a tragic vision into discussions of such suffering for women. It was proposed that a tragic vision of reality might aid theological and spiritual considerations of evil and suffering in a variety of ways. For instance, such a vision retains the profound inconsolability surrounding radical, unmerited suffering, while also acknowledging and exploring the notion that this type of suffering does not always arise from conscious wrongdoing or wicked intent. It reminds us that in seeking viable responses to suffering not all suffering is the same and, thus, that suffering requires more than one, universal response. Some types of suffering may be eradicated through human effort and social/political/cultural revision; but, other types of suffering resist all efforts to change the situation and must be approached from different angles that incorporate notions of human finitude, conflict, and fragility.

Furthermore, a tragic vision of reality, as discussed in chapter 4, helps us to recognize that our lives of contingency and vulnerability are, to a certain extent, inevitably and inescapably determined by forces out of our control, as well as by our own fragility of goodness. We are all caught, no matter how good our intentions, by the radical nature of our sin and circumscribed by both external and internal forces that undo our efforts to alleviate evil and suffering. One of the values, then, of seeing life through a tragic lens is that it does not lead to false hope in human actions, constructs, and institutions. It helps us recognize and acknowledge the complexity and depth of the evil to which suffering in our times is connected.

Nonetheless, it was also noted that a tragic vision of reality does not advocate a passive stance in the face of contingency and finitude. It stresses that, despite our limits, we must act, we must resist and defy that which seeks the destruction of one's dignity, virtue, and even one's very life. In utilizing a tragic vision within a Christian feminist theology of suffering, one does not negate the validity of human responsibility for some forms of evil. It views evil as both moral (that is, something that can be changed through human effort) and as natural and tragic. Thus, tragedy acknowledges that sin, cruelty, and indifference play a major role in evil and suffering, but it also places evil in a context that is more inclusive than human fault.

As noted in chapter 4, a tragic vision also, and perhaps most importantly, can point toward an experience of transformation for the radical sufferer. It can bring one to a shift in how she views her own and others' suffering—a shift that involves a reimagining of her images, metaphors, and experiences of God, and that helps her find new meaning, her own meaning, in the midst of affliction. Through a recognition and acknowledgment of one's insufficiency in the face of radical evil and suffering, the radical sufferer may come to a recognition of her need for something beyond the tragic structure of human life, and thus, perhaps, to an experience of unverifiable faith. What she may come to, through a tragic understanding of reality, is the realization that at some points, only God's grace can heal the depth and extent of sin, suffering, and tragedy that we experience.

With all these previous considerations in mind, I attempted in chapter 5 to outline some key elements to consider in a theological/spiritual response to the suffering discussed throughout this work. I call such a response a "mystical/political" spirituality that attempts to incorporate both voices regarding women's suffering that Patricia Wismer identified in chapter 3 (that the actual suffering of women should never be minimized and thus, we should never settle for suffering that can be eliminated, *and* that one can discover meaning in suffering), as well as both aspects of evil, as moral and tragic, identified by Tiina Allik in chapter 4.

From the political pole, a spirituality that attempts to address the concerns of women in pain must take ever more seriously the situation of sexism in our various cultural contexts, as well as how such sexism subtly operates even within religious values and institutions to hinder the flourishing of women within our society. It would also recognize and affirm support networks among women, but would also critically confront and change the prejudice and lateral sexism that occur *among* women.

Such a spirituality, incorporating a political pole, might also attempt to build community across differences, on the basis of mutuality, reciprocity, and interdependence (modeled on the Trinity itself), and work to envision effective ways of relating with others that do not dismiss or trivialize another's pain. A spirituality that attempts to address the concrete pain women experience would also enable the sufferer to develop meaningful, productive ties with others, to work in solidarity with others to deal with forms of suffering that can be modified or eliminated through social and political change.

Furthermore, such a spirituality would encourage the autonomy, self-actualization, and self-transcendence of women, as well as men, before a God who desires our wholeness. For instance, it might encourage women to utilize various forms of verbal and physical self-defense to help establish psychological distance between the sufferer and, say, a known perpetrator of the suffering. It might also emphasize the role of memory in effecting change, accentuate the essential value of expression and communication within experiences of suffering, and incorporate attention to the body and one's feelings in responding to situations of suffering.

Such a spirituality might, therefore, help women in pain regain a sense of self-esteem, dignity, and purpose through a refashioning of internal values and standards from which to judge self and others. It might include a reevaluation of traditional virtues (such as obedience and self-sacrifice), and a recovery of anger, cunning, wit, and moral courage as positive Christian womanly virtues. Such a refashioning might also incorporate a vision of oneself as a "partner" with God in actively effecting justice in the world, as well as in actively expressing God's compassion to self and others.

A spirituality that incorporates the political pole would also struggle to free itself from any ideology, including feminism, that becomes oppressive to one's growth toward wholeness in God. Thus, it might continuously employ techniques and practices of individual and collective discernment not only to determine the usefulness of various ideologies, but also to analyze and reevaluate one's images, metaphors, and understandings of God, the human person, and one's approach to suffering.

Moreover, it is my contention that much of the foregoing also needs a grounding in what I have termed a mystical or contemplative pole incorporated into one's spirituality. Such an approach incorporates the value of vigil before God—a waiting on God for healing, inspiration, and hope. Particularly in situations of radical suffering, when one has reached an impasse as defined by Constance FitzGerald, traditional techniques of prayer and contemplation might help the sufferer when she no longer feels capable of continuing on, much less of actively working on her and others' suffering. In my view, here, both God's grace and one's faith, working together, can meet tragedy on its own terms—in the realm of the unexpected, paradoxical, mysterious, and incomprehensible.

With this, we now arrive at the end of this long reflection on suffering. Throughout this endeavor this work has led me back into old memories, through deep waters, and to many unexpected places. I have attempted not only to confront some of my own intellectual and faith issues, but also to present the writings of others in their own voices, to allow them to "converse" with one another, and to integrate my own critiques and views with those voices. What Melanie May has said of the writing of her book on the "theopoetics of death and resurrection" resonates with my own underlying desires for this study. As she states:

> I write what I write the way I write to have a say in bringing
> hope and faith back into the world. I write to keep hope alive
> and to heal the fracture of faith on earth. And I write to wrest
> a blessing from the faithful Presence I name God, to be healed
> by the Risen One who I believe bodies forth hope for abundant life.[1]

If only all of theology, including this plunge into the deep waters of suffering, could do so much!

Furthermore, in this endeavor, I do not believe that I have found any universal, definitive answers to suffering, particularly for women, and really did not expect I would. What I have discovered is more of the nuance, ambiguity, and paradox of life and the mystery of suffering along the way. I have discovered, through an exploration of their complexity, that suffering and evil are truly mysteries that we need to wonder about continuously, ponder, explore, wrestle with, and transform with God's help. But, at the completion of this study, the question still remains: is there a value to suffering for women?

My own response is a qualified yes. For many, suffering surely crushes and leaves one desolate, immobile, hopeless, and suicidal.

---

[1]Melanie May, *A Body Knows: A Theopoetics of Death and Resurrection* (New York: Continuum, 1995) 22.

It can destroy a person's dignity, meaning in life, hope for the future, and even one's will to live. Suffering, for these, can end in death or a life that is a living death, and this suffering must be seen for what it is: horrible, death-dealing, inconsolable. And yet I, too, confirm that even this type of suffering must be resisted somehow, as many of the women writers in chapter 3 so movingly articulated. Perhaps, a form of this resistance appears when the community connected with the sufferer articulates and protests the pain that the sufferer herself can no longer convey.

On the other hand, for others, suffering leads to creative outbursts and production, the building of strength and fortitude, the awakening of new vistas to explore in oneself. To be able to resist (even in some small way), to voice a protest, to link voices and spirits with others who know what it means to face the limits of one's existence can help some who suffer. The value here seems to come in seeing a choice—a choice to be with the suffering differently rather than being overwhelmed and destroyed by it. The value, it seems, is in one's recognition that even in acute and chronic anguish, we might choose, at times, to be with our suffering differently. We might learn not to comply with our own suffering, not to allow it to become our "sovereign lord," but to stand apart from it, come to see it differently, and to act from that place. Adrienne Rich's words, taken from the poem quoted in the introduction, echo here. . . . "I believe I am choosing something new/not to suffer uselessly yet still to feel. . . ."

But even here, it seems, the value one finds does not remove the sorrow or anguish. It does not quell the "why" questions, and one remains inconsolable on a certain level, bearing witness in one's own life to the pain of the world. Yet this stance against suffering also does not necessarily perpetuate helplessness, despair, or nihilism. The value, here, seems to be that suffering can bring us to a type of reckoning—a reckoning with the reality of the situation, but also with our own choices regarding how to proceed, as well as with our own limitations to change or control the situation.

Moreover, the value in suffering for me is that it can bring us face-to-face with our limits and vulnerability as human beings, and shows us our inherent need for each other, and for something/someone greater than us individually and collectively. Suffering can open us to the reality that, as human persons, no matter how well-intentioned and faithful, we cannot "fix" on our own all the suffering that we encounter in this life. Because of the complexity, pervasiveness, and powerfulness of the evil that we perpetrate and encounter in our lives, we need to look beyond ourselves at times for "our own integrity, our own healing, our own wholeness." I believe that this needs to be done even in order to confront and effectively work at alleviating the evil we can do something to eradicate.[2] As Pamela Dickey Young states, so too, do I agree:

> I am not as confident as some that all the resources for the integrity I long for reside within myself. It is my experience of the transcendent, which I, as a Christian, call God, that draws me beyond myself to the possibility of integrated relationships with others and with that God. Integrity is relational. I find it only in relation to others, including . . . God, who is its very possibility.[3]

For without a sense of a greater reality, a context of larger sources of significance that the classical tragedies and Christian literature give voice to and that we interact with, we are locked into a closed environment of our own making, bound by our lacks and limitations, seeking control where we have little or none. The loss of the concept of divine transcendence (linked to divine immanence) in some feminist theological discussions places all the responsibility on us, and thus, denies our very real limits as human beings and can harm the very people that one seeks to help. Without a sense of the transcendent as well as the immanent in the midst of suffering, the potential for despair and hopelessness when all our best efforts fall short; when our institutions, ideologies, and values betray us; and even when our own virtue inevitably fails us can paralyze all subsequent efforts for change. Thus, in my own view, part of what suffering can give us is the very real knowledge in our bodies, minds, and spirits, of our need for the transcendent, for God.

What some of the writings covered in this study have suggested is that suffering, then, is not just something in human life to "get

---

[2]Pamela Dickey Young, "Beyond Moral Influence to an Atoning Life," *Theology Today* 52 (1995) 351.

[3]Ibid., 352.

over," to avoid, or even fully resolve. They suggest that suffering, particularly radical suffering, is often pivotal for the action of grace to become manifest in our lives. Why this is so remains to be wondered about and discussed more thoroughly in future work.[4]

But, given our persistent need for control over our experiences, our common blindness to the ever-present manifestations of God in our world, and our inherent limitations as created, embodied beings, the value of suffering may be that it leads us to recognize our radical vulnerability. This vulnerability is before the rest of the world, external and internal forces (some of which have harmful intent), and our own personal and collective fragility and limitations. Through this recognition of our vulnerability, perhaps suffering can also ultimately lead us to an openness before God, which dawns as a recognition of our need for and dependency on something or someone greater than oneself or the world of which one is a part. Often, we do not recognize our predicament or the grace that presses toward us in the midst of our suffering. But, writers such as Karl Rahner give voice to a reality upon which our hope in suffering can be built, as he states: "Grace is God himself, his communication in which he gives himself to us as the divinizing loving kindness which is himself."[5]

Perhaps, the value of suffering lies in this knowledge, but more so in the actual encounter with God in the very midst of our suffering and the choices that are opened up because of that experience. In this often surprising and paradoxical encounter with God, we can discover for ourselves that ultimately we are not alone, even at the depths of our despair. Thus, through suffering as a limit experience and experiences of God's presence in the midst of such limitation, we might come to hope in the face of utter despair, to trust that there is something beyond or greater or better than just this moment. We might come to place ourselves, with genuine

---

[4]One response that I received recently from British poet-novelist Sarah Connor is as follows: "I would suggest it is because grace cannot operate when we trust ourselves, our place in the world, our power. Grace is most manifest when we have nothing to rely upon, to place our trust in, to depend on. When we are reduced to the essential self. Then God can love us totally and completely. And then we can minister to the broken world," letter dated August 17, 1997.

[5]Karl Rahner, *Nature and Grace: Dilemmas in the Modern Church* (New York: Sheed and Ward, 1964) 128.

knowledge of our limitations, within a larger context of significance and meaning. We might come, through an actual encounter
with God in suffering, to trust that there is something/someone
worthy of that trust and hope. As with the interpretation of Job
that I offered in chapter 4 and as the psalmist said, "But at my vindication, I shall see your face; when I awake, I shall be satisfied, be-
holding your likeness."[6] Through an encounter with God, our
pain is not trivialized but transformed.

In the midst of our North American cultural milieu in which
many of us abhor discomfort and withdraw from the difficult,
some of the writers studied here challenge us to look directly at the
meaningfulness of suffering in our lives. They do not ignore the fact
of persistent, horrendous, and global suffering, or the ways that suffering particularly affects women in various concrete situations;
they know that our awareness of God's presence, grace, and providential care does not come easily, particularly in these postmodern
times.[7] But, in addition, what they do speak of is that we must look
ever more closely to the "phenomena" of God's love and compassion in our very midst, because we cannot resolve these crises of
suffering on our own. What they witness to is an encounter with
God and meaning that, somehow, for each of us, individually and
collectively, can transform that suffering which seeks to destroy us.

And so, I end this work with another of the Anne Sexton
poems that have framed this endeavor for me. Within this one,
"The Rowing Endeth," lies a notion of one value of suffering for
Christian women of faith as I see it—not as any explanation or
justification for suffering. But, that through suffering and despite
all our expectations to the contrary, we *can* come to an encounter
with One who knows our suffering, because of God's incarnation
in Christ and the Holy Spirit. In the very midst of our suffering, we
can come to an encounter with love, grace, and yes, even with joy:

[6]Psalm 17:16.

[7]Not the least of which is the breakdown of our "deep symbols" or "words of
power," that shape the values of our society and guide the life of faith, morality,
and action, as Edward Farley discusses in his recent work *Deep Symbols: Their
Postmodern Effacement and Reclamation* (Valley Forge, Penn.: Trinity Press
International, 1996). The five deep symbols that he deals with in this work are tradition, reality, obligation (duty), law, and hope. To this list, I would add faith and
tragedy as other symbols needing recovery and, what he calls, "reenchantment."

### THE ROWING ENDETH

I'm mooring my rowboat
at the dock of the island called God.
This dock is made in the shape of a fish
and there are many boats moored
at many different docks.
"It's okay," I say to myself,
with blisters that broke and healed
and broke and healed—
saving themselves over and over.
And salt sticking to my face and arms like
a glue-skin pocked with grains of tapioca.
I empty myself from my wooden boat
and onto the flesh of The Island.

"On with it!" He says and thus
we squat on the rocks by the sea
and play—can it be true—
a game of poker.
He calls me.
I win because I hold a royal straight flush.
He wins because He holds five aces.
A wild card had been announced
but I had not heard it
being in such a state of awe
when He took out the cards and dealt.
As he plunks down His five aces
and I sit grinning at my royal flush,
He starts to laugh,
the laughter rolling like a hoop out of His mouth
and into mine,
and such laughter that He doubles right over me
laughing a Rejoice-Chorus at our two triumphs.
Then I laugh, the fishy dock laughs
the sea laughs. The Island laughs.
The Absurd laughs.

Dearest dealer,
I with my royal straight flush,

love you so for your wild card,
that untamable, eternal, gut-driven *ha-ha*
and lucky love.[8]

---

[8]Anne Sexton, "The Rowing Endeth," in *The Complete Poems* (Boston: Houghton Mifflin, 1981) 473–4.

# Bibliography

Abernethy, Ann Greenwalt, et al. *Spinning a Sacred Yarn: Women Speak from the Pulpit.* New York: Pilgrim Press, 1982.

Allik, Tiina. "Human Finitude and the Concept of Women's Experience," *Modern Theology* 9 (1993) 67–85.

_____. "Narrative Approaches to Human Personhood: Agency, Grace, and Innocent Suffering," *Philosophy and Theology* 1 (1987) 305–33.

_____. "Religious Experience, Human Finitude, and the Cultural-Linguistic Model," *Horizons: Journal of the College Theology Society* 20 (1993) 241–59.

Amato, Joseph. *Victims and Values: A History and Theory of Suffering.* New York: Praeger Books, 1990.

Anczarski, Mary. "The Mystery of Suffering," *Catholic Worker* 59 (1992) 5.

Aristotle. *Aristotle's Poetics.* Trans. S. H. Butcher. New York: Hill and Wang, 1961.

Becker, Ernest. *The Denial of Death.* New York: The Free Press, 1973.

Bergant, Dianne. "A Look at Suffering," *The Bible Today* 29 (1991) 303–9.

Blomquist, Jean M. *Wrestling till Dawn: Awakening to Life in Times of Struggle.* Nashville: Upper Room Books, 1994.

*The Book of Job.* Trans. Stephen Mitchell. San Francisco: North Point Press, 1987.

Bouchard, Larry D. "Tragedy," in *Encyclopedia of Bioethics,* vol. 5. Ed. Warren Thomas Reich. Revised ed. New York: Macmillan Library Reference USA/Simon & Schuster Macmillan, 1995, 2490–6.

Bregman, L. "Suffering," in *Dictionary of Pastoral Care and Counseling.* Ed. Rodney J. Hunter. Nashville: Abingdon Press, 1990, 1230–2.

Brereton, Geoffrey. *Principles of Tragedy: A Rational Examination of the Tragic Concept in Life and Literature.* Coral Gables, Fla.: University of Miami Press, 1970.

Brès, Yvon. *La souffrance et le tragique: Essais sur le judéo-christianisme, les tragiques, Platon et Freud.* Paris: Presses Universitaires de France, 1992.

Bringle, Mary Louise. *Despair: Sickness or Sin?: Hopelessness and Healing in the Christian Life.* Nashville: Abingdon Press, 1990.

Brock, Rita Nakashima. *Journeys by Heart: A Christology of Erotic Power.* New York: Crossroad, 1988.

Brown, Joanne Carlson, and Rebecca Parker. "For God So Loved the World?" in *Christianity, Patriarchy, and Abuse: A Feminist Critique.* Ed. Joanne Carlson Brown and Carole R. Bohn. New York: Pilgrim Press, 1989, 1–30.

Bussert, Joy M. K. *Battered Women: From a Theology of Suffering to an Ethic of Empowerment.* New York: Lutheran Church in America, Division for Mission in North America, 1986.

Callahan, Sidney. "A Mother's Death: Is This What God Demands?" *Commonweal* 123 (May 17, 1996) 7–8.

Carr, Anne. "On Feminist Spirituality," in *Women's Spirituality: Resources for Christian Development.* Ed. Joann Wolski Conn. New York/Mahwah, N.J.: Paulist Press, 1986, 49–57.

_____. "The New Vision of Feminist Theology: Method," in *Freeing Theology: The Essentials of Theology in Feminist Perspective.* Ed. Catherine Mowry LaCugna. San Francisco: HarperSan Francisco, 1993, 5–29.

Cassell, Eric J. "The Importance of Understanding Suffering for Clinical Ethics," *Journal of Clinical Ethics* 2 (1991) 81–2.

_____. "Pain and Suffering," in *Encyclopedia of Bioethics,* vol. 4. Ed. Warren Thomas Reich. Revised ed. New York: Macmillan Library Reference USA/Simon & Schuster Macmillan, 1995, 1897–905.

Chopp, Rebecca S. "Feminism's Theological Pragmatics: A Social Naturalism of Women's Experience," *Journal of Religion* 67 (1987) 239–56.

_____. *Praxis of Suffering: An Interpretation of Liberation and Political Theologies.* Maryknoll, N.Y.: Orbis Books, 1986.

Cone, James H. "God and Black Suffering," in *The Spirituals and the Blues: An Interpretation.* New York: Seabury Press, 1992, 58–85.

Confoy, Maryanne. "Women's Experience and Theology," *St. Mark's Review* 151 (1992) 17–20.

Cousins, Ewert H. "What Is Christian Spirituality?" in *Modern Christian Spirituality: Methodological and Historical Essays.* Ed. Bradley Hanson. Atlanta: Scholars Press, 1990, 39–44.

Crowley, Paul, ed. "Evil and Hope," *Proceedings of the Fiftieth Annual Convention of the Catholic Theological Society of America* 50 (1995).

Downey, Michael. "Weakness and Vulnerability," in *The New Dictionary of Catholic Spirituality.* Ed. Michael Downey. Collegeville: The Liturgical Press, 1993, 1018–21.

Duffy, Stephen J. "Evil," in *The New Dictionary of Catholic Spirituality.* Ed. Michael Downey. Collegeville: The Liturgical Press, 1993, 361–4.

_____. "Our Hearts of Darkness: Original Sin Revisited," *Theological Studies* 49 (1988) 597–622.

Dupré, Louis. "Evil—a Religious Mystery: A Plea for a More Inclusive Model of Theodicy," *Faith and Philosophy* 7 (1990) 261–80.

Engel, Mary Potter. "Evil, Sin, and Violation of the Vulnerable," in *Lift Every Voice: Constructing Christian Theologies from the Underside.* Ed. Susan Brooks Thistlethwaite and Mary Potter Engel. San Francisco: Harper & Row, 1990, 152–64.

Farley, Margaret. "Power and Powerlessness: A Case in Point," *Proceedings of the Catholic Theological Society of America* 37 (1982) 116–8.

Farley, Wendy. "Resistance as a Theological Category: *The Cunning of History* Revisited," *Bridges* 3 (1991) 115–27.

_____. *Tragic Vision and Divine Compassion: A Contemporary Theodicy.* Louisville, Ky.: Westminster/John Knox Press, 1990.

Fatula, Mary Ann. "Suffering," in *The New Dictionary of Theology.* Ed. Joseph A. Komonchak, et al. Wilmington: Michael Glazier, 1988, 990–2.

Fischer, Kathleen. *Women at the Well: Feminist Perspectives on Spiritual Direction.* New York/Mahwah, N.J.: Paulist Press, 1988.

FitzGerald, Constance. "Impasse and Dark Night," in *Women's Spirituality: Resources for Christian Development.* Ed. Joann Wolski Conn. New York/Mahwah, N.J.: Paulist Press, 1986, 287–311.

Fortune, Marie F. "The Transformation of Suffering: A Biblical and Theological Perspective," in *Christianity, Patriarchy, and Abuse: A Feminist Critique.* Ed. Joanne Carlson Brown and Carole R. Bohn. New York: Pilgrim Press, 1989, 139–47.

Gallagher, Vera. "Thoughts from Death and Life," *Review for Religious* 52 (1993) 238–40.

Gear, Janet Christine. *Love in the Face of Suffering: A Study of Dorothee Sölle's Prophetic Mysticism.* M.A. thesis. Berkeley: Pacific School of Religion, 1996.

Giles, Mary E. "Reflections on Suffering in a Mystical-Feminist Key," *Journal of Spiritual Formation* 15 (1994) 137–48.

Grant, Jacquelyn. "Subjectification as a Requirement for Christological Construction," in *Lift Every Voice: Constructing Christian Theologies from the Underside.* Ed. Susan Brooks Thistlethwaite and Mary Potter Engel. San Francisco: Harper & Row, 1990, 201–14.

Gruba-McCallister, Frank. "Becoming Self through Suffering: The Irenaean Theodicy and Advanced Development," *Advanced Development Journal* 4 (1992) 49–57.

Halliwell, Stephen. "Human Limits and the Religion of Greek Tragedy," *Literature and Theology* 4 (1990) 169–80.

Harrison, Beverly Wildung. "The Power of Anger in the Work of Love," in *Making the Connections: Essays in Feminist Social Ethics.* Ed. Carol S. Robb. Boston: Beacon Press, 1985, 3–21.

Haughton, Rosemary. *The Passionate God.* New York/Mahwah, N.J.: Paulist Press, 1981.

Heyward, Isabel Carter. *The Redemption of God: A Theology of Mutual Relation.* Washington, D.C.: University Press of America, 1982.

_____. "Suffering, Redemption, and Christ: Shifting the Grounds of Feminist Christology," *Christianity and Crisis* 49 (December 11, 1989) 381–5.

Howe, Kathryn. "Spirituality of Suffering," *Pastoral Sciences* 12 (1993) 141–65.

Jaspers, Karl. *Tragedy Is Not Enough.* Trans. Harald A. T. Reiche, et al. Boston: Beacon Press, 1952.

John Paul II, Pope. "The Christian Meaning of Human Suffering" [Apostolic Letter *Salvifici doloris*], *Origins* 13 (February 23, 1984) 609–24.

Johnson, Elizabeth A. "Suffering God: Compassion Poured Out," in *She Who Is: The Mystery of God in Feminist Theological Discourse.* New York: Crossroad, 1992, 246–72.

Keshgegian, Flora A. "Suffering," in *Dictionary of Feminist Theologies.* Ed. Letty M. Russell and J. Shannon Clarkson. Louisville, Ky.: Westminster/John Knox Press, 1996, 278–80.

King, Ursula, ed. *Feminist Theology from the Third World.* Maryknoll, N.Y.: Orbis Books, 1994.

Kokolus, Cait. "Of Heartwounds and Hope," *Living Prayer* 26 (September/October 1993) 13–6.

Kollar, Nathan R. "Toward a Spirituality of Pain," *Spirituality Today* 42 (1990) 209–16.

Kwok Pui-Lan. "God Weeps with Our Pain," in *New Eyes for Reading: Biblical and Theological Reflections by Women from the Third World.* Ed. John S. Pobee and Barbel von Wartenberg-Potter. Geneva: World Council of Churches, 1986, 90–5.

Lee-Pollard, Dorothy A. "Powerlessness as Power: A Key Emphasis in the Gospel of Mark," *Scottish Journal of Theology* 40 (1987) 173–88.

Leifeld, Wendy. "In the Furnace of Affliction God's Comfort," *New Covenant* 23 (1994) 14–6.

Loades, Ann. "C. S. Lewis: Grief Observed, Rationality Abandoned, Faith Regained," *Journal of Literature and Theology* 3 (1989) 107–21.

Loewy, Erich H. "The Role of Suffering and Community in Clinical Ethics," *Journal of Clinical Ethics* 2 (1991) 83–7.

Lorde, Audre. "Eye to Eye: Black Women, Hatred, and Anger," in *Sister Outsider: Essays and Speeches.* Trumansburg, N.Y.: Crossing Press, 1984, 145–75.

Lowe, Walter. *Evil and the Unconscious.* Chico, Calif.: Scholars Press, 1983.

Mancuso, Theresa. "Suffering and the Quest for Happiness," *Living Prayer* 27 (July/August 1994) 15–20.

May, Melanie. *A Body Knows: A Theopoetics of Death and Resurrection.* New York: Continuum, 1995.

McAloon, Francis X. *Christianity and the Event of Suffering: The Conditions of Possibility for a Relatively Adequate Contemporary Theological Conversation.* M.S.T. thesis. Berkeley: Jesuit School of Theology at Berkeley, 1992.

Metz, Johannes Baptist. *Poverty of Spirit.* Trans. John Drury. Paramus, N.J./New York: Paulist Press, 1968.

Miller, Jerome. *The Way of Suffering: A Geography in Crisis.* Washington, D.C.: Georgetown University Press, 1988.

Moltmann-Wendel, Elizabeth. "Is There a Feminist Theology of the Cross?" in *The Scandal of a Crucified World: Perspectives on the Cross and Suffering.* Ed. Yacob Tesfai. Maryknoll, N.Y.: Orbis Books, 1994, 87–98.

Morris, David B. *The Culture of Pain.* Berkeley: University of California Press, 1991.

Noddings, Nel. *Women and Evil.* Berkeley: University of California Press, 1989.

Nussbaum, Martha C. *The Fragility of Goodness: Luck and Ethics in Greek Tragedy and Philosophy.* Cambridge, Mass./New York: Cambridge University Press, 1986.

O'Connor, Elizabeth. "Creative Suffering," in *Our Many Selves.* New York: Harper & Row, 1971, 93–198.

Osiek, Carolyn. "The Feminist and the Bible," in *Feminist Perspectives on Biblical Scholarship.* Ed. Adela Yarbro Collins. Chico, Calif.: Scholars Press, 1985, 97.

Poethig, Kathryn. *Suffering: An Interfaith Conversation* [Women's Theology Conference audiocassette tapes]. Berkeley: Center for Women and Religion, Graduate Theological Union, 1995.

Quinn, Philip L. "Agamemnon and Abraham: The Tragic Dilemma of Kierkegaard's Knight of Faith," *Literature and Theology* 4 (1990) 181–93.

_____ "Tragic Dilemmas, Suffering Love, and Christian Life," *Journal of Religious Ethics* 17 (1989) 151–83.

Rahner, Karl. "Why Does God Allow Us to Suffer?" in *Theological Investigations,* vol. 19: *Faith and Ministry.* Trans. Edward Quinn. New York: Crossroad, 1983, 194–208.

Rich, Adrienne. *The Dream of a Common Language: Poems 1974–1977.* New York: W. W. Norton & Company, 1983.

Richard, Lucien. *What Are They Saying about the Theology of Suffering?* New York/Mahwah, N.J.: Paulist Press, 1992.

Ricoeur, Paul. *Fallible Man: Philosophy of the Will.* Trans. Charles Kelbley. Chicago: Henry Regnery Company, 1965.

_____. *The Philosophy of Paul Ricoeur: An Anthology of His Works.* Ed. Charles E. Reagan and David Stewart. Boston: Beacon Press, 1978.

_____. *Symbolism of Evil.* Trans. Emerson Buchanan. Boston: Beacon Press, 1969.

_____. *Time and Narrative,* vol. 1. Trans. Kathleen McLaughlin and David Pellauer. Chicago: University of Chicago Press, 1984.

Ross, Susan A., and Mary Catherine Hilkert. "Feminist Theology: A Review of Literature," *Theological Studies* 56 (1995) 327–52.

Ruether, Rosemary Radford. *Sexism and God-Talk: Toward a Feminist Theology.* Boston: Beacon Press, 1983.

Ruffing, Janet K. "Physical Illness: A Mystically Transformative Element in the Life of Elizabeth Leseur," *Spiritual Life* 40 (1994) 220–9.

Ruprecht, Louis A. *Tragic Posture and Tragic Vision: Against the Modern Failure of Nerve.* New York: Continuum, 1994.

Saiving, Valerie. "The Human Situation: A Feminine View," *Journal of Religion* 40 (1960) 100–12. Reprinted in *Womanspirit Rising: A Feminist Reader in Religion*. San Francisco: Harper & Row, 1979, 25–42.

Sands, Kathleen M. *Escape from Paradise: Evil and Tragedy in Feminist Theology*. Minneapolis: Fortress Press, 1994.

Scarry, Elaine. *The Body in Pain: The Making and Unmaking of the World*. New York: Oxford University Press, 1985.

Scheler, Max. *The Nature of Sympathy*. Trans. Peter Heath. New Haven: Yale University Press, 1954.

_____. "On the Tragic," *Cross Currents* 4 (1954) 178–91.

Schneiders, Sandra M. *Beyond Patching: Faith and Feminism in the Catholic Church*. New York/Mahwah, N.J.: Paulist Press, 1991.

_____. "The Effects of Women's Experience on their Spirituality," in *Women's Spirituality: Resources for Christian Development*. Ed. Joann Wolski Conn. New York/Mahwah, N.J.: Paulist Press, 1986, 31–48.

_____. "Spirituality in the Academy," in *Modern Christian Spirituality: Methodological and Historical Essays*. Ed. Bradley Hanson. Atlanta: Scholars Press, 1990, 15–37.

Scott, Nathan A., ed. *The Tragic Vision and the Christian Faith*. New York: Association Press, 1957.

Sexton, Anne. *The Complete Poems*. Boston: Houghton Mifflin, 1981.

Shoemaker, M. E. "Pain Theory and Research," in *Dictionary of Pastoral Care and Counseling*. Ed. Rodney J. Hunter. Nashville: Abingdon Press, 1990, 818–9.

Sia, Marian F., and Santiago. *From Suffering to God: Exploring Our Images of God in Light of Suffering*. New York: St. Martin's Press, 1994.

Smith, Karen Sue. "Can You See the Good in Suffering?" [a reader survey], *U.S. Catholic* 59 (February 1994) 6–15.

Smith, Pamela A. "Chronic Pain and Creative Possibility: A Psychological Phenomenon Confronts Theologies of Suffering," in *Broken and Whole: Essays on Religion and the Body*. Ed. Maureen A. Tilley and Susan A. Ross. Annual Publication of the College Theology Society, vol. 39 (1993). Latham, N.Y.: University Press of America, 1995, 159–88.

Sölle, Dorothee. *The Strength of the Weak: Toward a Christian Feminist Identity*. Trans. Robert and Rita Kimber. Philadelphia: Westminster Press, 1984.

_____. *Suffering*. Trans. Everett R. Kalin. Philadelphia: Fortress Press, 1975.

Sparks, Richard. "Suffering," in *The New Dictionary of Catholic Spirituality*. Ed. Michael Downey. Collegeville: The Liturgical Press, 1993, 950–3.

Surin, Kenneth. "Evil, Problem of," in *Blackwell Encyclopedia of Modern Christian Thought*. Ed. Alister E. McGrath. Oxford, England/Cambridge, Mass.: Blackwell Publishers, 1993, 192–9.

———. "The Sign That Something Else Is Always Possible: Hearing and Saying 'Jesus Is Risen' and Hearing the Voices of Those Who Suffer: Some Textual/Political Reflections," *Literature and Theology* 4 (1990) 263–77.

Sutherland, Anne V. "Worldframes and God-Talk in Trauma and Suffering," *Journal of Pastoral Care* 49 (1995) 280–92.

Sutherland, Stewart R. "Christianity and Tragedy," *Literature and Theology* 4 (1990) 157–68.

Tamez, Elsa. "A Letter to Job," in *New Eyes for Reading: Biblical and Theological Reflections by Women from the Third World*. Ed. John S. Pobee and Barbel von Wartenberg-Potter. Geneva: World Council of Churches, 1986, 50–2.

Thornton, Sharon Garred. *Pastoral Care and the Reality of Suffering: Pastoral Theology from the Perspective of a Theology of the Cross*. Ph.D. dissertation. Berkeley: Graduate Theological Union, 1991.

Tilley, T. W. "Evil, Problem of," in *The New Dictionary of Theology*. Ed. Joseph A. Komonchak, et al. Wilmington: Michael Glazier, 1987, 360–3.

Townes, Emilie M., ed. *A Troubling in My Soul: Womanist Perspectives on Evil and Suffering*. Maryknoll, N.Y.: Orbis Books, 1993.

Trost, Lou Ann. "On Suffering, Violence, and Power," *Currents in Theology and Mission* 21 (1994) 35–40.

Weil, Simone. *Attente de Dieu*. Paris: Fayard, 1969. English translation: *Waiting for God*. Trans. Emma Craufurd. New York: Harper & Row, 1951.

Weitz, Morris. "Tragedy," in *Encyclopedia of Philosophy*, vol. 8. Ed. Paul Edwards. New York: Macmillan and The Free Press, 1967, 155–61.

Welch, Sharon. *A Feminist Ethic of Risk*. Minneapolis: Fortress Press, 1990.

Whitney, Barry L. *Theodicy: An Annotated Bibliography on the Problem of Evil, 1960–1990*. New York: Garland Publishers, 1993.

Williams, Delores S. *Sisters in the Wilderness: The Challenge of Womanist God-Talk*. Maryknoll, N.Y.: Orbis Books, 1993.

Wilson-Kastner, Patricia. *Faith, Feminism, and the Christ*. Philadelphia: Fortress Press, 1983.

Wismer, Patricia L. "Evil," in *New Handbook of Christian Theology*. Ed. Donald W. Musser and Joseph L. Price. Nashville: Abingdon Press, 1992, 173–5.

_____. "For Women in Pain," in *In the Embrace of God: Feminist Approaches to Theological Anthropology*. Ed. Ann O'Hara Graff. Maryknoll, N.Y.: Orbis Books, 1995, 138–58.

Young, Pamela Dickey. "Beyond Moral Influence to an Atoning Life," *Theology Today* 52 (1995) 344–55.

Young-Eisendrath, Polly. *The Gifts of Suffering: Finding Insight, Compassion, and Renewal*. Reading, Mass.: Addison-Wesley Publishing, 1996.

# Index

## A

abuse, 67, 90, 100–9, 141
  *See also* statistics
acceptance of suffering, 48, 98,
  101, 116–7, 125–30, 150, 173,
  217–24
  *See also* passivity
action, 49, 106, 109, 111, 124, 130,
  141, 164, 169, 172–3, 178, 182,
  190–1, 194, 198–9, 210–5, 225
affliction, 32–5
agency, 8, 22, 29, 34, 89, 108, 130,
  141–2, 148, 168, 173, 183, 203–4
Allik, Tiina, 165 n. 12, 176–7, 179,
  181–4, 187–8, 195, 197, 200–4,
  230
ambiguity, 67, 115, 120, 125–6,
  157, 172, 181, 199, 219, 221, 224
Andersen, Francis, 190–1
anger, 68, 103–4, 109, 139, 158, 215
Anselm of Canterbury, 45, 55
anthropology, 14, 41, 69, 95–6,
  156–8, 165–204, 207
Antigone, 170–1
anxiety, 25, 76–7, 176, 179–80,
  220–1
apathy, 20, 123, 131, 220
Aristotle, 60, 64, 164
Augustine of Hippo, 38–9, 64, 69,
  80, 86, 89, 104

## B

Baures, Mary Margaret, 217 n. 21
bearing suffering, 21–2, 93, 129
Becker, Ernest, 193, 218, 225
Bible, use in combating oppres-
  sion, 142–4
blame and blaming, 70, 72, 97,
  102–3, 106–7, 117, 153–4, 189
Blomquist, Jean, 117–20, 217, 223
body and embodiment, 109–15,
  138, 157, 176, 182, 215
Bouchard, Larry, 162, 164–5
Bregman, L., 31
Brock, Rita Nakashima, 79, 120
Brown, Joanne Carlson, 67, 90–2,
  95, 97, 99, 150, 225
Brueggemann, Walter, 36–7
Bussert, Joy M. K., 85, 102, 104–9,
  212

## C

Carr, Anne E., 57, 207, 209–12
Cassell, Eric J., 17, 19, 24–30,
  122–3, 194, 202
child abuse. *See* abuse
choice(s), 8, 22, 38–42, 61–2, 89,
  105, 109, 116, 123, 128, 162, 164,
  170, 178, 186–7, 199, 205, 212
Chopp, Rebecca, 9 n. 12, 58, 80
chorus, Greek, 164, 214

Cobb, John, 43–4
commonalities, 9–10
compassion, 34, 41, 103, 117, 137, 139, 195
    *See also* God, compassion
complicity with suffering, 33, 67, 220
concupiscence, 69, 182–3
Cone, James, 146
conflict, 29–30, 77–8, 170–80, 196
connection, 16–7, 32, 75, 113–4, 116, 209
    *See also* isolation
control, desire to and lack of, 19, 25, 103, 116, 171, 180, 187, 193–4, 201, 206
Copeland, M. Shawn, 140–3
Cousins, Ewert, 209
cross/paschal mystery, 49, 86–99, 106–8, 128, 142
culpability. *See* responsibility


**D**

Daly, Mary, 81, 83
defilement, 33, 145–6, 185
dehumanization, 34, 50–1, 69, 134–5, 146, 167
denial and avoidance of suffering, 18–9, 22, 55
    contrasted with confrontation with suffering, 117, 126–30
desire, 179–83, 220–1
despair, 30, 50, 63, 67, 77, 130, 136, 139, 198–9, 218, 235
discernment, 131, 208, 213
disobedience. *See* obedience
domestic violence. *See* abuse
dualism, 38, 64, 69, 78, 80–3, 104–5
Duffy, Stephen, 180, 188 n. 86, 189, 197 n. 102, 201

**E**

embodiment. *See* body
endurance, 21, 40, 42, 95, 98, 106–8, 125
Engel, Mary Potter, 68–9
eros. *See* sexuality
ethical vision of reality. *See* reality, ethical vision of
evil, 44, 94, 102, 136–8, 174, 184–9, 197–201, 224
    as a "something," 77, 81, 160, 185
    cultural/social, 30, 32, 47, 60–3, 67, 171
    privatization, 61
    reconsiderations by women, 59–85
    traditional views, 35–42, 64–78, 87–9
    types, 37, 60, 200

**F**

faith, 49, 55, 87, 94, 101, 106, 114, 117–8, 130, 148–9, 193, 200, 218, 221–4
    unverifiable, 188, 202, 224
Fall of man, 38–40, 62, 65–6, 69–72, 104, 137–9
fallibility, 166, 168, 170–1, 183–4, 194, 197–8
Farley, Edward, 236 n. 7
Farley, Wendy, 134–40, 164–81, 187–8, 195, 197
Fatula, Mary Ann, 23
fault. *See* responsibility
    *See also* blame and blaming; flaw
fear, 55, 67, 70, 74–6, 128, 164–5, 195
    *See also* anxiety; denial
feminism/feminist, 198, 212–3
    definition, 56–7
feminist theology, 54–8, 72, 78–81, 84, 198

of suffering, 120–43, 149–51
tasks, 57, 72
finitude/limitedness, 21, 109–11,
    115, 162–5, 168, 175–7, 182–4,
    191, 195–8, 203, 218–21, 223,
    235–6
    *See also* impasse
FitzGerald, Constance, 218–23,
    231
flaw, tragic, 166, 168, 184
Fortune, Marie F., 100–9, 212–3,
    225
fragility. *See* fallibility
freedom, 34, 44, 97, 128, 139, 147,
    168–72, 180 n. 60, 181, 185,
    187, 201, 210, 212
future, role of, in suffering, 28

G
Geertz, Clifford, 35
Giles, Mary, 212–3
God, 70–1, 102, 132–3, 206–10,
    234–8
    and suffering. *See* theodicy;
        Jesus Christ; cross
    compassion, 42, 49, 103, 137,
        213, 222–4
    encounter with. *See* meaning,
        encounter with
    goodness/benevolence, 35–50,
        71, 90, 96–7, 108, 155–6,
        222–4
    hiddenness, 34, 42–3, 71, 221
    honor, 91
    images of, 132–3, 188, 202, 213
    impassibility, 44, 88
    justness, 35–50, 70, 148, 155–6,
        223–4
    omnipotence. *See* power, divine
    omniscience, 107
    permitting suffering, 38–9, 80,
        101

presence, 109, 113–7, 120, 124,
    147, 200, 204, 213, 216, 235
revelation, 188–93
suffering God, 44–8, 91–3, 133,
    223–4
transcendence, 78, 80–1, 203–4,
    234
Goldstein, Valerie Saiving, 72–3,
    154
(the) good, 80–2, 95, 134, 138, 165,
    167, 173, 182, 191, 194, 199
"good news," 14–5, 106–7, 114
goods, 80, 182
    competing/conflicting, 77,
        170–4, 178, 191, 199
grace, 94, 115, 143, 158–9, 183,
    193, 203–4, 224, 235–6
Griffin, David, 43–4
guilt/guiltlessness, 30–1, 33,
    38–41, 66, 71, 91, 101–2, 138–9,
    145, 166, 185, 190
Gutiérrez, Gustavo, 47, 49

H
Halliwell, Stephen, 175–6, 202
*hamartia,* 166, 192
Hegel, G.W.F., 178
helplessness. *See* passivity
hero/ine, tragic, 164–6, 169–70,
    173–6, 186, 189–93
Heyward, Isabel Carter, 79, 86–9,
    96, 103–4, 213, 225
Hick, John, 41
*hubris,* 166, 192
human person/humanity. *See*
    anthropology
Hume, David, 35–6
Hunt, Mary, 78–9

I
imagination, xiv, 109–13, 124,
    198, 219–20

impasse, 218–23
  *See also* finitude
inclusivity, 211
inexpressibility. *See* language
injustice. *See* justice
innocent suffering. *See* radical
  suffering
insufficiency, 168, 176, 204
isolation, 16–7, 24, 61, 110, 121,
  131, 167, 206
  *See also* connection

**J**
Jaspers, Karl, 202 n. 111
Jesus Christ, 14, 62–3, 147
  anger, 103–4
  as model, 48, 91, 106
  incarnation, 93, 98
  ministry, 92
  necessity for suffering, 91–3
  resurrection, 107–8, 148
  suffering/redemptive suffering,
    40, 46, 93, 96, 98, 108
  *See also* cross; theodicy
Job, 29, 39, 42, 131–3, 188–93, 236
John of the Cross, Saint, 218–23
Johnson, Elizabeth, 44–5, 73
justice/injustice, 36, 80, 84, 107,
  135, 138, 148, 173, 188, 192, 195

**K**
Kant, Immanuel, 60,
Kasper, Walter, 21
Keshgegian, Flora A., 58 n. 11, 60,
  90

**L**
lament, 42–3, 122, 190, 214
language, 15–7, 122–3, 130, 133,
  141, 214–5
limits. *See* finitude
loss, 30–1, 74–5

love, 125–8, 209–10, 236–8
Lowe, Walter, 172, 180, 201
Luke, Helen M., 22 n. 26
Luther, Martin, 104

**M**
Martin, Clarice, 143–5
May, Melanie, 113–8, 216, 218,
  223, 225, 232
meaning, 27, 30, 35–6, 96, 141,
  201–2
  encounter with, 21, 109, 113–4,
    120, 124, 147, 190–3, 208,
    224, 235–6
  questions of, 2, 6, 12–4, 29, 36,
    88, 90, 95 n. 145, 100, 119,
    202–3
meaninglessness, 76, 168, 193,
  199. *See also* Sölle, Dorothee
memory, xiv–xvii, 142–3, 214
Merton, Thomas, 18
Moltmann, Jürgen, 51
Morris, David B., 17–21, 26–7,
  32–3, 194
mystery, 21, 115, 119, 188, 199
  of evil, 78, 83, 189
  suffering as, versus puzzle, 17,
    20, 194
mystics, 125, 127–9, 147, 218–23

**N**
Noddings, Nel, 60, 63, 65, 70–7,
  171
numbness, psychic, 19, 121
Nussbaum, Martha, 194

**O**
obedience, 38–41, 68–73, 103–5
  *See also* passivity
O'Connor, Elizabeth, 114, 116,
  119, 223
Osiek, Carolyn, 56–7

**P**

pain
  acute contrasted to chronic,
    32–3, 109–13
  and imagination, 109–13
  and suffering, 24–5, 30, 71, 74,
    147–8
  biomedical perspective, 24–30
  control, 19, 112, 116
  meaning and, 26–7, 112, 173
  process, 25–7
painlessness, 18
Parker, Rebecca, 67, 90–2, 95, 97,
  99, 150, 225
partnership with God, 143–5, 148,
  214
passivity/helplessness, 63, 74–6,
  87, 89, 94, 101, 107–8, 114, 121,
  127, 145, 147, 153
patriarchy, 56–8, 63–85, 198
persons, 23, 27–8, 31, 145–6
Philoctetes, 167, 198
physical abuse. *See* abuse
pity, 164–5
Plato, 64
possibility, 139, 193, 200, 218, 225
power/powerlessness, 79, 82, 85,
  119, 128–9, 135, 142, 167
  divine, 35–6, 38–50, 96–7, 99,
    107, 132–3, 137, 155–6, 183,
    191
  human, 36, 76, 103, 108, 121, 135,
    147, 169, 193, 214, 218–20
praxis–oriented approaches, 43,
  47–50, 144, 152–3
prayer, 122–3, 214
pride, 68, 73
Prometheus, 170
protest, 43, 48, 119, 122–4, 190,
  193, 198, 214, 223, 225
punishment, 39–40, 66, 70–1, 102,
  132, 134, 166

**R**

radical/tragic/innocent suffering,
  33, 39, 48, 51, 92, 131–9, 155,
  160–206
Rahner, Karl, 42, 182–3, 235
rationality, 78, 80, 122, 199, 223
reality
  affirmation of, 125–6
  ethical vision of, 190, 192, 194
  flight from, 125
  tragic structure of, 139, 174–89
  tragic vision of, 163–204
receptivity. *See* vulnerability
redemption, 15, 31, 40, 87–99,
  148, 159, 196–7, 203
  as liberation, 49, 89, 95, 142–5
relationality/relationship, 74, 116,
  155–8, 166, 175, 177, 207–11
  distortion of as sin, 61, 68–72, 85
  with God, 71, 86–9, 92, 94, 206
resistance, 48, 68, 94, 119, 122, 129–
  30, 139–45, 158, 173–4, 198, 225
responsibility, 43, 49–50, 62–3, 66,
  70, 76, 84–8, 97, 103, 152–4,
  168–70, 180, 185, 187, 196,
  200–2
  fault, 138, 166, 169, 172, 186,
    188, 190, 194, 202
Rich, Adrienne,
  "Splittings," 8, 233
Richard, Lucien, 19, 48–9
Ricoeur, Paul, 184–9, 195, 197, 202
Ruether, Rosemary Radford, 57,
  61–8, 70, 72, 78, 84, 171

**S**

Saiving, Valerie. *See* Goldstein,
  Valerie Saiving
salvation. *See* redemption
Sands, Kathleen, 68–9, 73, 77–84,
  104, 140, 164, 169, 172, 178–9,
  195–6, 198, 202

Scarry, Elaine, 15–6, 111–2
Scheler, Max, 162
Schneiders, Sandra, 56, 72–3, 206–7
self–conflict. *See* conflict
self–esteem, 141, 146, 214
self–hatred, 30–1, 33, 67, 136
self–identity, 29, 208, 212
self–purpose, 29, 34, 110, 182,
    208, 210, 214
self–sacrifice, 40, 103, 106
self–transcendence, 206, 208, 210,
    221
"servile will," 185–7
sexism, 56–8, 62–85, 198, 210–1
Sexton, Anne, xvi n. 1
    "The Big Boots of Pain," 3–5
    "Rowing," 11–2
    "The Rowing Endeth," 237–8
sexual abuse. *See* abuse
sexuality, 79–80, 82, 146
sin, 38–44, 60–96, 185, 197, 201
    gender differences, 72–8, 85, 154
    women's views, 65–85, 145–7,
        158
slavery, 34, 93, 136, 187
Smith, Karen Sue, 216
Smith, Pamela, 109–13, 156
Sobrino, Jon, 47
Sölle, Dorothee, 120–34, 188, 213,
    215–6, 220, 222–3
    acceptance contrasted to sub-
        mission, 125–30
    apathy, 20, 131
    blaming the victim, 70
    definitions/types of suffering,
        50, 130–3, 167–8, 204
    phases of suffering, 121–5, 129
    powerlessness, 76
    theology and suffering, 14
solidarity, 46, 49, 123, 143, 211,
    214, 222
soteriology. *See* redemption

Sparks, Richard, 14, 28, 37–43
spirituality, 205–25
    and suffering, 210–25
    and theology, 207
    Christian, 209–10
    definition, 206–10
    postbiblical, 81–3
Starhawk, 82
statistics, 1, 3, 6–7, 100, 160
Stewart, Maria, 144–5
sufferers
    attacked/despised, 16
    Job as an example of tragic,
        189–93
suffering
    and affliction, 32, 35
    and pain, 24–5, 30, 71, 74, 147–8
    as threat to integrity/well-
        being, 22–4, 27–31
    biomedical view, 24–30
    causes, 35–43, 47, 153, 166, 168,
        202
    definitions, 21–35, 41, 60, 147–8
    divine, 44–6, 48
    gender differences, 73
    hierarchy of, 131
    psychotherapeutic view, 30–1
    religious views, 35–49
    silence and, 121, 124, 131
    types, 50, 105, 126, 130–6,
        154–5, 168, 196
Surin, Kenneth, 38 n. 77, 43
surrender, 43, 118–9, 217–23

T
Tertullian, 65–6, 104
theodicy, 35–7, 69, 79, 91, 125–8,
    136, 152, 155–6, 200–1
    critiques, 86–99, 166–7
    typology, 37–43
        Augustinian/free–will model,
            38–9, 86, 89

dualistic model, 38
faith model, 42–3, 119
Irenaean model, 40–1, 86–9
punishment/retribution
    model, 39–40, 86–9
redemptive suffering/atone-
    ment model, 40, 89–99
remedial/instructive model,
    41–2
theological responses to suffering
liberation theologies, 46–50, 85,
    97, 154
process theology, 43–4, 85, 97
suffering–God approach, 44–6,
    95, 106
traditional, 35–43, 62–109
womanist, 140–9
*See also* feminist theology;
    names of specific theologians
Townes, Emilie M., 147–9
tragedy, 137–9, 161–204
and Christianity, 162–3, 165,
    181, 195–204
themes, 163–74
tragic suffering. *See* radical suffering
tragic vision of reality. *See* reality,
    tragic vision of
transformation, 56, 58, 92, 107–8,
    111–3, 119, 127, 198, 207,
    220–3, 236
Trinity, 98, 209–10
Trost, Lou Ann, 94, 98–9
trust, 68, 149

U

unmerited suffering. *See* radical
    suffering

V

value to suffering, 8, 21, 40–2,
    159, 232–8
victim(s)/victimization, 67, 91,
    108, 136, 143, 148, 214
vigil, 113, 216–8, 223
virtues, 142, 157–8, 215
vulnerability, 21, 44, 69, 112–3,
    115, 117–8, 128, 135, 172, 177,
    182–4, 197, 199, 216–21, 235

W

Weil, Simone, 16, 32–5, 42, 93,
    136, 220
Williams, Delores, 84, 145–7, 149
Wismer, Patricia L., 95 n. 145,
    149–51, 154, 156–8, 230
women, 9, 23, 53–160, 205–25
devaluation, 63–8, 72–3, 85,
    146, 154
focus on, 6–8
religious doctrines and, 105,
    108–9, 149
suffering servant role, 91, 106
subordination, 104–5
tragic vision and, 196–200
violence against, 99–109
*See also* feminism; feminist
    theology; patriarchy; sexism;
    sin
Woolf, Virginia, 15
world order, 170–2, 191–2
worship, 208–9

Y

Young, Pamela Dickey, 90–7, 197,
    234